Pro React

Cássio de Sousa Antonio

Pro React

ISBN-13 (pbk): 978-1-4842-1261-5

ISBN-13 (electronic): 978-1-4842-1260-8

Managing Director: Welmoed Spahr
Lead Editor: Louise Corrigan
Technical Reviewer: Jack Franklin and Tyler Merry
Editorial Board: Steve Anglin, Louise Corrigan, Jim DeWolf, Jonathan Gennick, Robert Hutchinson, Michelle Lowman, James Markham, Susan McDermott, Matthew Moodie, Jeff Olson, Jeffrey Pepper, Douglas Pundick, Ben Renow-Clarke, Gwenan Spearing
Coordinating Editor: Melissa Maldonado
Copy Editor: Mary Behr
Compositor: SPi Global
Indexer: SPi Global
Artist: SPi Global

Distributed to the book trade worldwide by Springer Science+Business Media New York, 233 Spring Street, 6th Floor, New York, NY 10013. Phone 1-800-SPRINGER, fax (201) 348-4505, e-mail orders-ny@springer-sbm.com, or visit www.springer.com. Apress Media, LLC is a California LLC and the sole member (owner) is Springer Science + Business Media Finance Inc (SSBM Finance Inc). SSBM Finance Inc is a Delaware corporation.

For information on translations, please e-mail rights@apress.com, or visit www.apress.com.

Apress and friends of ED books may be purchased in bulk for academic, corporate, or promotional use. eBook versions and licenses are also available for most titles. For more information, reference our Special Bulk Sales–eBook Licensing web page at www.apress.com/bulk-sales.

Any source code or other supplementary material referenced by the author in this text is available to readers at www.apress.com. For detailed information about how to locate your book's source code, go to www.apress.com/source-code/.

To my wife, Mel, for all the support, inspiration, and love.
You make it all worthwhile.

Contents at a Glance

Contents

About the Author

Cássio de Souza Antonio started programming 20 years ago with a Sinclair Spectrum and has since built a career as software engineer and technical manager in Brazil and USA. He has developed and contributed to projects for major brands such as Microsoft, Coca-Cola, Unilever, and HSBC, among others. His startup was acquired in late 2014. Currently Cássio works as a consultant. You can follow him on Twitter (@cassiozen).

About the Technical Reviewers

Jack Franklin is a speaker, author, and technical writer who spends most of his time writing or talking about JavaScript. He works as a Developer Evangelist at Pusher and is a keen open source contributor. He's a big fan of React and writes extensively on JavaScript at `www.javascriptplayground.com`. He can be found tweeting as `@Jack_Franklin`.

Tyler Merry is a UX Technologist for Universal Mind, where his focus is on bridging the gap between idea and implementation. Tyler approaches all problems through the filter of experimentation. He believes that the fastest and most accurate solution is working provocatively through multiple experiments and informal testing.

Through past work experiences with Coca-Cola, Sony, Pfizer, P&G, Ford, and Vail Resorts, he has learned the value of accuracy and communication. His work with early startups helped to reinforce the value of iteration, speed, and efficiency.

When not keeping up-to-date on web and UX trends, Tyler spends his time on his less-than-four-wheeled vehicles (bicycle, motorcycle, unicycle), or learning whatever skill catches his fancy for the day, like knitting, photography, or juggling.

Acknowledgments

I'd like to thank my parents, Sergio and Dete, for giving me freedom, independence, and love.

And a special thanks to the editorial staff at Apress for believing in this project, and for all the guidance and patience.

Introduction

React is an open source library for creating composable interfaces, and it is maintained by Facebook. Since its initial public release, the library has experienced a fast adoption rate and a vibrant community has sprung up around it.

The book will cover the library in detail and will discuss best practices for creating interfaces in a composable way. The React library itself is small, so the book will also cover additional tools and libraries in the React ecosystem (such as React Router and the Flux architecture) to provide the reader with enough knowledge to create complete applications.

Each topic is covered clearly and concisely, and is packed with the details you need to learn to be truly effective. The most important features are given a no-nonsense, in-depth treatment, and chapters include common problems and details on how to avoid them.

An Overview of This Book

Chapter 1 packs a lot of information to get you up and running with a basic React configuration and an overall understanding of how user interfaces are structured in React.

Chapter 2 gets deeper into JSX (React's JavaScript language extension used to declare the component markup together with JavaScript). It also examines how to take advantage of React's event system and virtual DOM implementation.

Chapter 3 deals with how to create complete applications by using components. You will learn about data flow in React applications and get to know components in depth (nesting components, exposing an API, props, and state).

Chapter 4 is about creating a rich experience for the end user. You will learn how to implement animations (with the help of React's add-on CSSTransitionGroup) and drag-and-drop (using an external library called React DnD).

Chapter 5 is all about routing. You will learn how to manage the URI and set application end points using one of the most-used libraries in the React community, the React Router.

Chapter 6 presents the Flux architecture. You will learn the architecture in detail, which problems it solves, and how to integrate it within a React application.

Chapter 7 is about performance tuning. Here, you will learn how to measure your application's performance. You will then understand how to optimize your code to obtain better performance for your application.

Chapter 8 covers isomorphic (or universal) React applications (or, how to render React on the server). This technique allows for a better perceived performance, search engine optimization, and graceful degradation (when the app works even if the local JavaScript is disabled).

Finally, Chapter 9 covers testing. You will learn how components can be tested using React's Test Utils. You will also learn about Jest, the testing framework made by Facebook that is the preferred way to test React projects.

Who This Book Is For

The content in this book is intended for intermediate level JavaScript developers, programmers that already have experience creating front-end apps using some jQuery or maybe even some Backbone/Angular, and who need better tools and knowledge to solve the increasingly common problem of structuring complex front-end applications.

Source Code

The code for the examples shown in this book is available online in the Source Code section of the Apress web site. Visit `www.apress.com`, click Source Code, and look for this book's title. You can also download the source code from this book's home page. In addition, all the sample code and some practical extras are available on GitHub (`pro-react.github.io`).

Contacting the Author

Thank you for buying this book. I hope you enjoy reading it and that you find it a valuable resource. I welcome your personal feedback, questions, and comments regarding this book's content and source code. You can contact me at `proreactbook@gmail.com`.

Good luck! I am looking forward to your React applications!

CHAPTER 1

■ ■ ■

Getting Started

React is an open-source project created by Facebook. It offers a novel approach towards building user interfaces in JavaScript. Since its initial public release, the library has experienced a fast adoption rate and has created a vibrant community around it.

Over the course of the book, you will learn everything you need to know to get the benefits of React in your projects. since React is only concerned about rendering the UI and makes no assumptions about the rest of your technology stack, this book will you walk through the routing and application architectures that fit in the library's patterns.

In this chapter, we will go through a few topics at a high level so you can start building applications as quickly as possible. The topics we'll cover include the following:

- A complete definition of React and an overview of its benefits

- How to use JSX, a JavaScript syntax extension used in React for expressing UI

- How to create React components, complete with props and state

Before You Get Started

React fits in the modern JavaScript development ecosystem. To code along with the examples in this book, you will need to have Node.js and npm installed. You should also be familiar with functional JavaScript paradigms as well as some of the language's newest features, such as arrow functions and classes.

Node.js and npm

JavaScript was born to run on the browser, but Node.js makes it possible to run JavaScript programs on your local computer and on a server through its open source command line tool. Together with npm (Node Package Manager), Node.js has become invaluable for local development of JavaScript-heavy applications, allowing a developer to create scripts for running tasks (such as copying and moving files or starting a local development server, for example) and to automatically download dependencies.

If you don't have Node.js installed, take your time to install it now by downloading the installer for Windows, Mac or Linux at https://nodejs.org/.

JavaScript ES6

JavaScript is a live language that has been evolving over the years. Recently the community agreed on a set of improvements for the language. Some of the most recent browsers have already implemented such features, and the React community makes extensive use of them (arrow functions, classes, and the spread operator, to

1

name a few). React also encourages the use of functional patterns in JavaScript, so it's important that you're familiar with how functions and context works in the language and that you understand methods such as map, reduce, and assign. If you are a little hazy on some of these details, online appendixes on these subjects are provided on the Apress website (www.apress.com/) and on the book's GitHub page (http://pro-react.github.io/).

Defining React

To get a clear understanding of what exactly React is, I like to define it as this:
> *React is an engine for building composable user interfaces using JavaScript and (optionally) XML.*
> Let's break down this statement to analyze each part:

> > **React is an engine:** React's site defines it as a library, but I like to use the term "engine" because it helps convey one of React's core strengths: its approach to reactive UI rendering. This approach separates state (all the internal data that defines the application at a given point in time) from the UI presented to the user. With React, you declare how state is represented as visual elements of the DOM and from then on the DOM is automatically updated to reflect state changes.

> > The term "engine" was first used to describe React by Justin Deal because it reminded him of the similarity between reactive rendering and the way game engines work (https://zapier.com/engineering/react-js-tutorial-guide-gotchas/).

> > **for creating composable user interfaces:** Reducing the complexity of creating and maintaining user interfaces is at the heart of React. It embraces the concept of breaking the UI into components, self-contained concern-specific building blocks, which are easy to reuse, extend, and maintain.

> > **using JavaScript and (optionally) XML:** React is a pure JavaScript library that can be used on the browser, the server, and mobile devices. As you will see in this chapter, it has an optional syntax that allows you to use XML to describe your UI. As strange as it may look at first, it turns out that XML is great for describing user interfaces: it's declarative, it's easy to spot the relationship between elements, and it's easy to visualize the overall structure of your UI.

React's Benefits

There are a lot of JavaScript MVC frameworks out there. So why did Facebook build React and why would you want to use it? In the next three sections, we'll explore some of its benefits in order to answer this question.

Reactive Rendering is Simple

In the early days of web development, way before the concept of single page applications, for every interaction the user performed on a page (like hitting a button), a whole new page was sent from the server, even if this new page was only a slightly different version of the page the user was on. That made for a terrible experience from the point of view of the user, but for the developer it was very easy to plan what exactly the user would see at a given interaction or a given point.

Single page applications are constantly fetching new data and transforming parts of the DOM as the user interacts. As interfaces grow more complex, it gets more and more complicated to examine the current state of the application and make the necessary punctual changes on the DOM to update it.

One technique used by many JavaScript frameworks (especially before React appeared) to tackle this increasing complexity and keep the interface in sync with state is data binding, but this approach comes with disadvantages in maintainability, scalability, and performance.

Reactive rendering is easier to use than traditional data binding. It lets us write in a declarative way how components should look and behave. And when the data changes, React conceptually renders the whole interface again.

Since its not viable for performance reasons to actually trash and re-render the entire interface every time state data changes, React uses an in-memory, lightweight representation of the DOM called "virtual DOM."

Manipulating the in-memory representation of the DOM is faster and more efficient than manipulating the real DOM. When the state of the application changes (as the result of an user interaction or data fetching, for example) React quickly compares the current state of the UI with the desired state and computes the minimal set of real DOM mutations to achieve it. This makes React very fast and efficient. React apps can easily run at 60fps, even on mobile devices.

Component-Oriented Development Using Pure JavaScript

In a React application, everything is made of components, which are self-contained, concern-specific building blocks. Developing applications using components allows a "divide and conquer" approach where no particular part needs to be especially complex. They are kept small and because they can be combined, it's easy to create complex and more feature-rich components made of smaller components.

React components are written in plain JavaScript, instead of template languages or the HTML directives traditionally used for web application UIs. This is for a good reason: templates can be limiting because they dictate the full set of abstractions that you are allowed to use to build your UI. React's use of a full-featured programming language to render views is a big advantage to the ability to build abstractions.

Additionally, by being self-contained and using a unifying markup with its corresponding view logic, React components lead to a separation of concerns. In the early days of the Web, different languages were created to force a separation of concerns: HTML for content structure, CSS for styling, and JavaScript for behavior. This separation worked very well when it was introduced because the pervading style of web page at the time was a static presentation. But now that interfaces are magnitudes more interactive and complex, display logic and markup have inevitably become tied together; the separation between markup, styling, and JavaScript turned into just a separation of technologies, not a separation of concerns.

React assumes that display logic and markup are highly cohesive; they both show the UI and encourage the separation of concerns by creating discrete, well-encapsulated, and reusable components for each concern.

Flexible Abstraction of the Document Model

React has its own lightweight representation of the UI that abstracts away the underlying document model. The most notable advantage of this approach is that it enables the use of the same principles to render HTML for the Web as well as native iOS and Android views. This abstraction also leads to other interesting points:

- Events behave in a consistent, standards-compliant way in all browsers and devices, automatically using delegation.

- React components can be rendered on the server for SEO and perceived performance.

Building Your First React App

You now know that components are the building block of React UIs, but what do they look like? How do you create one? At the bare minimum, a React component is simply a JavaScript class with a render method that returns a description of the component's UI, like so:

```
class Hello extends React.Component {
  render() {
    return (
      <h1>Hello World</h1>
    )
  }
}
```

You probably noticed the HTML tags in the middle of the JavaScript code. As mentioned, React has a syntax extension to JavaScript called JSX that lets us write XML (and consequently HTML) inline with code.

JSX is optional but it has been widely accepted as the standard way of defining UIs in React components because of its declarative syntax, expressiveness, and the fact that it gets converted to plain JavaScript function calls, means that it doesn't alter the language semantics.

We will get in more detail about JSX in the next chapter, but the important thing to consider now is that React requires a "transformation" step (or transpilation, if you will) where JSX gets transformed into JavaScript.

In the modern JavaScript development ecosystem, there are a lot of tools that can handle this step. Let's take a moment to discuss how to set up a development workflow for React projects.

React Development Workflow

Long gone are the days where we could write all JavaScript in a single file, manually download one or two JavaScript libraries, and glue everything together one a page. And while it's certainly possible to download or even copy and paste the React library as a minified JavaScript file and start running components immediately, transforming JSX at runtime, nobody does this, except for small demos and prototypes.

In even the most basic scenarios, we want a development workflow that allow us to do the following:

- Write JSX and transform it into regular JavaScript on the fly

- Write code in a module pattern

- Manage dependencies

- Bundle JavaScript files and use source maps for debugging

With this in mind, the basic project structure for a React project contains the following:

1. A **source folder**, to contain all your JavaScript modules.

2. An index.html **file**. In React applications, the HTML page tends to be almost empty. It is responsible only for loading the application's JavaScript and providing a div (or any other element, actually) that is used by React to render the application's components into.

3. A package.json **file**. The package.json is a standard npm manifest file that holds various information about the project, such a name, description, information about the author, etc. It lets the developer specify dependencies (that can get automatically downloaded and installed) and define script tasks.

4. A **module packager or build tool**, which will be used for JSX transformation and module/dependency bundling. The usage of modules helps organize JavaScript code by splitting it into multiple files, each one declaring its own dependencies. The module bundler then automatically packs everything together in the correct load order. There are a lot of tools that handle this intermediary step, including Grunt, Gulp, and Brunch, among others. You can easily find recipes for React in any of those tools, but in general, the React community has adopted webpack as the preferred tool for this job. At its core, webpack is a module bundler, but it can also put the source code through loaders that can transform and compile it.

Figure 1-1 shows the mentioned files and folders structure.

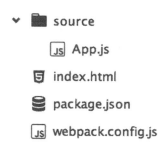

Figure 1-1. *Minimum React project files and folders structure*

■ **Tip**   You will find an appendix entirely dedicated to setting up a React project using webpack in the online materials for this book. The appendix covers webpack in detail and shows how to set up advanced options such as hot reloading React components. The online appendixes are available at Apress site (www.apress.com) and at this book's GitHub page (pro-react.github.io).

Getting Started Quickly

To keep focus on learning the React library, a React app boilerplate pack is provided with this book. Download it from apress.com or from the direct GitHub page at https://github.com/pro-react/react-app-boilerplate. The boilerplate project comes with all the basic files and configurations needed to start developing immediately. After downloading it, all you have to do is install the dependencies and run the development server to test the project in the browser. To automatically install all the dependencies, open the terminal or command prompt and run npm install. To run the development server, simply type npm start.

You're ready to go. Feel free to skip the next topic and go straight to building your first React component.

Or, Do It Yourself

If you want to get your hands dirty, you can manually create the basic project structure in five steps. Since the focus of this book is on the React library, we won't get into many details or look into optional configurations for now, but you can read more about them in the online appendixes or look the source files for the React app boilerplate project. Both can be downloaded from the Apress website (www.apress.com/) or from this book's GitHub page (http://pro-react.github.io/).

1. Start by creating the source folder (common names are source or app). This folder will only contain JavaScript modules. Static assets that don't go through the module bundler (which includes index.html, images and, for now, CSS files) will be saved in the root folder.

2. In the root folder of your project, create the index.html file. It should look like Listing 1-1.

    Listing 1-1. Simple HTML Page That Loads the Bundled JavaScript and Provides a Root Div in Which to Render React Components

    ```html
    <!DOCTYPE html>
    <html>
      <head>
        <title>First React Component</title>
      </head>
      <body>
        <div id="root"></div>
        <script type="text/javascript" src="bundle.js"></script>
      </body>
    </html>
    ```

3. Create the package.json file by running npm init on the terminal or command prompt and following the instructions. You will use npm for dependency management (downloading and installing all required libraries). Your project's dependencies include React, the Babel compiler for JSX transforming (loader and core), and webpack (including the webpack dev server). Edit your package.json file so it looks like Listing 1-2 and then run npm install.

    Listing 1-2. Dependencies on a Sample package.json

    ```json
    {
      "name": "your-app-name",
      "version": "X.X.X",
      "description": "Your app description",
      "author": "You",
      "devDependencies": {
        "babel-core": "^5.8.*",
        "babel-loader": "^5.3.*",
        "webpack": "^1.12.*",
        "webpack-dev-server": "^1.10.*"
      },
      "dependencies": {
        "react": "^0.13.*"
      }
    }
    ```

4. Moving on, you need to configure webpack, your module bundler of choice. Listing 1-3 shows the configuration file. Let's walk through it. First, the entry key points to the main application module.

Listing 1-3. The webpack.config.js File

```
module.exports = {
  entry: [
    './source/App.js'
  ],
  output: {
    path: __dirname,
    filename: "bundle.js"
  },
  module: {
    loaders: [{
      test: /\.jsx?$/,
      loader: 'babel'
    }]
  }
};
```

The next key, output, tells webpack where to save the single JavaScript file containing all the modules packed in the correct order.

Finally, in the the module loaders section, you pass all .js files through Babel, the JavaScript compiler that transforms all JSX into plain JavaScript code. Bear in mind that Babel does more than that, though; it allows the usage of modern JavaScript syntax such as arrow functions and classes.

5. Now it's time for the finishing touches. The project structure is done. The necessary command to start a local server (which will be needed to test in the browser) is 'node_modules/.bin/webpack-dev-server', but to avoid having to to type this long command in every time, you can edit the package.json you created in step 3 and turn this long command into a task, as shown in Listing 1-4.

Listing 1-4. Adding the Start Script to package.json

```
{
  "name": "your-app-name",
  "version": "X.X.X",
  "description": "Your app description",
  "author": "You",
  "scripts": {
    "start": "node_modules/.bin/webpack-dev-server --progress"
  },
  "devDependencies": {
    "babel-core": "^5.8.*",
    "babel-loader": "^5.3.*",
    "webpack": "^1.12.*",
    "webpack-dev-server": "^1.10.*"
  },
  "dependencies": {
    "react": "^0.13.*"
  }
}
```

With this set up, the next time you want to run the local development server, simply type npm start.

Creating Your First Component

With a basic project structure in place that manages dependencies, provides a module system, and transforms JSX for you, you can now recreate the Hello World component and render it on the page. You will keep the same code for the component, but add an import statement to make sure the React library gets included in the bundled JavaScript.

```
import React from 'react';

class Hello extends React.Component {
  render() {
    return (
      <h1>Hello World</h1>
    );
  }
}
```

Next, you will use React.render to display your component on the page, as shown here and in Figure 1-2:

```
React.render(<Hello />, document.getElementById('root'));
```

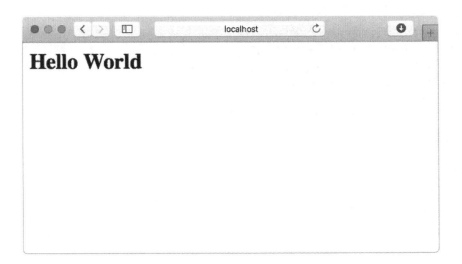

Figure 1-2. *Your first component rendered in the browser*

■ **Tip**   While it's possible to render directly into a document body, it's usually a good idea to render into a child element (usually a div). Many libraries and even browser extensions attach nodes to the document body, and since React needs to fully manage the DOM tree under its control, this can cause unpredictable issues.

Saving a little typing

A commom technique used by many developers to save a little typing is to use destructuring assignemt in the module import, in order to have direct access to the modules internal functions and classes. In our previous example, we could use it to avoid typing "React.Component":

```
import React, { Component } from 'react';

class Hello extends Component {
  render() {
    return (
      <h1>Hello World</h1>
    );
  }
}
```

It surely does not have a really big impact in this example, but the cumulative impact in bigger projects justifies its usage.

■ **Note**   Destructuring assignment is part of the specification for the next version of javascript. This and other future version topics that can already be used in React are covered in the online Appendix C.

Dynamic Values

In JSX, values written between curly braces ({}) are evaluated as a JavaScript expression and rendered in the markup. If you want to render a value from a local variable, for example, you could do this:

```
import React, { Component } from 'react';

class Hello extends Component {
  render() {
    var place = "World";
    return (
      <h1>Hello {place}</h1>
    );
  }
}

React.render(<Hello />, document.getElementById("root"));
```

Composing Components

React favors the creation of simple reusable components that are nested and combined to create complex UIs. Now that you've seen the basic structure of a React component, let's make sense of how they can be composed together.

Props

A key factor to make components reusable and composable is the ability to configure them, and React provides properties (or props, in short) for doing so. Props are the mechanism used in React for passing data from parent to child components. They can't be changed from inside the child component; props are passed and "owned" by the parent.

In JSX, props are provided as tag attributes much like in HTML. As an example, let's build a simple grocery list composed of two components, the parent GroceryList component and the child GroceryItem component:

```
import React, { Component } from 'react';

// Parent Component
class GroceryList extends Component {
  render() {
    return (
      <ul>
        <ListItem quantity="1" name="Bread" />
        <ListItem quantity="6" name="Eggs" />
        <ListItem quantity="2" name="Milk" />
      </ul>
    );
  }
}

// Child Component
class ListItem extends Component {
  render() {
    return (
      <li>
        {this.props.quantity}× {this.props.name}
      </li>
    );
  }
}

React.render(<GroceryList />,document.getElementById("root"));
```

Besides using named props, it's also possible to reference the content between the opening and closing tags using props.children:

```
import React, { Component } from 'react';

// Parent Component
class GroceryList extends Component {
  render() {
    return (
      <ul>
        <ListItem quantity="1">Bread</ListItem>
        <ListItem quantity="6">Eggs</ListItem>
        <ListItem quantity="2">Milk</ListItem>
```

```
        </ul>
      );
    }
}

// Child Component
class ListItem extends Component {
  render() {
    return (
      <li>
        {this.props.quantity}× {this.props.children}
      </li>
    );
  }
}

React.render(<GroceryList />, document.getElementById('root'));
```

Presenting the Kanban Board App

Throughout this book you're going to build several small components and sample code for each topic. You're also going to build one complete application, a Kanban-style project management tool.

In a Kanban board, project activities correspond to cards (Figure 1-3). Cards are assembled into lists according to their status and are supposed to progress from one list to the next, mirroring the flow of a feature from idea to implementation.

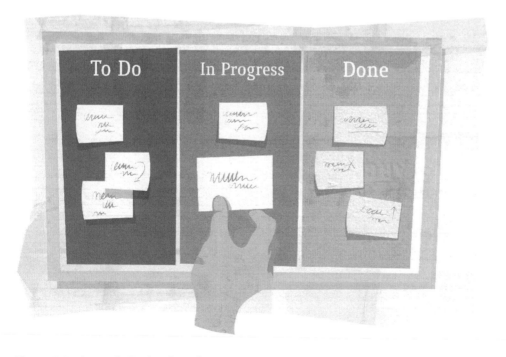

Figure 1-3. *A sample Kanban board*

There are many Kanban-style project management apps available online. Trello.com is a prominent example, although your project will be simpler. Your final project will look like Figure 1-4 and the data model the Kanban app will consume is shown in Listing 1-5.

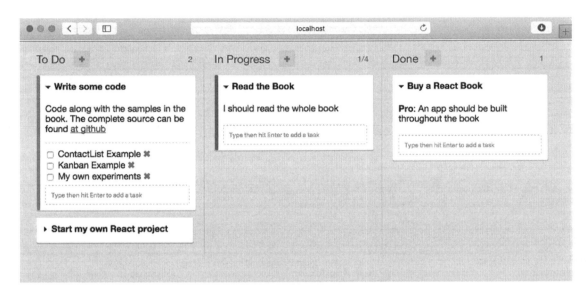

Figure 1-4. *The Kanban app you'll build in the next chapters*

Listing 1-5. The Kanban App Data Model

```
[
  { id:1,
    title: "Card one title",
    description: "Card detailed description.",
    status: "todo",
    tasks: [
      {id: 1, name:"Task one", done:true},
      {id: 2, name:"Task two", done:false},
      {id: 3, name:"Task three", done:false}
    ]
  },
  { id:2,
    title: "Card Two title",
    description: "Card detailed description",
    status: "in-progress",
    tasks: []
  },
  { id:3,
    title: "Card Three title",
    description: "Card detailed description",
    status: "done",
    tasks: []
  },
];
```

Defining Component Hierarchy

The first thing to understand is how to break the interface into nested components. Here are three things to consider.

1. Remember that components should be small and have a single concern. In other words, a component should ideally only do one thing. If it ends up growing, it should be broken into smaller subcomponents.

2. Analyse the project's wireframes and layout because they give many clues about component hierarchy.

3. Look at your data model. Interfaces and data models tend to adhere to the same information architecture, which means the work of separating your UI into components is often trivial. Just break it up into components that represent exactly one piece of your data model.

If you apply these concepts to the Kanban app, you will come to the composition shown in Figure 1-5.

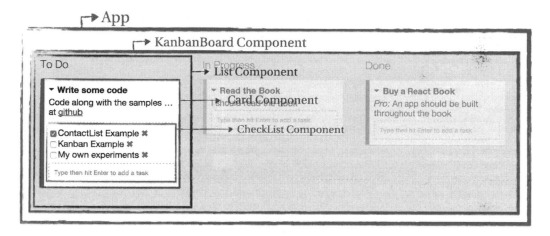

Figure 1-5. *The hierarchy of components in the Kanban App*

The Importance of Props

Props are of key importance in component composition. They are the mechanism used in React for passing data from parent to child components. Props can't be changed from inside the component; they are passed and "owned" by the parent.

Building the Components

Having figured out the interface hierarchy, it's time to build the components. There are two main approaches to building the components: top-down or bottom-up. That is, you can either start with building the components higher up in the hierarchy (such as the App component) or with the ones lower in it (like the CheckList component). To get an insight of all the props being passed down and how they are used in child components, you will start building your Kanban components from top-down.

Additionaly, to keep the project organized and to make it easy to maintain and implement new features, you're going to keep each component in its own JavaScript file.

App Module (App.js)

You will keep the app.js file really simple for now. It will only contain the data and it will only render a KanbanBoard component. In this first iteration of your Kanban app, the data will be hard-coded on a local variable, but in future chapters you will fetch it from an API. See Listing 1-6.

Listing 1-6. A Simple app.js File

```javascript
import React from 'react';
import KanbanBoard from './KanbanBoard';

let cardsList = [
  {
    id: 1,
    title: "Read the Book",
    description: "I should read the whole book",
    status: "in-progress",
    tasks: []
  },
  {
    id: 2,
    title: "Write some code",
    description: "Code along with the samples in the book",
    status: "todo",
    tasks: [
      {
        id: 1,
        name: "ContactList Example",
        done: true
      },
      {
        id: 2,
        name: "Kanban Example",
        done: false
      },
      {
        id: 3,
        name: "My own experiments",
        done: false
      }
    ]
  },
];

React.render(<KanbanBoard cards={cardsList} />, document.getElementById('root'));
```

KanbanBoard Component (KanbanBoard.js)

The KanbanBoard component will receive the data as props and will be responsible for filtering the status to create three list components: "To Do," "In Progress," and "Done". See Listing 1-7.

■ **Note** As stated in the beginning of this chapter, React's components are written in plain JavaScript. They don't have the loops on branching helpers that you may find on template libraries such as Mustache, for example, but that's not bad news since you have a full-featured programming language at your fingertips. In the next components, you will use filter and map functions to work with data from the cards array.

Listing 1-7. The KanbanBoard Component

```
import React, { Component } from 'react';
import List from './List';

class KanbanBoard extends Component {
render(){
    return (
      <div className="app">

        <List id='todo' title="To Do" cards={
          this.props.cards.filter((card) => card.status === "todo")
        } />

        <List id='in-progress' title="In Progress" cards={
          this.props.cards.filter((card) => card.status === "in-progress")
        } />

        <List id='done' title='Done' cards={
          this.props.cards.filter((card) => card.status === "done")
        } />

      </div>
    );
  }
}
export default KanbanBoard;
```

List Component (List.js)

The List component will just display the list's name and render all the card components within it. Notice that you will map the cards array received via props and pass individual information such as the title and description down to the card component, also as props. See Listing 1-8.

Listing 1-8. The List Component

```
import React, { Component } from 'react';
import Card from './Card';

class List extends Component {
  render() {
    var cards = this.props.cards.map((card) => {
      return <Card id={card.id}
                   title={card.title}
                   description={card.description}
                   tasks={card.tasks} />
    });

    return (
      <div className="list">
        <h1>{this.props.title}</h1>
        {cards}
      </div>
    );
  }
}

export default List;
```

Card Component (Card.js)

The Card is the component with which the user will interact most. Each card has a title, a description and a checklist, as shown in Figure 1-6 and Listing 1-9.

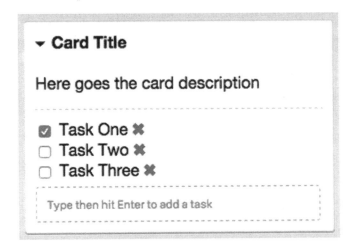

Figure 1-6. The Kanban app's card

Listing 1-9. The Card Component

```
import React, { Component } from 'react';
import CheckList from './CheckList';

class Card extends Component {
  render() {
    return (
      <div className="card">
        <div className="card__title">{this.props.title}</div>
        <div className="card__details">
          {this.props.description}
          <CheckList cardId={this.props.id} tasks={this.props.tasks} />
        </div>
      </div>
    );
  }
}

export default Card;
```

Notice the use of the `className` attribute within the Card component. Since JSX is JavaScript, identifiers such as `class` are discouraged as XML attribute names, hence the use of `className`. This subject will be further discussed in the next chapter.

Checklist Component (CheckList.js)

Finally, there is the component that makes the bottom part of the card, the checklist. Notice that you're still missing the form to create new tasks; you will work on this later. See Listing 1-10.

Listing 1-10. The Checklist Component

```
import React, { Component } from 'react';

class CheckList extends Component {
  render() {
    let tasks = this.props.tasks.map((task) => (
      <li className="checklist__task">
        <input type="checkbox" defaultChecked={task.done} />
        {task.name}
        <a href="#" className="checklist__task--remove" />
      </li>
    ));
```

```
    return (
      <div className="checklist">
        <ul>{tasks}</ul>
      </div>
    );
  }
}

export default CheckList;
```

Finishing Touches

The React components are done. To make things look pretty, now let's write some CSS to style the interface (see Listing 1-11). Don't forget to create an HTML file to load the JavaScript and CSS files, and a div for React to render into (an example is shown in Listing 1-12).

Listing 1-11. CSS File

```css
*{
  box-sizing: border-box;
}

html,body,#app {
  height:100%;
  margin: 0;
  padding: 0;
}

body {
  background: #eee;
  font-family: "Helvetica Neue", Helvetica, Arial, sans-serif;
}

h1{
  font-weight: 200;
  color: #3b414c;
  font-size: 20px;
}

ul {
  list-style-type: none;
  padding: 0;
  margin: 0;
}

.app {
  white-space: nowrap;
  height:100%;
}
```

```css
.list {
  position: relative;
  display: inline-block;
  vertical-align: top;
  white-space: normal;
  height: 100%;
  width: 33%;
  padding: 0 20px;
  overflow: auto;
}

.list:not(:last-child):after{
  content: "";
  position: absolute;
  top: 0;
  right: 0;
  width: 1px;
  height: 99%;
  background: linear-gradient(to bottom, #eee 0%, #ccc 50%, #eee 100%) fixed;
}

.card {
  position: relative;
  z-index: 1;
  background: #fff;
  width: 100%;
  padding: 10px 10px 10px 15px;
  margin: 0 0 10px 0;
  overflow: auto;
  border: 1px solid #e5e5df;
  border-radius: 3px;
  box-shadow: 0 1px 0 rgba(0, 0, 0, 0.25);
}

.card__title {
  font-weight: bold;
  border-bottom: solid 5px transparent;
}

.card__title:before {
  display: inline-block;
  width: 1em;
  content: '▶';
}

.card__title--is-open:before {
  content: '▼';
}
```

```
.checklist__task:first-child {
  margin-top: 10px;
  padding-top: 10px;
  border-top: dashed 1px #ddd;
}

.checklist__task--remove:after{
  display: inline-block;
  color: #d66;
  content: "+";
}
```

Listing 1-12. HTML File

```
<!DOCTYPE html>
<html>
<head>
  <title>Kanban App</title>
  <link rel="stylesheet" href="style.css">
</head>
<body>
  <div id="root"></div>
  <script type="text/javascript" src="bundle.js"></script>
</body>
</html>
```

If you followed along, you should see something similar to Figure 1-7.

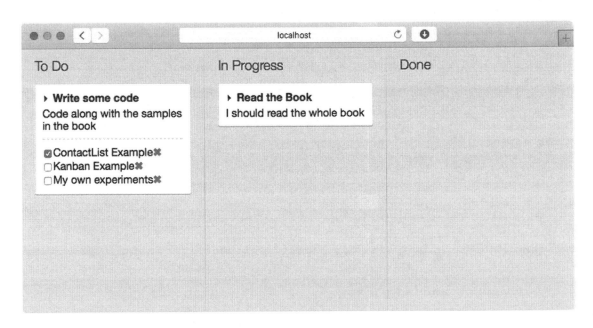

Figure 1-7. *The composed components interface*

Introducing State

So far you've seen that props are received by the component and are immutable. This leads to static components. If you want to add behavior and interactions, a component needs to have mutable data to represent its state. React's components can have mutable data inside this.state. Note that this.state is private to the component and can be changed by calling this.setState().

Now comes an important aspect of React's components: when the state is updated, the component triggers the reactive rendering, and the component itself and its children will be re-rendered. As mentioned, this happens very quickly due to React's use of a virtual DOM.

Kanban App: Togglable Cards

To illustrate state in components, let's add a new functionality to your Kanban app. You're going to make the cards toggle. Users will be able to show or hide details about the card.

It's possible to set a new state at any time, but if you want the component to have an initial state, you can set it on the class constructor. Currently, the Card component doesn't have a constructor, only a render method. Let's add a constructor function to define a new key called showDetails in the component's state (note that the import/export statements and the contents of the render method were omitted for brevity). See Listing 1-13.

Listing 1-13. Togglable Cards

```
class Card extends Component {
  constructor() {
    super(...arguments);
    this.state = {
      showDetails: false
    };
  }

  render() {
    return ( ... );
  }
}
```

In this sequence, you change the JSX in the render method to only render the card's details if the state property showDetails is true. To make this, you declare a local variable called cardDetails, and only assign actual data if the current state showDetails is true. On the return statement, you simply return the value of this variable (which will be empty if showDetails is false). See Listing 1-14.

Listing 1-14. The render method of the Card Component

```
render() {
  let cardDetails;
  if (this.state.showDetails) {
    cardDetails = (
      <div className="card__details">
        {this.props.description}
        <CheckList cardId={this.props.id} tasks={this.props.tasks} />
      </div>
    );
  };
```

21

```
  return (
    <div className="card">
      <div className="card__title">{this.props.title}</div>
      {cardDetails}
    </div>
  );
}
```

To finish, Let's add a click event handler to change the internal state. Use the JavaScript ! (not) operator to toggle the Boolean property showDetails (if it's currently true, it will became false and vice-versa), as shown in Listing 1-15.

Listing 1-15. Click Event Handler

```
render() {
  let cardDetails;
    if (this.state.showDetails) {
      cardDetails = (
        <div className="card__details">
          {this.props.description}
          <CheckList cardId={this.props.id} tasks={this.props.tasks} />
        </div>
      );
    };

  return (
    <div className="card">
      <div className="card__title" onClick={
          ()=>this.setState({showDetails: !this.state.showDetails})
      }>{this.props.title}</div>
      {cardDetails}
    </div>
  );
}
```

When running the example on the browser, all contacts will start closed and can be toggled on click (Figure 1-8).

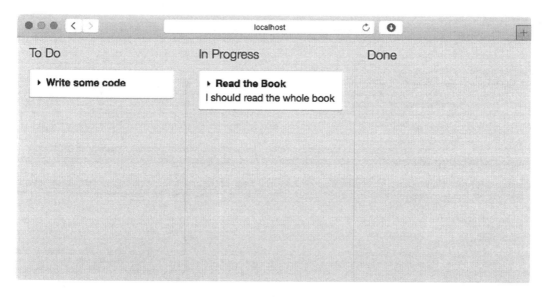

Figure 1-8. *Togglable Kanban Cards*

Summary

This chapter explored what React is and what benefits it brings to the universe of web development (primarily a very performant, declarative approach to structure your application user interface into components). You also created your first components and witnessed all the basic concepts of React's components: the render method, JSX, props, and state.

CHAPTER 2

■ ■ ■

Inside the DOM Abstraction

In the previous chapter, you saw that React abstracts away the DOM, providing a simpler programming model, better performance, and the possibility to render components on the server and even power native mobile apps.

This chapter will cover JSX, the JavaScript language extension used to describe the UI.

Events in React

React implements a synthetic event system that brings consistency and high performance to React applications and interfaces.

It achieves consistency by normalizing events so that they have the same properties across different browsers and platforms.

It achieves high performance by automatically using event delegation. React doesn't actually attach event handlers to the nodes themselves. Instead, a single event listener is attached to the root of the document; when an event is fired, React maps it to the appropriate component element. React also automatically removes the event listeners when a component unmounts.

DOM Event Listeners

HTML has always provided a beautiful and easy-to-understand event handling API for tag attributes: onclick, onfocus, etc. The problem with this API (and the reason why it is not used in professional projects) is that it's full of undesirable side effects: it pollutes the global scope, it's hard to track in the context of a big HTML file, it can be slow, and it can lead to memory leaks, just to name a few issues.

JSX makes use of a similarly easy-to-use and understand API but removes the undesired side effects from the HTML counterpart. Callback functions are scoped to the component (which, as you've seen, is responsible for just one part of the UI and tends to contain small markup), and it's smart enough to use event delegation and auto manage unmounting. Notice, however, that there are some minor differences in contrast with the original HTML implementation. In React, the properties are camel cased ("onClick" instead of "onclick"). Built to be consistent across browsers and devices, it implements a subset of all the variations found in different versions of different browsers. Tables 2-1 through 2-4 show the available events.

Table 2-1. *Touch and Mouse Events*

onTouchStart	onTouchMove	onTouchEnd	onTouchCancel	
onClick	onDoubleClick	onMouseDown	onMouseUp	onMouseOver
onMouseMove	onMouseEnter	onMouseLeave	onMouseOut	onContextMenu
onDrag	onDragEnter	onDragLeave	onDragExit	onDragStart
onDragEnd	onDragOver	onDrop		

Table 2-2. *Keyboard Events*

onKeyDown	onKeyUp	onKeyPress

Table 2-3. *Focus and Form Events*

onFocus	onBlur	
onChange	onInput	onSubmit

Table 2-4. *Other Events*

onScroll	onWheel	onCopy	onCut	onPaste

Kanban App: Managing the DOM Event

In the last iteration of the Kanban app, you added the following inline function (using the fat arrow =>) inside the onClick event handler:

```
<div className="card__title" onClick={
  ()=>this.setState({showDetails: !this.state.showDetails})
}>
```

This is practical but not very flexible. Let's change this implementation to use a new method called toggleDetails inside the class to handle the event:

```
class Card extends Component {
  constructor() {
    super(...arguments);
    this.state = {
      showDetails: false
    };
  }

  toggleDetails() {
    this.setState({showDetails: !this.state.showDetails});
  }
```

```
  render() {
    let cardDetails;
      if (this.state.showDetails) {
        cardDetails = (
          <div className="card__details">
            {this.props.description}
            <CheckList cardId={this.props.id} tasks={this.props.tasks} />
          </div>
        );
      }

    return (
      <div className="card">
        <div className="card__title" onClick={this.toggleDetails.bind(this)}>
          {this.props.title}
        </div>
        {cardDetails}
      </div>
    )
  }
}
```

■ **Note**   Earlier React versions (specifically prior to the use of ES6 classes) had a built-in "magic" feature that bound all methods to `this` automatically. Since this could be confusing for JavaScript developers that are not used to this feature in other classes, it was removed. In the current versions, the developer has to explicitly bind the function to context. This can be done in different ways, the simplest one being to simply use `.bind(this)` to generate a bound function. Bind and other functional JavaScript methods are discussed in Appendix B.

Digging Deeper in JSX

JSX is React's optional extension to the JavaScript syntax used for writing declarative XML-style syntax inside JavaScript code.

For web projects, React's JSX provides a set of XML tags that are similar to HTML, but there are other use cases in which another set of XML tags are used to describe the user interface (such as React with SVG, React Canvas, and React Native).

When transpiled (converted to plain JavaScript, so the browser or server can interpret the code), the XML is transformed into a function call to the React Library.

This

```
<h1>Hello World</h1>
```

becomes

```
React.createElement("h1", null, "Hello World");
```

The use of JSX is optional. However, embracing it has the following benefits:

- XML is great for representing UIs in element trees with attributes.
- It's more concise and easier to visualize the structure of your application.
- It's plain JavaScript. It doesn't alter the language semantics.

JSX vs. HTML

For web usage, JSX looks like HTML, but it's not an exact implementation of the HTML specification. React's creators went so far to make JSX similar enough to HTML so it could be used to describe web interfaces properly, but without losing sight of the fact that it should also conform to JavaScript style and syntax.

Differences Between JSX and HTML

There are three important aspects you should be aware of when writing HTML syntax with JSX:

1. Tag attributes are camel cased.
2. All elements must be balanced.
3. The attribute names are based on the DOM API, not on the HTML language specs.

Let's review them now.

Tag Attributes Are Camel Cased

For example, in HTML, the input tag can have an optional `maxlength` attribute:

```
<input type="text" maxlength="30" />
```

In JSX, the attribute is written as `maxLength` (note the uppercase "L"):

```
return <input type="text" maxLength="30" />
```

All Elements Must be Balanced

Since JSX is XML, all elements must be balanced. Tags such as `<br>` and `<img>`, which don't have ending tags, need to be self-closed. So, instead of `<br>`, use `<br/>` and instead of `<img src="...">`, use `<img src="..." />`.

Attribute Names are Based on the DOM API

This can be confusing, but it is actually very easy. When interacting with the DOM API, tag attributes may have different names than those you use in HTML. One of such example is `class` and `className`.

For example, given this regular HTML

```
<div id="box" class="some-class"></div>
```

if you want to manipulate the DOM and change its class name using plain JavaScript, you would do something like

```
document.getElementById("box").className="some-other-class"
```

As far as JavaScript is concerned, that attribute is called `className`, not `class`. Since JSX is just a syntax extension to JavaScript, it conforms to the attribute names as defined in the DOM. That same `div` should be expressed in JSX as

```
return <div id="box" className="some-class"></div>
```

JSX Quirks

JSX can be tricky sometimes. This section groups small techniques, tips, and strategies to deal with common problems you may face when building components with JSX.

Single Root Node

React components can only render a single root node. To understand the reasons for this limitation, let's look at this sample return from a render function:

```
return(
  <h1>Hello World</h1>
)
```

It is transformed into a single statement:

```
return React.createElement("h1", null, "Hello World");
```

On the other hand, the following code isn't valid:

```
return (
  <h1>Hello World</h1>
    <h2>Have a nice day</h2>
 )
```

To be clear, this is not a JSX limitation, but rather a JavaScript characteristic: a return statement can only return a single value, and in the previous code we were trying to return two statements (two calls to `React.createElement`). The alternative is very simple: as you would do in plain JavaScript, wrap all return values in a root object.

```
return (
  <div>
    <h1>Hello World</h1>
    <h2>Have a nice day</h2>
  </div>
)
```

This works perfectly because it would be transformed into

```
return React.createElement("div", null,
    React.createElement("h1", null, "Hello World"),
    React.createElement("h2", null, " Have a nice day"),
 )
```

thus returning a single value, and done via valid JavaScript.

Conditional Clauses

If statements doesn't fit well in JSX, but what may be seen as a JSX limitation is actually a consequence of the fact that JSX is just plain JavaScript. To better explain, let's start by reviewing how JSX gets transformed into plain JavaScript.

JSX like

```
return (
    <div className="salutation">Hello JSX</div>
)
```

gets transformed into JavaScript like

```
return (
    React.createElement("div", {className: "salutation"}, "Hello JSX");
)
```

However, if you try to write an if clause in the middle of the JSX, like

```
<div className={if (condition) { "salutation" }}>Hello JSX</div>
```

it would be transformed into an invalid JavaScript expression, as shown here and in Figure 2-1:

```
React.createElement("div", {className: if (condition) { "salutation"}}, "Hello JSX");
```

```
> React.createElement("div", {className: if (condition) { "salutation"}}, "Hello JSX");
⊗    ▶Uncaught SyntaxError: Unexpected token if
```

Figure 2-1. Syntax error when trying to use an if expression inside JSX

What Are the Alternatives?

Although not being possible to use an "if" statement inside JSX, there are alternatives to render content conditionally, including using ternary expressions and assigning conditionally to a variable (null and undefined values are treated by React and outputs nothing when escaped in JSX).

Use Ternary Expressions

If you have a very simple expression, you can use the ternary form:

```
render() {
  return (
    <div className={condition ? "salutation" : ""}>
      Hello JSX
    </div>
  )
}
```

This will be transformed into a valid JS:

```
React.createElement("div", {className: condition ? "salutation" : ""}, "Hello JSX");
```

The ternary form also works for conditionally rendering entire nodes:

```
<div>
  {condition ?
    <span>Hello JSX</span>
  : null}
</div>
```

Move the Condition Out

If a ternary expression isn't robust enough for your case, the alternative is to not use conditionals in the middle of JSX. Simply move the conditional's clauses outside (as you did in Chapter 2 for hiding or showing the ContactItem details).

Instead of

```
render() {
  return (
    <div className={if (condition) { "salutation" }}>
      Hello JSX
    </div>
  )
}
```

move the conditional outside of JSX, like

```
render() {
  let className;
  if(condition){
    className = "salutation";
  }
  return (
    <div className={className}>Hello JSX</div>
  )
}
```

React knows how to handle undefined values and won't even create a class attribute in the div tag if the condition is false.

Kanban App: Indicating Whether a Card Is Open or Closed

In the first chapter, you used this technique of moving the condition out for toggling the Card details. Let's also use the ternary form to add a className conditionally to the Card Title (some of the original code is omitted for brevity). The results are shown in Figure 2-2.

```
class Card extends Component {
  constructor() { ... }
  toggleDetails() { ... }

  render() {
    let cardDetails;
      if (this.state.showDetails) {
        cardDetails = (
          <div className="card__details">
            {this.props.description}
            <CheckList cardId={this.props.id} tasks={this.props.tasks} />
          </div>
        );
      }

    return (
      <div className="card">
        <div className={
              this.state.showDetails? "card__title card__title--is-open" : "card__title"
          } onClick={this.toggleDetails.bind(this)}>
            {this.props.title}
        </div>
        {cardDetails}
      </div>
    )
  }
}
```

Figure 2-2. *Conditional class*

Blank Space

This is a very small and quick tip: in HTML, browsers usually render a space between elements in multiple lines. React's JSX will only render a space if you specifically tell it to do so. For example, the following JSX will render as shown in Figure 2-3.

```
return (
  <a href="http://google.com">Google</a>
  <a href="http://facebook.com">Facebook</a>
)
```

GoogleFacebook

Figure 2-3. *JSX doesn't produce a space between lines*

To explicitly insert a space, you can use an expression with an empty string {" "}:

```
return(
  <a href="http://google.com">Google</a>{" "}
  <a href="http://facebook.com">Facebook</a>
)
```

This renders the desired output, as shown in Figure 2-4.

Google Facebook

Figure 2-4. *Using an expression to render a space*

Comments in JSX

Another quirk derived from the fact that JSX isn't HTML is the lack of support for HTML comments (e.g. `<!-- comment -->`). Although traditional HTML tag comments are not supported, since JSX is made of JavaScript expressions, it's possible to use regular JS comments. You just need to be careful to put {} around the comments when you are within the child section of a tag.

```
let content = (
  <Nav>
    {/* child comment, put {} around */}
    <Person
      /* multi
         line
         comment */
      name={window.isLoggedIn ? window.name : ''} // end of line comment
    />
  </Nav>
);
```

Rendering Dynamic HTML

React has built-in XSS attack protection, which means that by default it won't allow HTML tags to be generated dynamically and attached to JSX. This is generally good, but in some specific cases you might want to generate HTML on the fly. One example would be rendering data in markdown format to the interface.

■ **Note**   Markdown is a format that allows you to write using an easy-to-read, easy-to-write plain text format. For example, surrounding text with double asterisks will make it strong (bold).

React provides the dangerouslySetInnerHTML property to skip XSS protection and render anything directly.

Kanban App: Rendering Markdown

Let's see this in action by enabling markdown on the Kanban app Card's description. You will start by changing the card descriptions on your data model to include some markdown formatting.

```
let cardsList = [
  {
    id:1,
    title: "Read the Book",
    description: "I should read the **whole** book",
    status: "in-progress",
    tasks: []
  },
  {
    id:2,
    title: "Write some code",
    description: "Code along with the samples in the book. The complete source can be found ↵
                 at [github](https://github.com/pro-react)",
    status: "todo",
    tasks: [
      {id: 1, name:"ContactList Example", done:true},
      {id: 2, name:"Kanban Example", done:false},
      {id: 3, name:"My own experiments", done:false}
    ]
  },
];
```

You will need a JavaScript library to convert the markdown used in the card descriptions to HTML. There are many open source libraries available. In this example, you're going to use one called marked (https://github.com/chjj/marked).

If you're following along with this book's examples and using a module system, import the library on your package.json and install it (both can be done with the single command npm install --save marked). Don't forget to import the marked module on the beginning of your file.

Using the marked module, your code will look like this:

```
import React, { Component } from 'react';
import CheckList from './CheckList';
import marked from 'marked';
```

Then, you're going to use the function marked() provided by the library to convert the markdown to HTML (I have omitted some code not pertinent to this example for brevity):

```
class Card extends Component {
  constructor() {...}
  toggleDetails() {...}

  render() {
    let cardDetails;
      if (this.state.showDetails) {
        cardDetails = (
          <div className="card__details">
            {marked(this.props.description)}
            <CheckList cardId={this.props.id} tasks={this.props.tasks} />
          </div>
        );
      }

    return (
      <div className="card">
        <div className={
              this.state.showDetails? "card__title card__title--is-open" : "card__title"
            } onClick={this.toggleDetails.bind(this)>
            {this.props.title}
        </div>
        {cardDetails}
      </div>
    )
  }
}
```

But as expected, React by default won't allow any HTML tags to be rendered inside your JSX so the output will look like Figure 2-5.

35

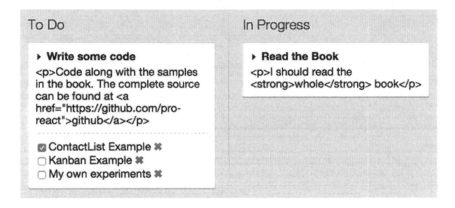

Figure 2-5. *React escaping HTML by default*

Using dangerouslySetInnerHTML, you can achieve the desired final result, as shown here and in Figure 2-6:

```
cardDetails = (
  <div className="card__details">
    <span dangerouslySetInnerHTML={{__html:marked(this.props.description)}} />
    <CheckList cardId={this.props.id} tasks={this.props.tasks} />
  </div>
);
```

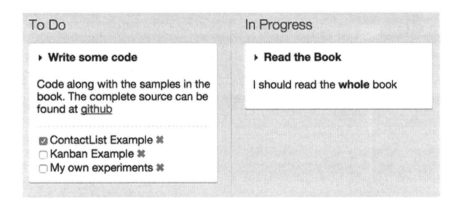

Figure 2-6. *React rendering dynamically generated HTML with dangerouslySetInnerHTML*

React Without JSX

JSX brings a concise and familiar syntax for describing UIs as tree structures. It does so by enabling the use of XML inside JavaScript code without altering the semantics of JavaScript. React was designed with JSX in mind; however, it's absolutely possible to use React without JSX. Although you'll continue using JSX for all the examples in this book, this section will briefly explore how to work with React without JSX.

React Elements in Plain JavaScript

You can create React elements in plain JavaScript using React.createElement, which takes a tag name or component, a properties object, and variable number of optional child arguments.

```
let child1 = React.createElement('li', null, 'First Text Content');
let child2 = React.createElement('li', null, 'Second Text Content');
let root = React.createElement('ul', { className: 'my-list' }, child1, child2);
React.render(root, document.getElementById('example'));
```

Element Factories

For convenience, React provides short-hand factory functions under React.DOM for common HTML tags. Let's put this together with a more advanced example:

```
React.DOM.form({className:"commentForm"},
  React.DOM.input({type:"text", placeholder:"Name"}),
  React.DOM.input({type:"text", placeholder:"Comment"}),
  React.DOM.input({type:"submit", value:"Post"})
)
```

The above is equivalent to the following JSX:

```
<form className="commentForm">
  <input type="text" placeholder="Name" />
  <input type="text" placeholder="Comment" />
  <input type="submit" value="Post" />
</form>
```

Using destructuring assignment, it's possible to tidy things up for a more concise syntax:

```
import React, { Component } from 'react';
import {render} from 'react-dom';

let {
  form,
  input
} = React.DOM;

class CommentForm extends Component {
  render(){
    return form({className:"commentForm"},
      input({type:"text", placeholder:"Name"}),
      input({type:"text", placeholder:"Comment"}),
      input({type:"submit", value:"Post"})
    )
  }
}
```

Custom Factories

It's also possible to create factories for custom components, like so:

```
let Factory = React.createFactory(ComponentClass);
...
let root = Factory({ custom: 'prop' });
render(root, document.getElementById('example'));
```

Inline Styling

By authoring React components using JSX, you're combining UI definition (content markup) and interaction (JavaScript) in the same file. As discussed, the separation of concerns in this scenario comes from discrete, well-encapsulated, and reusable components for each concern. But there's another important factor to user interfaces besides content and interaction: styling.

React provides the capacity to write inline styles using JavaScript. At first, the idea to write styles in JavaScript can seem a little strange, but it can provide some benefits over traditional CSS:

- Scoped styles without selectors

- Avoids specificity conflicts

- Source order independence

Note that JavaScript is highly expressive and so by using it you automatically gain variables, functions, and full range of control flow constructs.

Defining Inline Styles

In React's components, inline styles are specified as a JavaScript object. Style names are camel cased in order to be consistent with DOM properties (e.g. node.style.backgroundImage). Additionally, it's not necessary to specify pixel units - React automatically appends the correct unit behind the scenes. The following example shows an example of inline styling in React:

```
import React, { Component } from 'react';
import {render} from 'react-dom';

class Hello extends Component {
  render() {
    let divStyle = {
      width: 100,
      height: 30,
      padding: 5,
      backgroundColor: '#ee9900'

    };
    return <div style={divStyle}>Hello World</div>
  }
}
```

Kanban App: Card Color via Inline Styling

While it's possible to completely ditch CSS in favor of inline styling using JavaScript, generally an hybrid approach is more appropriate, where CSS (or CSS preprocessors such as Sass or Less) is used for major style definitions and inline styling inside React components is used for dynamic, state-based appearance.

In the next steps, you're going to add custom color to mark a card.

1. **Add color to your data model.** First, let's change the CardsList array to insert the colors:

```
let cardsList = [
  {
    id:1,
    title: "Read the Book",
    description: "I should read the book",
    color: '#BD8D31',
    status: "in-progress",
    tasks: []
  },
  {
    id:2,
    title: "Write some code",
    description: "Code along with the samples ... at [github](https://github.com/pro-react)",
    color: '#3A7E28',
    status: "todo",
    tasks: [
      {id: 1, name:"ContactList Example", done:true},
      {id: 2, name:"Kanban Example", done:false},
      {id: 3, name:"My own experiments", done:false}
    ]
  },
];
```

2. **Pass the color as props to the Card component.** The Card's parent component is the List component. Currently, the List component passes three attributes as props to the Card component: title, description, and tasks. You need to add color as another attribute:

```
class List extends Component {
  render() {
    let cards = this.props.cards.map((card) => {
      return <Card id={card.id}
                title={card.title}
                description={card.description}
                color={card.color}
                tasks={card.tasks} />
    });

    return (
      ...
    )
  }
}
```

3. **Create a** div **with inline style in the Card component.** Finally, you need to create an object containing all the style rules and the div that will use the style object inline:

```
class Card extends Component {
  constructor() {...}
  toggleDetails() {...}

  render() {
    let cardDetails;
    if (this.state.showDetails) {...}

    let sideColor = {
      position: 'absolute',
      zIndex: -1,
      top: 0,
      bottom: 0,
      left: 0,
      width: 7,
      backgroundColor: this.props.color
    };

    return (
      <div className="card">
        <div style={sideColor}/>
        <div className={
              this.state.showDetails? "card__title card__title--is-open" : "card__title"
          } onClick={this.toggleDetails.bind(this)}>
          {this.props.title}
        </div>
        {cardDetails}
      </div>
    )
  }
}
```

Figure 2-7 shows the rendered result.

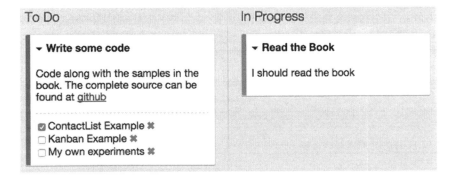

Figure 2-7. *Inline styles for dynamic card colors*

Working With Forms

In React, a component's internal state is kept to minimum because every time the state changes, the component is rendered again. The purpose of this is to have an accurate representation of the component state in your JavaScript code and let React keep the interface in sync.

For this reason, form components such as <input>, <textarea>, and <option> differ from their HTML counterparts because they can be mutated via user interactions.

React provides two ways of handling forms as components and lets you choose based on your app characteristics or personal preference. The two available ways to handle a form field are as a controlled component or an uncontrolled component.

Controlled Components

A form component with a value or checked prop is called a controlled component. In a controlled component, the value rendered inside the element will always reflect the value of the prop. By default the user won't be able to change it.

That's the case for your Kanban cards checklist. If you try clicking one of the task's checkboxes, it won't change. They are reflecting the value hardcoded in your cardsList array and will only change if you change the array itself.

Before heading back to the Kanban project, though, let's see another example. Start with a Search component that contains an input field:

```
import React, { Component } from 'react';
import {render} from 'react-dom';

class Search extends Component {
  render() {
    return (
      <div>
        Search Term: <input type="search" value="React" />
      </div>
    )
  }
}

render(<Search />, document.body);
```

This will render a form field displaying an immutable value of "React." Any user input will have no effect on the rendered element because React has declared the value to be "React," as shown in Figure 2-8.

Figure 2-8. *The form element*

CHAPTER 2 ■ INSIDE THE DOM ABSTRACTION

To be able to make this value change, you need to handle it as a component state. This way, any changes to the state value will be reflected in the interface.

```
class Search extends Component {
  constructor() {
    super();
    this.state = {
      searchTerm: "React"
    };
  }

  render() {
    return (
      <div>
        Search Term:
        <input type="search" value={this.state.searchTerm} />
      </div>
    )
  }
}
```

You could even give the end user the ability to update the state value using the onChange event.

```
class Search extends Component {
  constructor() {
    super();
    this.state = {
      searchTerm: "React"
    };
  }

  handleChange(event) {
    this.setState({searchTerm: event.target.value});
  }

  render() {
    return (
      <div>
        Search Term:
        <input type="search" value={this.state.searchTerm}
               onChange={this.handleChange.bind(this)} />
      </div>
    )
  }
}
```

This may look like a convoluted way to deal with forms, but it has the following advantages:

- It stays true to the React way of handling components. The state is kept out of the interface, and is entirely managed in your JavaScript code.

- This pattern makes it easy to implement interfaces that respond to or validate user interactions. For example, you could very easily limit the user input to 50 characters:

```
this.setState({searchTerm: event.target.value.substr(0, 50)});
```

Special Cases

There are a few special cases to remember when creating controlled form components: TextArea and Select.

TextArea

In HTML, the value of <textarea> is usually set using its children:

```
<textarea>This is the description.</textarea>
```

For HTML, this easily allows developers to supply multiline values. However, since React is JavaScript, you do not have string limitations (you use \n if you want newlines, for example). To keep consistent across other form elements, React uses the value prop to set <textarea> values:

```
<textarea value="This is a description." />
```

Select

In HTML, you set the selected option using the "selected" attribute on the option tag. In React, in order to make components easier to manipulate, the following format is adopted instead:

```
<select value="B">
 <option value="A">Mobile</option>
 <option value="B">Work</option>
 <option value="C">Home</option>
</select>
```

Uncontrolled Components

Controlled components adhere to React's principles and have their advantages. While uncontrolled components are an anti-pattern for how most other components are constructed in React, sometimes you don't need to oversee the user input field by field.

This is especially true in longer forms, where you want to let the user fill in the fields and then process everything when the user is done.

Any input that does not supply a value is an uncontrolled component, and the value of the rendered element will reflect the user's input. For example,

```
return (
  <form>
    <div className="formGroup">
      Name: <input name="name" type="text" />
    </div>
    <div className="formGroup">
      E-mail: <input name="email" type="mail" />
    </div>
    <button type="submit">Submit</button>
  </form>
)
```

will render two input fields that start off with an empty value. Any user input will be immediately reflected by the rendered elements.

■ **Tip**   If you want to set up an initial value for an uncontrolled form component, use the `defaultValue` prop instead of `value`.

It's still possible to handle uncontrolled component forms using onSubmit, like so:

```
handleSubmit(event) {
  console.log("Submitted values are: ",
              event.target.name.value,
              event.target.email.value);
  event.preventDefault();
}

render() {
  return (
    <form onSubmit={this.handleSubmit}>
      <div className="formGroup">
        Name: <input name="name" type="text" />
      </div>
      <div className="formGroup">
        E-mail: <input name="email" type="mail" />
      </div>
      <button type="submit">Submit</button>
    </form>
  )
}
```

Kanban App: Creating a Task Form

Regarding your Kanban app, you already have controlled components: the tasks checkboxes. Let's add an uncontrolled component this time: a text field to include new tasks.

```
class CheckList extends Component {
  render(){
    let tasks = this.props.tasks.map((task) => (...));
    return (
      <div className="checklist">
        <ul>{tasks}</ul>
        <input type="text"
               className="checklist--add-task"
               placeholder="Type then hit Enter to add a task" />
      </div>
    )
  }
}
```

Since you didn't specify a value prop, the user can freely write inside the text field. In the next chapter, you will wire the form fields in the checklist to add and mark tasks as done.

To finish, let's add some CSS to style the form element:

```
.checklist--add-task {
  border: 1px dashed #bbb;
  width: 100%;
  padding: 10px;
  margin-top: 5px;
  border-radius: 3px;
}
```

Virtual DOM Under the Hood

As you've seen so far, one of React's key design decisions is to make the API seem like it re-renders the whole app on every update. DOM manipulation is a slow task for a variety of reasons, so in order to make this possible in a performant way, React implements a virtual DOM. Instead of updating the actual DOM every time the application state changes, React simply creates virtual tree that looks like the DOM state that you want. Then it figures out how to make the DOM look like this efficiently without recreating all of the DOM nodes.

This process of finding the minimum number of changes that must be made in order to make the virtual DOM tree and the actual DOM tree identical is called reconciliation, and in general it is a very complex and extremely expensive operation. Even after many iterations and optimizations, this remains a very difficult and time-consuming problem. To make this tractable, React makes a few assumptions about how typical applications work that allow for a much faster algorithm in practical use cases. Some assumptions include:

- When comparing nodes in the DOM tree, if the nodes are of different types (say, changing a div to a span), React is going to treat them as two different sub-trees, throw away the first one, and build/insert the second one.

- The same logic is used for custom components. If they are not of the same type, React is not going to even try to match what they render. It is just going to remove the first one from the DOM and insert the second one.

- If the nodes are of the same type, there are two possible ways React will handle this:

  - If it's a DOM element (such as changing `<div id="before" />` to `<div id="after" />`), React will only change attributes and styles (without replacing the element tree).

  - If it's a custom component (such as changing `<Contact details={false} />` to `<Contact details={true} />`), React will not replace the component. Instead, it will send the new properties to the current mounted component. This will end up triggering a new `render()` on the component, and the process will reinitiate with the new result.

Keys

Although React's Virtual DOM and differing algorithms are very smart, in order to be fast, React makes some assumptions and takes a naive approach in some cases. Lists of repeating items are especially tricky to handle. To understand why, let's start with an example. Listings 2-1 and 2-2 represent a previous and current render.

Listing 2-1. Example List

`<li>Orange</li> <li>Banana</li>`

Listing 2-2. Example List After New Render

`<li>Apple</li> <li>Orange</li>`

The difference between the two lists seems pretty obvious, but which is the best approach to transform one list into the other? Adding a new item (Apple) to the beginning of the list and deleting the last one (Banana) is a possible operation, but changing the last item's name and position is also a possibility. In bigger lists, different possibilities arise and each of them can possibly cause side effects. Considering that nodes can be inserted, deleted, substituted, and moved, it is pretty hard to determine best approaches for all possible cases with an algorithm.

For this reason, React introduced the key attribute. Keys are unique identifiers that allow for fast lookups between trees for finding insertions, deletions, substitutions, and moves. Every time you create components in a loop, it's a good idea to provide a key for each child in order to help the React Library match and avoid performance bottlenecks.

Kanban App: Keys

Your previous Kanban app example is already warning about child elements without keys in the browser console (see Figure 2-9).

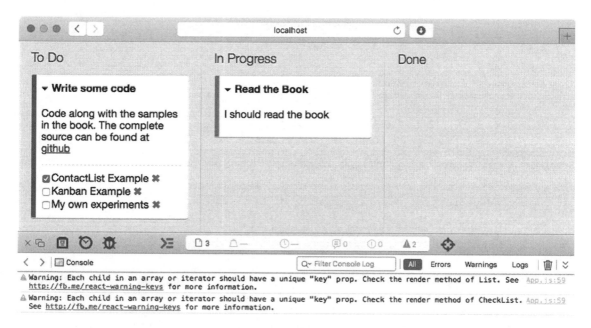

Figure 2-9. *A React warning about missing key props on the List and Checklist components*

The key prop can contain any value that is unique and constant. Your card's data contains an ID for each card. Let's use it as the *key* prop in the List component:

```
class List extends Component {
  render() {
    let cards = this.props.cards.map((card) => {
      return <Card key={card.id}
                   id={card.id}
                   title={card.title}
                   description={card.description}
                   color={card.color}
                   tasks={card.tasks} />
    });

    return (
      <div className="list">
        <h1>{this.props.title}</h1>
        {cards}
      </div>
    )
  }
}
```

You also have an array in Checklist. Let's add a key there, too:

```
class CheckList extends Component {
  render(){
    let tasks = this.props.tasks.map((task) => (
      <li key={task.id} className="checklist__task">
        <input type="checkbox" defaultChecked={task.done} />
        {task.name}{' '}
        <a href="#" className="checklist__task--remove" />
      </li>
    ));
    return (...);
  }
}
```

Refs

In the React way of working, when rendering a component, you're always dealing with the virtual DOM. If you change a component's state or send new props to a child, for example, they are reactively rendered to the virtual DOM. React will then update the actual DOM after the reconciliation phase.

This means that as developers you're never touching the real DOM. In some cases, though, you may find yourself wanting to "reach out" for the actual DOM markup rendered by a component. Think twice before manipulating the actual DOM because in almost every case there's a clearer way to structure your code within the React model. However, for the few cases where it still might be necessary or beneficial, React provides an escape hatch known as refs.

Refs can be used as a string prop on any component, like so:

```
<input ref="myInput" />
```

The referenced DOM markup can then be accessed via this.refs, like so:

```
let input = this.refs.myInput;
let inputValue = input.value;
let inputRect = input.getBoundingClientRect();
```

In this book, we will use refs very sparingly because there are few circumstances where they are really necessary. As an example, let's create a component consisting of only a text input and a button that, when clicked, focuses the text input:

```
class FocusText extends Component {
  handleClick() {
    // Explicitly focus the text input using the raw DOM API.
    this.refs.myTextInput.focus();
  }
  render() {
    // The ref attribute adds a reference to the component to
    // this.refs when the component is mounted.
```

```
  return (
    <div>
      <input type="text" ref="myTextInput" />
      <input
        type="button"
        value="Focus the text input"
        onClick={this.handleClick.bind(this)}
      />
    </div>
  );
}
}
```

Summary

In this chapter, you examined the details about React's DOM abstraction and the techniques the library uses to achieve fast performance, like event delegation and its diff and reconciliation characteristics (including the need for key props). You also learned about JSX in depth (and how React can be used without JSX, if desired), inline styles, and forms.

CHAPTER 3

■ ■ ■

Architecting Applications with Components

The previous chapters provided an overview of React. You saw that React is all about bringing a component-based architecture to interface building. You understood the evolutionary approach of bringing HTML together with JavaScript to describe components and achieve separation of concerns not by separating technologies or languages, but by having discreet, isolated, reusable, and composable components.

This chapter will cover how to structure a complex user interface made of nested components. You will see the importance of exposing a component API through propTypes, understand how data flows in a React application, and explore techniques on how to compose components.

Prop Validation

When creating components, remember that they can be composed into bigger components and reused (in the same project, in other projects, by other developers). Therefore, it is a good practice to make explicit in your components which props can be used, which ones are required, and which types of values they accept. This can be done by declaring propTypes. propTypes help document your components, which benefits future development in two ways.

1. You can easily open up a component and check which props are required and what type they should be.

2. When things get messed up, React will give you an error message in the console, saying which props are wrong/missing and the render method that caused the problem.

propTypes are defined as a class constructor property. For example, given this Greeter React component

```
import React, { Component } from 'react';
import { render } from 'react-dom';

class Greeter extends Component {
  render() {
    return (
      <h1>{this.props.salutation}</h1>
    )
  }
}

render(<Greeter salutation="Hello World" />, document.getElementById('root'));
```

51

the *salutation* prop needs to be a string and is required (you can't render unless a salutation is provided). To achieve this, you have to define the propTypes as a class constructor property, like this:

```
import React, { Component, PropTypes } from 'react';
import { render } from 'react-dom';

class Greeter extends Component {
  render() {
    return (
      <h1>{this.props.salutation}</h1>
    )
  }
}
Greeter.propTypes = {
  salutation: PropTypes.string.isRequired
}

render(<Greeter salutation="Hello World" />, document.getElementById('root'));
```

If the requirements of the propTypes are not met when the component is instantiated, a `console.warn` will be logged. For example, if you try to render a Greeter component without any props

```
React.render(<Greeter />, document.getElementById('root'));
```

the warning will be

```
Warning: Failed propType: Required prop `salutation` was not specified in `Greeter`.
```

For optional props, simple leave the `.isRequired` off, in which case the prop type will only be checked by React if a value is provided.

Default Prop Values

You can also provide a default prop value in case none is provided. The syntax is similar: define a `defaultProps` object as a constructor property.

You could, for example, leave the prop *salutation* optional (by removing the isRequired) and give it a default value of "Hello World":

```
class Greeter extends Component {
  render() {
    return (
      <h1>{this.props.salutation}</h1>
    )
  }
}

Greeter.propTypes = {
  salutation: PropTypes.string
}
```

```
Greeter.defaultProps = {
  salutation: "Hello World"
}
```

```
render(<Greeter />, document.getElementById('root'));
```

Now, if no salutation prop is provided, your component will render a default "Hello World". If a salutation is provided, though, it needs to be of type string.

As said earlier, you are not required to use propTypes in your application, but they provide a good way to describe the API of your component, and it is a good practice to always declare them.

Built-in propType Validators

React propTypes export a range of validators that can be used to make sure the data you receive is valid. By default, all of the propTypes in Tables 3-1 through 3-3 are optional, but you can chain with isRequired to make sure a warning is shown if the prop isn't provided.

Table 3-1. *JavaScript Primitives PropTypes*

Validator	Description
PropTypes.array	Prop must be an array.
PropTypes.bool	Prop must be a Boolean value (true/false).
PropTypes.func	Prop must be a function.
PropTypes.number	Prop must be a number (or a value that can be parsed into a number).
PropTypes.object	Prop must be an object.
PropTypes.string	Prop must be a string.

Table 3-2. *Combined Primitives PropTypes*

Validator	Description

PropTypes.oneOfType	An object that could be one of many types, such as
	
	`PropTypes.oneOfType([`
	`  PropTypes.string,`
	`  PropTypes.number,`
	`  PropTypes.instanceOf(Message)`
	`])`

PropTypes.arrayOf	Prop must be an array of a certain type, such as `PropTypes.arrayOf(PropTypes.number)`
PropTypes.objectOf	Prop must be an object with property values of a certain type, such as `PropTypes.objectOf(PropTypes.number)`

PropTypes.shape	Prop must be an object taking on a particular shape. It needs the same set of properties, such as
	
	`PropTypes.shape({`
	`  color: PropTypes.string,`
	`  fontSize: PropTypes.number`
	`})`

Table 3-3. *Special PropTypes*

Validator	Description
PropTypes.node	Prop can be of any value that can be rendered: numbers, strings, elements, or an array.
PropTypes.element	Prop must be a React element.
PropTypes.instanceOf	Prop must be instance of a given class (this uses JS's instanceof operator.), such as PropTypes.instanceOf(Message).
PropTypes.oneOf	Ensure that your prop is limited to specific values by treating it as an enum, like PropTypes.oneOf(['News', 'Photos']).

Kanban App: Defining Prop Types

The correct approach is to declare a component's propTypes as soon as you create the component itself, but given that you just learned about them and their importance, let's review all of the Kanban App's components and declare its propTypes (as shown in Listings 3-1 to 3-4).

Listing 3-1. PropTypes for the KanbanBoard Component

```
import React, { Component, PropTypes } from 'react';
import List from './List';

class KanbanBoard extends Component {
  render() {...}
};
KanbanBoard.propTypes = {
  cards: PropTypes.arrayOf(PropTypes.object)
};

export default KanbanBoard;
```

Listing 3-2. PropTypes for the List Component

```
import React, { Component, PropTypes } from 'react';
import Card from './Card';

class List extends Component {
  render() {...}
};
List.propTypes = {
  title: PropTypes.string.isRequired,
  cards: PropTypes.arrayOf(PropTypes.object)
};

export default List;
```

Listing 3-3. PropTypes for the Card Component

```
import React, { Component, PropTypes } from 'react';
import marked from 'marked';
import CheckList from './CheckList';

class Card extends Component {
  constructor() {...}
  toggleDetails() {...}
  render() {...}
};
Card.propTypes = {
  id: PropTypes.number,
  title: PropTypes.string,
  description: PropTypes.string,
  color: PropTypes.string,
  tasks: PropTypes.arrayOf(PropTypes.object)
};

export default Card;
```

Listing 3-4. PropTypes for the Checklist Component

```
import React, { Component, PropTypes } from 'react';

class CheckList extends Component {
  render() {...}
};
CheckList.propTypes = {
  cardId: PropTypes.number,
  tasks: PropTypes.arrayOf(PropTypes.object)
};


export default CheckList;
```

Custom PropType Validators

As mentioned, React offers a great suite of built-in propType validators that cover pretty much every basic use case, but there may still be some scenarios where one might need a more specific validator.

Validators are basically just functions that receive a list of properties, the name of the property to check, and the name of the component. The function must then return either nothing (if the tested prop was valid) or an instance of an Error suitable for the invalid prop.

Kanban App: Defining a Custom PropType Validator

In your Kanban app, the Card component has a title, a description, and other properties. By way of an example, you're going to write a validator that will warn if the card title is longer than 80 characters. The code is shown in Listing 3-5, and a sample card failing the custom propType validator is represented in Figure 3-1.

Listing 3-5. Custom PropType Validator on the Card Component

```
import React, { Component, PropTypes } from 'react';
import marked from 'marked';
import CheckList from './CheckList';

let titlePropType = (props, propName, componentName) => {
  if (props[propName]) {
    let value = props[propName];
    if (typeof value !== 'string' || value.length > 80) {
      return new Error(
        `${propName} in ${componentName}  is longer than 80 characters`
      );
    }
  }
}

class Card extends Component {
  constructor() {...}
  toggleDetails() {...}
  render() {...}
}
Card.propTypes = {
  id: PropTypes.number,
  title: titlePropType,
  description: PropTypes.string,
  color: PropTypes.string,
  tasks: PropTypes.arrayOf(PropTypes.object)
};

export default Card;
```

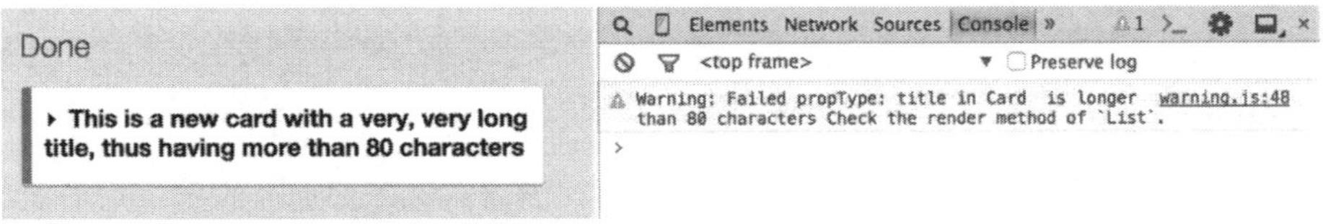

Figure 3-1. *A new card failing the custom propType validation*

■ **Note**   In this sample code, you use the new JavaScript ES6 syntax for string interpolation. You can learn more about this and other ES6 language features used throughout this book in the online Appendix C.

Component Composition Strategies and Best Practices

This section will cover strategies and best practices for creating React applications by composing components. You will discuss how to achieve state management, data fetching, and control over user interactions in a structured and organized way.

Stateful and Pure Components

So far you've seen that components can have data as props and state.

- **Props** are a component's configuration. They are received from above and immutable as far as the component receiving them is concerned.

- **State** starts with a default value defined in the component's constructor and then suffers from mutations in time (mostly generated from user events). A component manages its own state internally, and every time the state changes, the component is rendered again.

In React's components, state is optional. In fact, in most React applications the components are split into two types: those that manage state (stateful components) and those that don't have internal state and just deal with the display of data (pure components).

The goal of pure components is to write them so they only accept props and are responsible for rendering those props into a view. This makes it easier to reuse and test those components.

However, sometimes you need to respond to user input, a server request, or the passage of time. For this, you use state. Stateful components usually are higher on the component hierarchy and wrap one or more stateful or pure components.

It's a good practice to keep most of an app's components stateless. Having your application's state scattered across multiple components makes it harder to track. It also reduces predictability because the way your application works becomes less transparent. There's also the potential to introduce some very hard-to-untangle situations in your code.

Which Components Should Be Stateful?

Recognizing which components should own state is often the most challenging part for React newcomers to understand. When in doubt, follow this four-step checklist. For each piece of state in your application,

- Identify every component that renders something based on that state.

- Find a common owner component (a single component above all the components that need the state in the hierarchy).

- Either the common owner or another component higher up in the hierarchy should own the state.

- If you can't find a component where it makes sense to own the state, create a new component simply to hold the state and add it somewhere in the hierarchy above the common owner component.

To illustrate this concept, let's build a very simple contact app, as shown in Figure 3-2.

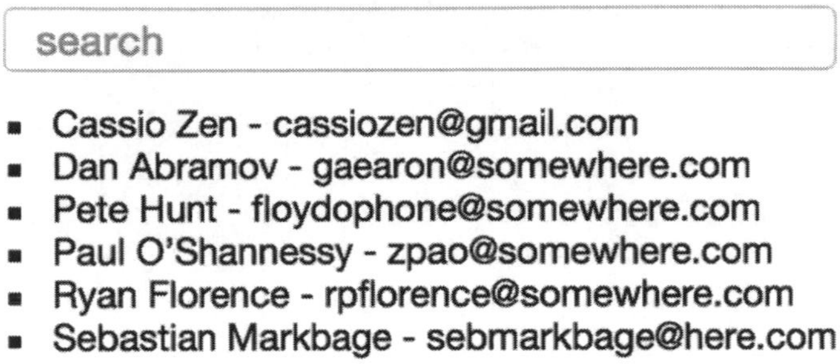

Figure 3-2. *The sample contacts app with search*

The component hierarchy is

- **ContactsApp**: The main component
  - **SearchBar**: Shows an input field so the user can filter the contacts
  - **ContactList**: Loops through data, creating a series of ContactItems
    - **ContactItem**: Displays the contact data

In the code, the contact list data is stored in a global variable. In a real app, the data would probably be fetched remotely, but for the sake of simplicity, it will be hard-coded on this example. Listing 3-6 shows the complete code including the ContactsApp, SearchBar, ContactList, and ContactItem components (as well as their propTypes).

Listing 3-6. ContacsApp Code

```
import React, { Component, PropTypes } from 'react';
import { render } from 'react-dom';

// Main component. Renders a SearchBar and a ContactList
class ContactsApp extends Component {
  render(){
    return(
      <div>
        <SearchBar />
        <ContactList contacts={this.props.contacts} />
      </div>
    )
  }
}
ContactsApp.propTypes = {
  contacts: PropTypes.arrayOf(PropTypes.object)
}
```

```
class SearchBar extends Component {
  render(){
    return <input type="search" placeholder="search" />
  }
}

class ContactList extends Component {
  render(){
    return(
      <ul>
        {this.props.contacts.map(
          (contact) => <ContactItem key={contact.email}
                                    name={contact.name}
                                    email={contact.email} />
        )}
      </ul>
    )
  }
}
ContactList.propTypes = {
  contacts: PropTypes.arrayOf(PropTypes.object)
}

class ContactItem extends Component {
  render() {
    return <li>{this.props.name} - {this.props.email}</li>
  }
}
ContactItem.propTypes = {
  name: PropTypes.string.isRequired,
  email: PropTypes.string.isRequired,
}

let contacts = [
  { name: "Cassio Zen", email: "cassiozen@gmail.com" },
  { name: "Dan Abramov", email: "gaearon@somewhere.com" },
  { name: "Pete Hunt", email: "floydophone@somewhere.com" },
  { name: "Paul O'Shannessy", email: "zpao@somewhere.com" },
  { name: "Ryan Florence", email: "rpflorence@somewhere.com" },
  { name: "Sebastian Markbage", email: "sebmarkbage@here.com" },
]

render(<ContactsApp contacts={contacts} />, document.getElementById('root'));
```

At this moment, all of your application's components are pure; they only render data received via props. However, you need to add the filter behavior to your app, and you will need to store mutable state to achieve that. Let's run through the checklist to figure out where state in this application should live.

ContactList needs to filter the contacts based on state, and SearchBar needs to display the search text. The common owner component is ContactsApp.

It conceptually makes sense for the filter text to live as a state in ContactsApp. The ContactsApp in turn will pass the filter text down as props. The SearchBar component will use it as value for the input field and the ContactList will use it to filter the contacts. Let's implement this component by component (as shown in Listings 3-7 through 3-9). In Listing 3-8, the SearchBar component will receive the filterText as a prop and set the input field value to this prop. The input field now is a controlled form component (as seen in Chapter 2). In Listing 3-9, the ContactList component also receives filterText as a prop and filters the contacts to show based on its value.

Listing 3-7. Updated Stateful ContactsApp Component

```
class ContactsApp extends Component {
  constructor(){
    super();
    this.state={
      filterText: ''
    };
  }
  render(){
    return(
      <div>
        <SearchBar filterText={this.state.filterText} />
        <ContactList contacts={this.props.contacts}
                     filterText={this.state.filterText}/>
      </div>
    )
  }
}
ContactsApp.propTypes = {...}
```

Listing 3-8. The SearchBar Component

```
class SearchBar extends Component {
  render(){
    return <input type="search" placeholder="search"
                  value={this.props.filterText} />
  }
}
// Don't forget to add the new propType requirements
SearchBar.propTypes = {
  filterText: PropTypes.string.isRequired
}
```

Listing 3-9. The ContactList Component

```
class ContactList extends Component {
  render(){
    let filteredContacts = this.props.contacts.filter(
      (contact) => contact.name.indexOf(this.props.filterText) !== -1
    );
```

```
      return(
        <ul>
          {filteredContacts.map(
            (contact) => <ContactItem key={contact.email}
                                      name={contact.name}
                                      email={contact.email} />
          )}
        </ul>
      )
    }
}
```

Now your application has only one stateful component on the top of the hierarchy and three pure components that display data received via props. The ContactList component filters the data to show based on the `filterText` prop (you can try right now by changing the ContactsApp's `filterText` state on the code), but the user can't type anything on the search field because it can't change its state from inside the SearchBar component; the state is owned by the parent component.

In the next section, you will learn how child (pure) components can communicate back to parent (stateful) components.

Data Flow and Component Communication

In a React application, data flows down in the hierarchy of components: React makes this data flow explicit to make it easy to understand how your program works.

In non-trivial apps, though, nested child components need to communicate with the parent component. One method to achieve this is through callbacks passed by parent components as props.

Let's use the ContactApp example to illustrate this. State belongs to the topmost ContactApp component and is passed down as props to SearchBar and ContactList.

You want to make sure that whenever the user changes the search form, you update the state to reflect the user input. Since components should only update their own state, ContactApp will pass a callback to SearchBar that will fire whenever the state should be updated. You can use the onChange event on the inputs to be notified of it. On the ContactsApp, you create a local function to change the filterText state and pass this function down as a prop to the searchBar (Listing 3-10).

Listing 3-10. Creating a local function

```
class ContactsApp extends Component {
  constructor(){...}

  handleUserInput(searchTerm){
    this.setState({filterText:searchTerm})
  }

  render(){
    return(
      <div>
        <SearchBar filterText={this.state.filterText}
                   onUserInput={this.handleUserInput.bind(this)} />
```

```
        <ContactList contacts={this.props.contacts}
                     filterText={this.state.filterText}/>
      </div>
    )
  }
}
ContactsApp.propTypes = {
  contacts: PropTypes.arrayOf(PropTypes.object)
}
```

The SearchBar component receives the callback as a prop and calls on the onChange event of the input field (Listing 3-11).

Listing 3-11. Receiving the callback and calling in the onChange

```
class SearchBar extends Component {
  handleChange(event){
    this.props.onUserInput(event.target.value)
  }

  render(){
    return <input type="search"
                  placeholder="search"
                  value={this.props.filterText}
                  onChange={this.handleChange.bind(this)} />
  }
}
SearchBar.propTypes = {
  onUserInput: PropTypes.func.isRequired,
  filterText: PropTypes.string.isRequired
}
```

The search in action and the complete code are shown in Figure 3-3 and Listing 3-12.

- Pete Hunt - floydophone@somewhere.com
- Paul O'Shannessy - zpao@somewhere.com

Figure 3-3. *The Contacts app's filter in action*

Listing 3-12. The Complete Contact App Code

```
import React, { Component, PropTypes } from 'react';
import { render } from 'react-dom';

// Main (stateful) component.
// Renders a SearchBar and a ContactList
// Passes down filterText state and handleUserInput callback as props
```

```
class ContactsApp extends Component {
  constructor(){
    super();
    this.state={
      filterText: ''
    };
  }

  handleUserInput(searchTerm){
    this.setState({filterText:searchTerm})
  }

  render(){
    return(
      <div>
        <SearchBar filterText={this.state.filterText}
                   onUserInput={this.handleUserInput.bind(this)} />
        <ContactList contacts={this.props.contacts}
                     filterText={this.state.filterText}/>
      </div>
    )
  }
}
ContactsApp.propTypes = {
  contacts: PropTypes.arrayOf(PropTypes.object)
}


// Pure component that receives 2 props from the parent
// filterText (string) and onUserInput (callback function)
class SearchBar extends Component {
  handleChange(event){
    this.props.onUserInput(event.target.value)
  }

  render(){
    return <input type="search"
                  placeholder="search"
                  value={this.props.filterText}
                  onChange={this.handleChange.bind(this)} />
  }
}
SearchBar.propTypes = {
  onUserInput: PropTypes.func.isRequired,
  filterText: PropTypes.string.isRequired
}

// Pure component that receives both contacts and filterText as props
// The component is responsible for actualy filtering the
// contacts before displaying them.
```

```
// It's considered a pure component because given the same
// contacts and filterText props the output will always be the same.
class ContactList extends Component {
  render(){
    let filteredContacts = this.props.contacts.filter(
      (contact) => contact.name.indexOf(this.props.filterText) !== -1
    );
    return(
      <ul>
        {filteredContacts.map(
          (contact) => <ContactItem key={contact.email}
                                    name={contact.name}
                                    email={contact.email} />
        )}
      </ul>
    )
  }
}
ContactList.propTypes = {
  contacts: PropTypes.arrayOf(PropTypes.object),
  filterText: PropTypes.string.isRequired
}

class ContactItem extends Component {
  render() {
    return <li>{this.props.name} - {this.props.email}</li>
  }
}
ContactItem.propTypes = {
  name: PropTypes.string.isRequired,
  email: PropTypes.string.isRequired
}

let contacts = [
  { name: "Cassio Zen", email: "cassiozen@gmail.com" },
  { name: "Dan Abramov", email: "gaearon@somewhere.com" },
  { name: "Pete Hunt", email: "floydophone@somewhere.com" },
  { name: "Paul O'Shannessy", email: "zpao@somewhere.com" },
  { name: "Ryan Florence", email: "rpflorence@somewhere.com" },
  { name: "Sebastian Markbage", email: "sebmarkbage@here.com" },
]

render(<ContactsApp contacts={contacts} />, document.getElementById('root'));
```

Component Lifecycle

When creating React components, it's possible to declare methods that will be automatically called in certain occasions throughout the lifecycle of the component. Understanding the role that each component lifecycle method plays and the order in which they are invoked will enable you to perform certain actions when a component is created or destroyed. It also gives you the opportunity to react to props or state changes accordingly.

Moreover, an implicit knowledge about the lifecycle methods is also necessary for performance optimizations (covered in Chapter 7) and to organize your components in a Flux architecture (covered in Chapter 6).

Lifecycle Phases and Methods

To get a clear idea of the lifecycle, you need to differentiate between the initial component creation phase, state and props changes, triggered updates, and the component's unmouting phase. Figures 3-4 to 3-7 demonstrate which methods are called on each phase.

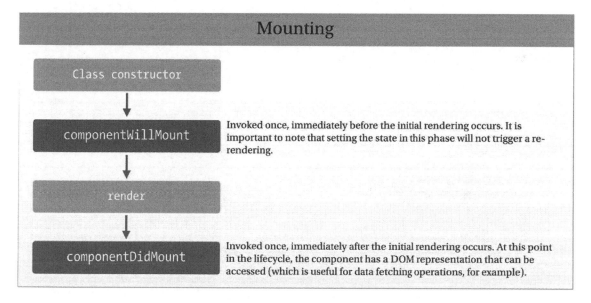

Figure 3-4. *Lifecycle methods invoked on the mounting cycle*

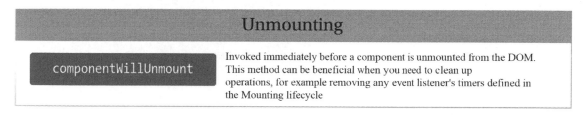

Figure 3-5. *Lifecycle method invoked on the unmounting cycle*

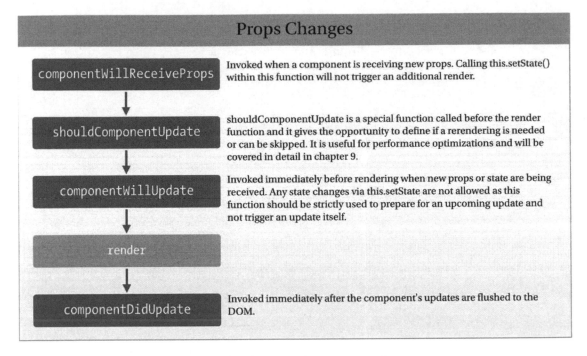

Figure 3-6. *Lifecycle methods invoked when the props of a component change*

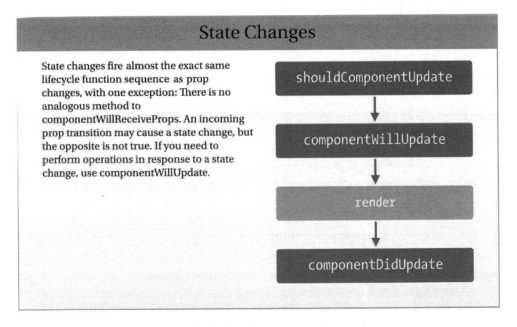

Figure 3-7. *Lifecycle methods invoked when the component's state change*

Lifecycle Functions in Practice: Data Fetching

To illustrate the usage of lifecycle methods in practice, imagine you want to change your last Contacts application to fetch the contacts data remotely. Data fetching is not really a React subject; it's just plain JavaScript, but the important aspect to notice is that you do have to fetch the data on a specific lifecycle of the component, the componentDidMount lifecycle method.

Since this chapter is about strategies and good practices for component composition, it is also worth noting that you should avoid adding data fetching logic to a component that already has other responsibilities. A good practice, instead, is to create a new stateful component whose single responsibility is communicating with the remote API, and passing data and callbacks down as props. Some people call this type of component a *container component*.

You will use the idea of a container component in your Contacts app, so instead of adding the data-fetching logic to the existing ContactsApp component, you will create a new component called ContactsAppContainer on top of it. The old ContactsApp won't be changed in any way. It will continue to receive data via props.

■ **Note**   In this sample code, you use the new window.fetch function, which is an easier way to make web requests and handle responses than using XMLHttpRequest. At the time of this writing, only Chrome and Firefox support this new standard, so install and import the whatwg-fetch polyfill from npm. (Polyfill is browser fallback that allows specific functionality to work in browsers that do not have the support for that functionality built in.)

```
npm install --save whatwg-fetch
```

Let's start by moving the hard-coded data to a json file (the json file must be in the public or static folder, so it will be served by the development server), as shown in Figure 3-8. Your project folder structure may vary; the important thing to notice is that the file is in the public or static folder that will be served by the web server.

Figure 3-8. *The new contacts.json file*

The new `ContactsAppContainer` component is shown in Listing 3-13. No other components were changed, except that instead of rendering `ContactsApp` you now render `ContactsAppContainer` to the document (as shown in the last lines of the listing).

Listing 3-13. The New ContactsAppContainer

```
import React, { Component, PropTypes } from 'react';
import { render } from 'react-dom';
import 'whatwg-fetch';

class ContactsAppContainer extends Component {
  constructor(){
    super();
    this.state={
      contacts: []
    };
  }

  componentDidMount(){
    fetch('./contacts.json')
    .then((response) => response.json())
    .then((responseData) => {
      this.setState({contacts: responseData});
    })
```

```
      .catch((error) => {
        console.log('Error fetching and parsing data', error);
      });
    }

    render(){
      return (
        <ContactsApp contacts={this.state.contacts} />
      );
    }
  }

// No changes in any of the components bellow
class ContactsApp extends Component {
  constructor(){...}
  handleUserInput(searchTerm){...}
  render(){...}
}
ContactsApp.propTypes = {...}

class SearchBar extends Component {
  handleChange(event){...}
  render(){...}
}
SearchBar.propTypes = {...}

class ContactList extends Component {
  render(){...}
}
ContactList.propTypes = {...}

class ContactItem extends Component {
  render() {...}
}
ContactItem.propTypes = {...}

// You now render ContactAppContainer, instead of ContactsApp
render(<ContactsAppContainer />, document.getElementById('root'));
```

That's all for remote data fetching. If you reload the Contacts app in the browser, it will look like nothing has changed, but underneath it is now loading the contacts data from an external source.

A Brief Talk About Immutability

React provides a setState method to make changes to the component internal state. Be careful to always use the setState method to update the state of your component's UI and never manipulate this.state directly. As a rule of thumb, treat this.state as if it were immutable.

There are different reasons for this. For one, by manipulating this.state directly you are circumventing React's state management, which not only works against the React paradigm but can also be potentially dangerous because calling setState() afterwards may replace the mutation you made. Furthermore, manipulating this.state directly minimizes the possibilities for future performance improvements in the application.

You will learn about performance improvements in later chapters but in many cases it deals with object comparison and checking weather a `JavaScript` object has changed or not. As it turns out, this is a pretty expensive operation in JavaScript that can generate a lot of overhead, but there's a simpler and faster way: if any time an object is changed it's replaced instead edited in place, then the check is orders of magnitude faster (because you can simply compare object references, such as object1 === object2).

That's the basic idea of *immutability*. Instead of changing an object, replace it.

Immutability in Plain JavaScript

The main idea behind immutability is just to replace the object instead of changing it, and while this is absolutely possible in plain JavaScript, it's not the norm. If you're not careful, you may unintentionally mutate objects directly instead of replacing them. For example, let's say you have this stateful component that displays data about a voucher for an airline travel (the `render` method is omitted in this example because you are only investigating the component's state):

```javascript
import React, { Component } from 'react';
import { render } from 'react-dom';

class Voucher extends Component {
  constructor() {
    super(...arguments)
    this.state = {
      passengers:[
        'Simmon, Robert A.',
        'Taylor, Kathleen R.'
      ],
      ticket:{
        company: 'Dalta',
        flightNo: '0990',
        departure: {
          airport: 'LAS',
          time: '2016-08-21T10:00:00.000Z'
        },
        arrival: {
          airport: 'MIA',
          time: '2016-08-21T14:41:10.000Z'
        },
        codeshare: [
          {company:'GL', flightNo:'9840'},
          {company:'TM', flightNo:'5010'}
        ]
      }
    }
  }

  render() {...}
}
```

Now, suppose you want to add a passenger to the passengers array. If you're not careful, you may unintentionally mutate the component state directly. For example,

```
let updatedPassengers = this.state.passengers;
updatedPassengers.push('Mitchell, Vincent M.');
this.setState({passengers:updatedPassengers});
```

The problem in this sample code, as you may have guessed, is that in JavaScript, objects and arrays are passed by reference. This means that when you say updatedPassengers=this.state.passengers you're not making a copy of the array; you are just creating a new reference to the same array that is in the current component's state. Furthermore, by using the array method push, you end up mutating its state directly.

To create actual array copies in JavaScript, you need to use non-destructive methods, that is, methods that will return an array with the desired mutations instead of actually changing the original one. map, filter, and concat are just a few examples of non-destructive array methods. Let's reapproach the earlier problem of adding a new passenger to the array, this time using the Array's concat method:

```
// updatedPassengers is a new array, returned from concat
let updatedPassengers = this.state.passengers.concat('Mitchell, Vincent M.');
this.setState({passengers:updatedPassengers});
```

There are also alternatives for generating new objects with mutations in JavaScript, like using Object.assign. Object.assign works by merging all properties of all given objects to the target object:

```
Object.assign(target, source_1, ..., source_n)
```

It first copies all enumerable properties of source 1 to the target, then those of source_2, etc. For example, to change the flightNo on the ticket state key, you could do this:

```
// updatedTicket is a new object with the original properties of this.state.ticket
// merged with the new flightNo.
let updatedTicket = Object.assign({}, this.state.ticket, {flightNo:'1010'});
this.setState({ticket:updatedTicket});
```

■ **Note** At the time of this writing, only Chrome and Firefox supported the new method Object.assign, but the good news is that Babel (the ES6 compiler you're using together with Webpack) already provides the polyfill for other browsers. All you need to do is install with 'npm install --save babel-polyfill' and import it with import 'babel-polyfill'.

Nested Objects

Although an array's non-destructive methods and Object.assign will do the job on most cases, it gets really tricky if your state contains nested objects or arrays. This is because of a characteristic of the JavaScript language: objects and arrays are passed by reference, and neither the array's non-destructive methods nor Object.assign make deep copies. In practice, this means the the nested objects and arrays in your newly returned object will only be references to the same objects and arrays on the old object.

Let's see this in practice, given the ticket object you were working on:

```
let originalTicket={
  company: 'Dalta',
  flightNo: '0990',
  departure: {
    airport: 'LAS',
    time: '2016-08-21T10:00:00.000Z'
  },
  arrival: {
    airport: 'MIA',
    time: '2016-08-21T14:41:10.000Z'
  },
  codeshare: [
    {company:'GL', flightNo:'9840'},
    {company:'TM', flightNo:'5010'}
  ]
}
```

If you create a ticket object with the Object.assign, like

```
let newTicket = Object.assign({}, originalTicket, {flightNo '5690'}}
```

You will end up with two objects in memory, as shown in Figure 3-9.

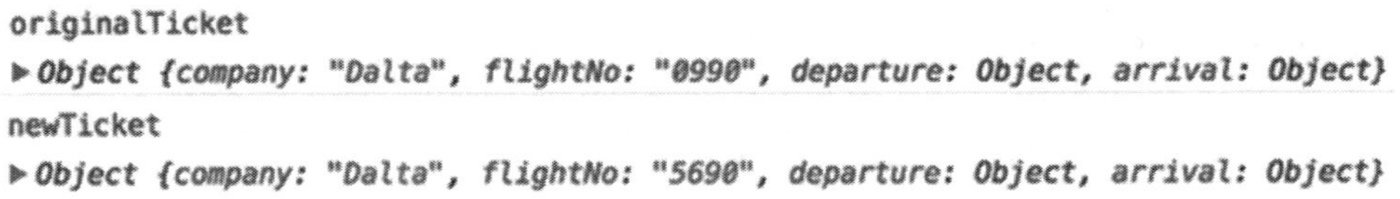

```
originalTicket
▶ Object {company: "Dalta", flightNo: "0990", departure: Object, arrival: Object}
newTicket
▶ Object {company: "Dalta", flightNo: "5690", departure: Object, arrival: Object}
```

Figure 3-9. *Note that originalTicket and newTicket have different flightNo properties*

However, given the default JavaScript behavior of passing arrays and objects by reference, the departure and arrival objects on newTicket aren't separate copies; they're references to the same originalTicket object. If you try to change the arrival object on newTicket, for example,

```
newTicket.arrival.airport="MCO"
```

Figure 3-10 shows both object representations now.

```
originalTicket
▼ Object {company: "Dalta", flightNo: "0990", departure: Object, arrival: Object} ▣
  ▼ arrival: Object
      airport: ("MCO")
      time: "2016-08-21T14:41:10.000Z"
newTicket
▼ Object {company: "Dalta", flightNo: "5690", departure: Object, arrival: Object} ▣
  ▼ arrival: Object
      airport: ("MCO")
      time: "2016-08-21T14:41:10.000Z"
```

Figure 3-10. *originalTicket and newTicket arrival keys references the same object*

Again, this has nothing to do with React; it's just the default JavaScript behavior, but this default behavior can and will impact React if you want to mutate a component state with nested objects. You could try making a deep clone of the original object, but this isn't a good option because it is expensive in performance and even impossible to do in some cases. The good news is that there is a simple solution: the React add-ons package provides a utility function (called immutability helper) that helps update more complex and nested models.

React Immutability Helper

React's add-on package provides an immutability helper called update. The update function works on regular JavaScript objects and arrays and helps manipulates these objects as if they were immutable: instead of actually changing the object, it always return a new, mutated object.

To begin with, you'll need to install and require the library:

```
npm install –save react-addons-update
```

Then, in your javascript file, import is using

```
import update from 'react-addons-update';
```

The update method accepts two parameters. The first one is the object or array that you want to update. The second parameter is an object that describes WHERE the mutation should take place and WHAT kind of mutation you want to make. So, given this simple object:

```
let student = {name:'John Caster', grades:['A','C','B']}
```

to create a copy of this object with a new, updated grade, the syntax for update is

```
let newStudent = update(student, {grades:{$push: ['A']}})
```

The object {grades:{$push: ['A']}} informs, from left to right, that the update function should

1. Locate the key grades ("where" the mutation will take place).

2. Push a new value to the array ("what" kind of mutation should happen).

If you want to completely change the array, you use the command $set instead of $push:

```
let newStudent = update(student, {grades:{$set: ['A','A','B']}})
```

There's no limit to the amount of nesting you can do. Let's head back to your voucher ticket object, where you were having trouble creating a new object with a different arrival information. The original object was

```
let originalTicket={
  company: 'Dalta',
  flightNo: '0990',
  departure: {
    airport: 'LAS',
    time: '2016-08-21T10:00:00.000Z'
  },
  arrival: {
    airport: 'MIA',
    time: '2016-08-21T14:41:10.000Z'
  },
  codeshare: [
    {company:'GL', flightNo:'9840'},
    {company:'TM', flightNo:'5010'}
  ]
}
```

The information you want to change (airport) is nested three levels deep. In React's update addon, all you need to do is keep nesting objects with their names on the objects that describe the mutation:

```
let newTicket = update(originalTicket, {
                        arrival: {
                          airport: {$set: 'MCO'}
                        }
                      });
```

Now only the new Ticket has the arrival airport set to "MCO". The original ticket maintains the original arrival airport, as shown in Figure 3-11.

```
originalTicket
▼ Object {company: "Dalta", flightNo: "0990", departure: Object, arrival: Object} 🔳
  ▼ arrival: Object
      airport: "MIA"
      time: "2016-08-21T14:41:10.000Z"

newTicket
▼ Object {company: "Dalta", flightNo: "5690", departure: Object, arrival: Object} 🔳
  ▼ arrival: Object
      airport: "MCO"
      time: "2016-08-21T14:41:10.000Z"
```

Figure 3-11. *originalTicket and newTicket now don't share the same arrival nested object*

Array Indexes

It's also possible to use array indexes to find WHERE a mutation should happen. For example, if you want to mutate the first codeshare object (the array elopement at index 0),

```
let newTicket = update(originalTicket,{
                        codeshare: {
                          0: { $set: {company:'AZ', flightNo:'7320'} }
                        }
                      });
```

Figure 3-12 shows the different objects with the newTicket array mutated.

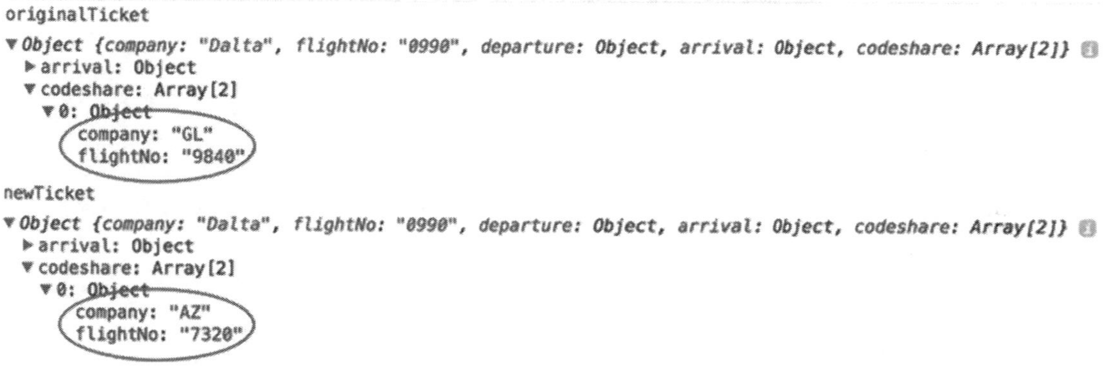

Figure 3-12. *Changes by array index using React's immutability helpers*

Available Commands

The available commands to determinate "what" kind of mutation should happen are shown in Table 3-4.

Table 3-4. *React Immutability Helper Commands*

Command	Description

$push	Similar to Array's push, it adds one or more elements to the end of an array. Example:
	
	```let initialArray = [1, 2, 3];```
	```let newArray = update(initialArray, {$push: [4]});```
	```// => [1, 2, 3, 4]```

$unshift	Similar to Array's unshift, it adds one or more elements to the beginning of an array. Example:
	
	```let initialArray = [1, 2, 3];```
	```let newArray = update(initialArray, {$unshift: [0]});```
	```// => [0,1, 2, 3]```

(continued)

Table 3-4. (*continued*)

Command	Description
$splice	Similar to Array's splice, it changes the content of an array by removing and/or adding new elements. The main syntactical difference here is that you should provide an array of arrays as a parameter, each individual array containing the splice parameters to operate on the array. Example:

	`let initial Array = [1, 2, 'a'];`
	`let newArray = update(initialArray, {$splice: [[2,1,3,4]]});`
	`// => [1, 2, 3, 4]`

$set	Replace the target entirely.
$merge	Merge the keys of the given object with the target. Example:

	`let ob. = {a: 5, b: 3};`
	`let newObj = update(obj, {$merge: {b: 6, c: 7}});`
	`// => {a: 5, b: 6, c: 7}`

$apply	Pass in the current value to the given function and update it with the new returned value. Example:

	`let obj = {a: 5, b: 3};`
	`let newObj = update(obj, {b: {$apply: (value) => value*2 }});`
	`// => {a: 5, b: 6}`

Kanban App: Adding (a Little) Complexity

To put all the new knowledge about components composition and state management in practice, you will connect the Kanban App Connect to an external API. You will fetch all the application's data from the server and manipulate tasks (delete, create, and toggle).

Fetching the Initial Cards from the External API

You will start by creating a new component at the top of your hierarchy. This container component will be used for data fetching/persistence. Create a new file named KanbanBoardContainer.js with a basic React component structure (as shown in Listing 3-14).

Listing 3-14. The New KanbanBoardContainer.js

```
import React, { Component } from 'react';
import KanbanBoard from './KanbanBoard';

class KanbanBoardContainer extends Component {
  constructor(){
    super(...arguments);
    this.state = {
      cards:[],
    };
  }
```

```
  render() {
    return <KanbanBoard cards={cards} />
  }
}

export default KanbanBoardContainer;
```

In the sequence, you fetch the data from the Kanban API Server. As you did earlier in this chapter, you use the new `window.fetch` function available on the latest generation of browsers. To make sure your app will run on other browsers as well, install the `fetch polyfill` from npm and save it as a dependency of the project:

```
npm install --save whatwg-fetch
```

For convenience, an online API for testing is provided at `http://kanbanapi.pro-ract.com`.

If you prefer to run locally, you can download the Kanban API Server from `www.apress.com` or from the book's github page at `https://github.com/pro-react`.

The only difference between the online API at `kanbanapi.pro-react.com` and the API Server is that to use the former you need to pass an authorization header (so the server can uniquely identify you and serve your own cards and tasks). The authorization can be any string that uniquely identifies your app or yourself (such a generic combination of characters or your e-mail address, for example). In both cases, a standard set of cards and tasks are already available on your first use so you can start testing immediately.

■ **Note**   The online Kanban rest API at `kanbanapi.pro-react.com` is provided for educational purposes only. As such, stored information will be reset after 24 hours of inactivity.

Also, please be careful about storing sensitive information on the `kanbanapi.pro-react.com` server. Although the server employs standard security measures, it is by definition not private.

The online API's terms of use statement is available at `http://kanbanapi.pro-react.com/terms`.

Let's start fetching the initial data for the application on the KanbanBoardContainer component, as shown in Listing 3-15. Note that you also add custom headers to the fetch command to make sure the server will respond properly.

Listing 3-15. Fetching Data Code

```
import React, { Component } from 'react';
import KanbanBoard from './KanbanBoard';
import 'whatwg-fetch';

// If you're running the server locally, the URL will be, by default, localhost:3000
// Also, the local server doesn't need an authorization header.
const API_URL = 'http://kanbanapi.pro-react.com';
const API_HEADERS = {
  'Content-Type': 'application/json',
  Authorization: 'any-string-you-like'// The Authorization is not needed for local server
};
```

```
class KanbanBoardContainer extends Component {
  constructor(){
    super(...arguments);
    this.state = {
      cards: []
    };
  }

  componentDidMount(){
    fetch(API_URL+'/cards', {headers: API_HEADERS})
    .then((response) => response.json())
    .then((responseData) => {
      this.setState({cards: responseData});
    })
    .catch((error) => {
      console.log('Error fetching and parsing data', error);
    });
  }

  render() {
    return <KanbanBoard cards={this.state.cards} />
  }
}

export default KanbanBoardContainer;
```

You create a new container component that fetches data remotely and passes to its corresponding pure component. All you need to do now is change the original App.js file to render the new KanbanBoardContainer, instead of rendering KanbanBoard directly:

```
import React from 'react';
import {render} from 'react-dom';
import KanbanBoardContainer from './KanbanBoardContainer';

render(<KanbanBoardContainer />, document.getElementById('root'));
```

If you test right now, it will look like nothing happened at all. The difference is that the Kanban app is live, so the data is no longer hard-coded.

Wiring Up the Task Callbacks as Props

Now let's create three functions to manipulate the tasks: addTask, deleteTask, and toggleTask. Since tasks belong to a card, all functions need to receive the cardId as a parameter. The addTask will receive the new task text, while both deleteTask and toggleTask should receive the taskId and the taskIndex (the position inside the card's array of tasks). You will pass the three functions down the whole hierarchy of components as props.

As a small trick to save a little typing, instead of creating one prop to pass each new function, you create a single object that references the three functions and pass it as a single prop. The code is shown in Listing 3-16.

Listing 3-16. The New Methods for Manipulating Tasks

```
class KanbanBoardContainer extends Component {
  constructor(){...}
  componentDidMount(){...}

  addTask(cardId, taskName){

  }

  deleteTask(cardId, taskId, taskIndex){

  }

  toggleTask(cardId, taskId, taskIndex){

  }

  render() {
    return (
      <KanbanBoard cards={this.state.cards}
                   taskCallbacks={{
                           toggle: this.toggleTask.bind(this),
                           delete: this.deleteTask.bind(this),
                              add: this.addTask.bind(this) }} />
    )
  }
}
```

Now there's some repetitive work to be done: all the components between the top of the hierarchy and the CheckList component (that is, the KanbanBoard, List and Card components) must receive the taskCallbacks prop from its parent and pass it along as a prop to its children. Despite looking like a repetitive task, this will make very clear how the communication is flowing from component to component. Listings 3-17, 3-18, and 3-19 show the updated code for those three components.

Listing 3-17. KanbanBoard Component Receiving and Passing the taskCallbacks Prop

```
class KanbanBoard extends Component {
  render() {
    return (
      <div className="app">

        <List title="To Do" taskCallbacks={this.props.taskCallbacks} cards={
          this.props.cards.filter((card) => card.status === "todo")
        } />

        <List title="In Progress" taskCallbacks={this.props.taskCallbacks} cards={
          this.props.cards.filter((card) => card.status == "in-progress")
        } />
```

```
      <List title="Done" taskCallbacks={this.props.taskCallbacks} cards={
        this.props.cards.filter((card) => card.status == "done")
      } />

    </div>
  )
  }
}
KanbanBoard.propTypes = {
  cards: PropTypes.arrayOf(PropTypes.object),
  taskCallbacks: PropTypes.object
}
```

Listing 3-18. List Component Receiving and Passing the taskCallbacks Prop

```
class List extends Component {
  render() {

    let cards = this.props.cards.map((card) => {
      return <Card key={card.id} taskCallbacks={this.props.taskCallbacks} {...card} />
    });

    return (...)
  }
}
List.propTypes = {
  title: PropTypes.string.isRequired,
  cards: PropTypes.arrayOf(PropTypes.object),
  taskCallbacks: PropTypes.object,
}
```

In Listing 3-18, it's worth noticing the use of the spread operator to reduce some typing when passing props to the Card component. To learn more about the spread operator, reference the online appendixes.

Listing 3-19. Card Component Receiving and Passing the taskCallbacks Prop

```
class Card extends Component {
  constructor() {...}
  toggleDetails() {...}
  render() {
    let cardDetails;
    if (this.state.showDetails) {
      cardDetails = (
        <div className="card__details">
          <span dangerouslySetInnerHTML={{__html:marked(this.props.description)}} />
          <CheckList cardId={this.props.id}
                     tasks={this.props.tasks}
                     taskCallbacks={this.props.taskCallbacks} />
        </div>
      );
    }
```

```
    let sideColor = {...}
    return (...)
  }
}
Card.propTypes = {
  id: PropTypes.number,
  title: titlePropType,
  description: PropTypes.string,
  color: PropTypes.string,
  tasks: PropTypes.array,
  taskCallbacks: PropTypes.object,
}
```

Finally, when in the Checklist component, you make use of taskCallbacks.taskCallbacks.delete and taskCallbacks.toggle, which can be directly associated with element event handlers:

```
class CheckList extends Component {
  render() {
    let tasks = this.props.tasks.map((task, taskIndex) => (
      <li key={task.id} className="checklist__task">
        <input type="checkbox" checked={task.done} onChange={
          this.props.taskCallbacks.toggle.bind(null, this.props.cardId, task.id, taskIndex)
        } />
        {task.name}{' '}
        <a href="#" className="checklist__task--remove" onClick={
          this.props.taskCallbacks.delete.bind(null, this.props.cardId, task.id, taskIndex)
        } />
      </li>
    ));

    return (...);
  }
}
```

To add a new task, however, you do some pre-processing inside the component before invoking the taskCallbacks.add callback. You do so for two reasons: to check if the user pressed the Enter key, and to clear the input field after invoking the callback function:

```
class CheckList extends Component {
  checkInputKeyPress(evt){
    if(evt.key === 'Enter'){
      this.props.taskCallbacks.add(this.props.cardId, evt.target.value);
      evt.target.value = '';
    }
  }
```

```
  render() {
    let tasks = this.props.tasks.map((task, taskIndex) => (...));

    return (
      <div className="checklist">
        <ul>{tasks}</ul>
        <input type="text"
               className="checklist--add-task"
               placeholder="Type then hit Enter to add a task"
               onKeyPress={this.checkInputKeyPress.bind(this)}  />
      </div>
    )
  }
}
```

The complete code for the CheckList component is shown in Listing 3-20.

Listing 3-20. The Complete CheckList Component Wired Up to Invoke All Task Callbacks

```
import React, { Component, PropTypes } from 'react';

class CheckList extends Component {
  checkInputKeyPress(evt){
    if(evt.key === 'Enter'){
      this.props.taskCallbacks.add(this.props.cardId, evt.target.value)
      evt.target.value = '';
    }
  }

  render() {
    let tasks = this.props.tasks.map((task, taskIndex) => (
      <li key={task.id} className="checklist__task">
        <input type="checkbox" checked={task.done} onChange={
          this.props.taskCallbacks.toggle.bind(null, this.props.cardId, task.id, taskIndex)
        } />
        {task.name}{' '}
        <a href="#" className="checklist__task--remove" onClick={
          this.props.taskCallbacks.delete.bind(null, this.props.cardId, task.id, taskIndex)
        } />
      </li>
    ));

    return (
      <div className="checklist">
        <ul>{tasks}</ul>
        <input type="text"
               className="checklist--add-task"
               placeholder="Type then hit Enter to add a task"
               onKeyPress={this.checkInputKeyPress.bind(this)}  />
      </div>
    )
  }
}
```

```
CheckList.propTypes = {
  cardId: PropTypes.number,
  taskCallbacks: PropTypes.object,
  tasks: PropTypes.array
};
export default CheckList;
```

Manipulating Tasks

In this last part, you make the actual manipulations of the tasks in the KanbanAppContainer state and persist all changes on the server through the API. In all three methods (deleteTask, toggleTask, and addTask), you need to make sure not to manipulate the current state directly, so you will use React's immutability helpers. Don't forget to install them using npm install --save react-addons-update.

There is one problem, though: since you filtered the cards in the KanbanList component, you don't have access to their original indexes anymore (and their indexes will be required to use the immutability helpers). So you can use the new findIndex() array method that runs a testing function on each element and returns the index of the element that satisfies the testing function.

■ **Note** At the time of this writing, only Chrome and Firefox supported the new methods
array.prototype.find and array.prototype.findIndex, so make sure to install babel-polyfill:

npm install --save babel-polyfill

Then, in your file, import it using:

import 'babel-polyfill'

Let's start coding the methods, beginning with the deleteTask method. You start by finding the index of the card you want by its ID. Then you create a new mutated object without the deleted task using the immutability helpers. Finally, you setState for the mutated object and use Fetch to inform the server of the change.

```
deleteTask(cardId, taskId, taskIndex){
    // Find the index of the card
    let cardIndex = this.state.cards.findIndex((card)=>card.id == cardId);

    // Create a new object without the task
    let nextState = update(this.state.cards, {
                        [cardIndex]: {
                          tasks: {$splice: [[taskIndex,1]] }
                        }
                    });

    // set the component state to the mutated object
    this.setState({cards:nextState});
```

```
    // Call the API to remove the task on the server
    fetch(`${API_URL}/cards/${cardId}/tasks/${taskId}`, {
      method: 'delete',
      headers: API_HEADERS
    });
  }
```

Toggling a task will happen in a similar fashion, but instead of splicing the array, you walk the object hierarchy up to the done property of the task and directly manipulate its value using a function:

```
toggleTask(cardId, taskId, taskIndex){
    // Find the index of the card
    let cardIndex = this.state.cards.findIndex((card)=>card.id == cardId);
    // Save a reference to the task's 'done' value
    let newDoneValue;
    // Using the $apply command, you will change the done value to its opposite
    let nextState = update(this.state.cards, {
                        [cardIndex]: {
                          tasks: {
                            [taskIndex]: {
                              done: { $apply: (done) => {
                                  newDoneValue = !done
                                  return newDoneValue;
                                }
                              }
                            }
                          }
                        }
                    });

    // set the component state to the mutated object
    this.setState({cards:nextState});

    // Call the API to toggle the task on the server
    fetch(`${API_URL}/cards/${cardId}/tasks/${taskId}`, {
        method: 'put',
        headers: API_HEADERS,
        body: JSON.stringify({done:newDoneValue})
    });
  }
```

As you may imagine, adding a new task works in a similar way. The only thing to notice is that since all tasks need an ID, you must generate a temporary ID for the task until it's persisted to the server and it returns the definitive ID. Then you must update the task ID. The temporary ID can be as simple as the current time in milliseconds:

```
addTask(cardId, taskName){
    // Find the index of the card
    let cardIndex = this.state.cards.findIndex((card)=>card.id == cardId);

    // Create a new task with the given name and a temporary ID
    let newTask = {id:Date.now(), name:taskName, done:false};
```

```
   // Create a new object and push the new task to the array of tasks
   let nextState = update(this.state.cards, {
                     [cardIndex]: {
                        tasks: {$push: [newTask] }
                     }
                  });

   // set the component state to the mutated object
   this.setState({cards:nextState});

   // Call the API to add the task on the server
   fetch(`${API_URL}/cards/${cardId}/tasks`, {
     method: 'post',
     headers: API_HEADERS,
     body: JSON.stringify(newTask)
   })
   .then((response) => response.json())
   .then((responseData) => {
     // When the server returns the definitive ID
     // used for the new Task on the server, update it on React
     newTask.id=responseData.id
     this.setState({cards:nextState});
   });
 }
```

Basic Optimistic Updates Rollback

You may have notice that you've made all the changes in the UI optimistically, that is, without actually waiting for the server to respond if the changes were saved. Being optimistic is important for perceived performance: when users interact with an online app, they don't want to wait for things to happen. They don't care that their tasks need to be stored in a remote database. Everything should appear to happen instantly. But what happens if the server fails? You need to make some new tries, revert back the UI changes, notify the user, and so on...

Optimistic updating and rollback is not a trivial task and can unfold in many outcomes, but it's easy to cover the basic rollback scenario right now because of a side effect of working with immutable structures: you can keep a reference to the old state and revert it back in case of problems.

For all three task callbacks, the code will be the same. First, keep a reference to the original state of the component:

```
// Keep a reference to the original state prior to the mutations
// in case you need to revert the optimistic changes in the UI
let prevState = this.state;
```

In the sequence, use setState to revert back to the original state if the fetch command fails OR if the server response status was not ok:

```
fetch(..., {...})
.then((response) => {
  if(!response.ok){
    // Throw an error if server response wasn't 'ok'
    // so you can revert back the optimistic changes
```

```
    // made to the UI.
    throw new Error("Server response wasn't OK")
  }
})
.catch((error) => {
  console.error("Fetch error:",error)
  this.setState(prevState);
});
```

To test, you can simply shut down the local API server (or disconnect from the Internet if you are using the online API) and try to make any changes to the tasks.

The complete for the KanbanAppContainer component is shown in Listing 3-21.

Listing 3-21. The Complete KanbanBoardContainer Code with the Task Manipulation Methods

```
import React, { Component } from 'react';
import update from 'react-addons-update';
import KanbanBoard from './KanbanBoard';
// Polyfills
import 'babel-polyfill';
import 'whatwg-fetch';

const API_URL = 'http://kanbanapi.pro-react.com';
const API_HEADERS = {
  'Content-Type': 'application/json',
  Authorization: 'any-string-you-like'// The Authorization is not needed for local server
};

class KanbanBoardContainer extends Component {
  constructor(){
    super(...arguments);
    this.state = {
      cards:[],
    };
  }

  componentDidMount(){
    fetch(`${API_URL}/cards`, {headers:API_HEADERS})
    .then((response) => response.json())
    .then((responseData) => {
      this.setState({
        cards: responseData
      })

      window.state = this.state;
    });
  }

  addTask(cardId, taskName){
    // Keep a reference to the original state prior to the mutations
    // in case you need to revert the optimistic changes in the UI
    let prevState = this.state;
```

```javascript
    // Find the index of the card
    let cardIndex = this.state.cards.findIndex((card)=>card.id == cardId);

    // Create a new task with the given name and a temporary ID
    let newTask = {id:Date.now(), name:taskName, done:false};
    // Create a new object and push the new task to the array of tasks
    let nextState = update(this.state.cards, {
                    [cardIndex]: {
                        tasks: {$push: [newTask] }
                    }
                });

    // set the component state to the mutated object
    this.setState({cards:nextState});

    // Call the API to add the task on the server
    fetch(`${API_URL}/cards/${cardId}/tasks`, {
        method: 'post',
        headers: API_HEADERS,
        body: JSON.stringify(newTask)
    })
    .then((response) => {
        if(response.ok){
            return response.json()
        } else {
            // Throw an error if server response wasn't 'ok'
            // so you can revert back the optimistic changes
            // made to the UI.
            throw new Error("Server response wasn't OK")
        }
    })
    .then((responseData) => {
        // When the server returns the definitive ID
        // used for the new Task on the server, update it on React
        newTask.id=responseData.id
        this.setState({cards:nextState});
    })
    .catch((error) => {
        this.setState(prevState);
    });
}

deleteTask(cardId, taskId, taskIndex){
    // Find the index of the card
    let cardIndex = this.state.cards.findIndex((card)=>card.id == cardId);

    // Keep a reference to the original state prior to the mutations
    // in case you need to revert the optimistic changes in the UI
    let prevState = this.state;
```

```
    // Create a new object without the task
    let nextState = update(this.state.cards, {
                    [cardIndex]: {
                        tasks: {$splice: [[taskIndex,1]] }
                    }
                });

    // set the component state to the mutated object
    this.setState({cards:nextState});

    // Call the API to remove the task on the server
    fetch(`${API_URL}/cards/${cardId}/tasks/${taskId}`, {
        method: 'delete',
        headers: API_HEADERS
    })
    .then((response) => {
        if(!response.ok){
            // Throw an error if server response wasn't 'ok'
            // so you can revert back the optimistic changes
            // made to the UI.
            throw new Error("Server response wasn't OK")
        }
    })
    .catch((error) => {
        console.error("Fetch error:",error);
        this.setState(prevState);
    });
}

toggleTask(cardId, taskId, taskIndex){
    // Keep a reference to the original state prior to the mutations
    // in case you need to revert the optimistic changes in the UI
    let prevState = this.state;

    // Find the index of the card
    let cardIndex = this.state.cards.findIndex((card)=>card.id == cardId);
    // Save a reference to the task's 'done' value
    let newDoneValue;
    // Using the $apply command, you will change the done value to its opposite,
    let nextState = update(
                    this.state.cards, {
                        [cardIndex]: {
                            tasks: {
                                [taskIndex]: {
                                    done: { $apply: (done) => {
                                        newDoneValue = !done
                                        return newDoneValue;
                                    }
                                }
                            }
                        }
                    }
                });
```

```
    // set the component state to the mutated object
    this.setState({cards:nextState});

    // Call the API to toggle the task on the server
    fetch(`${API_URL}/cards/${cardId}/tasks/${taskId}`, {
        method: 'put',
        headers: API_HEADERS,
        body: JSON.stringify({done:newDoneValue})
    })
    .then((response) => {
      if(!response.ok){
        // Throw an error if server response wasn't 'ok'
        // so you can revert back the optimistic changes
        // made to the UI.
        throw new Error("Server response wasn't OK")
      }
    })
    .catch((error) => {
      console.error("Fetch error:",error)
      this.setState(prevState);
    });
  }

  render() {
    return (
      <KanbanBoard cards={this.state.cards} taskCallbacks={{
          toggle: this.toggleTask.bind(this),
          delete: this.deleteTask.bind(this),
          add: this.addTask.bind(this) }} />
    )
  }
}

export default KanbanBoardContainer;
```

Summary

In this chapter, you studied how to structure complex UIs in React. You learned that in a React application, data always flows in a single direction, from parent to child components. For communication, a parent component can pass a callback function down as props so child components can report back.

You also saw that components can be much easier to reuse and reason about if you divide them into two categories: stateful components (which manipulate internal state) and pure components (which don't have an internal state and only display data received via props). It's a good practice to structure your application so that it has fewer stateful components (usually on the top levels of your application component hierarchy) and more pure components.

Finally, you saw why it's important to treat the component state as immutable, always using this.setState to make changes on it (and you learned how to use React's immutable helpers to generate mutated, shallow copies of this.state).

CHAPTER 4

■ ■ ■

Sophisticated Interactions

Having the correct expected functionality, fast load times, and a great perceived performance is not enough for an application by today's standards. The interface must also be refined, smooth, and include sophisticated interactions such as animated elements and drag-and-drop interactions.

Animation in React

React provides a default way of dealing with animations with its high level ReactCSSTransitionGroup (part of the add-ons module). The ReactCSSTransitionGroup is not full stack animation library. It doesn't feature value interpolation, timeline management, or chaining, for example, but it does facilitate the integration of CSS transitioning with React by allowing you to trigger CSS transitions and animations when components are added or removed from the DOM. CSS transitions and animations are standard browser mechanisms that provide a way to interpolate from one CSS style configuration to another.

In the next two sections, you will take an overall look on how CSS animation works and how to use ReactCSSTransitionGroup to perform component animations.

CSS Transition and Animation 101

To use ReactCSSTransitionGroup, you need to be familiar with setting up CSS transitions and animations, and you need to know how to trigger them with JavaScript. Let's briefly cover this subject before moving to integration with React components. If you already understand CSS transitions, feel free to skip straight to the React-specific content in the next section.

There are two categories of animations in CSS: CSS transitions and CSS keyframe animations.

- CSS transitions are animations made by interpolating values between two distinct states, a start state and an end state.

- CSS keyframe animations allow for more complex animations with control over intermediary steps besides start and end using keyframes.

CSS Transitions

CSS transitions provide a way to animate (or interpolate, to be more precise) the transition between CSS properties. For example, if you change the color of an element from grey to red, usually the change is instantaneous. With CSS transitions enabled, changes occur smoothly over a given period of time.

CSS transitions are controlled with the `transition` property. It tells the browser that the properties within that selector should have their values interpolated over time, creating an animated effect. The transition property accepts up to four attributes:

- The element property name to animate (such as color or width). If omitted, all properties that can be animated will transition.

- Duration of the animation.

- Optional timing function to control the acceleration curve (such as ease-in and ease-out).

- Optional delay before the animation starts.

Let's create a button-shaped HTML link that that changes the background color when the mouse is over it. In Listing 4-1, notice the presence of the `.button` and `.button:hover` selectors, which contain different values for the properties `background-color` and `box-shadow`, as well as the transition attribute defining the duration of the animation. Figure 4-1 illustrates the process of the button animating to the hovered state.

Listing 4-1. CSS Transition Attribute

```
<!DOCTYPE html>
<html>
  <head>
    <meta charset="utf-8">
    <title>Hover Transition</title>
    <style media="screen">
      a{
        font-family: Helvetica, Arial, sans-serif;
        text-decoration: none;
        color:#ffffff;
      }

      .button{
        padding: 0.75rem 1rem;
        border-radius: 0.3rem;
        box-shadow: 0;
        background-color: #bbbbbb;
      }

      .button:hover{
        background-color: #ee2222;
        box-shadow: 0 4px #990000;
        transition: 0.5s;
      }
    </style>
  </head>
  <body>
      <a href="#" class="button"> Hover Me! </div>
  </body>
</html>
```

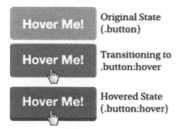

Figure 4-1. *A representation of what the hover animation looks like*

Note About Prefixes

As of the time of writing, some WebKit-based browsers still required the use of a prefix on the name of the properties of both kinds of animations, keyframes and transitions. Until they adopt the standard version, you'll want to include both unprefixed and prefixed versions in your code.

For example, for the hover button you should include

```
.button:hover{
  background-color: #ee2222;
  box-shadow: 0 4px #990000;
  webkit-transition: 0.5s;
  transition: 0.5s;
}
```

For simplicity, the examples in this book are unprefixed.

Keyframe Animations

Transition-based animations only provide control over two points of the animation: the beginning state and the final state. All the intermediary steps are interpolated by the browser. Another method of creating CSS animations is the keyframe property, which gives you more specific control over the intermediate steps of the animation sequence than you get when letting the browser handle everything automatically.

To use keyframes, you specify your animation steps in a separate block of CSS, with a @keyframes rule and a name, such as:

```
@keyframes pulsing-heart {
  0% { transform: none; }
  50% { transform: scale(1.4); }
  100% { transform: none; }
}
```

The block above is a set of keyframes named pulsing-heart. It defines three keyframes: one at the very beginning of the animation (represented by 0%), one at the middle of the animation (50%), and one at the end.

A keyframes definition can be later referenced in any style definition through the `animation` property. The `animation` property accepts the name of the set of keyframes, the animation duration, and other optional configurations (such as repetitions). As an example, let's create a simple heart that pulses when the mouse is over it.

```html
<!DOCTYPE html>
<html>
  <head>
    <meta charset="utf-8">
    <title>Pulsing Heart</title>
    <style media="screen">
    body{
      text-align: center;
    }
    @keyframes pulsing-heart {
      0% { transform: none; }
      50% { transform: scale(1.4); }
      100% { transform: none; }
    }

    .heart {
      font-size: 10rem;
      color: #FF0000;
    }

    .heart:hover {
      animation: pulsing-heart .5s infinite;
      transform-origin: center;
    }
    </style>
  </head>
  <body>
    <div>
    <div class="heart">&hearts; </div>
    </div>
  </body>
</html>
```

Programmatically Starting CSS Transitions and Animations

Since the pseudo selectors only cover the most basic interaction scenarios, you will want to use JavaScript to have more flexibility over when to trigger the CSS transitions and animations. This is usually done through class swapping: you create two separate classes for the same element, containing different property values between them. The HTML element starts using just one of these classes, and via JavaScript you dynamically remove the old class reference and add a new one, which will trigger the CSS animated transition.

Let's try this out with a very basic sketch of a side menu that is triggered by a "hamburger" menu on the page header, as shown in Figure 4-2.

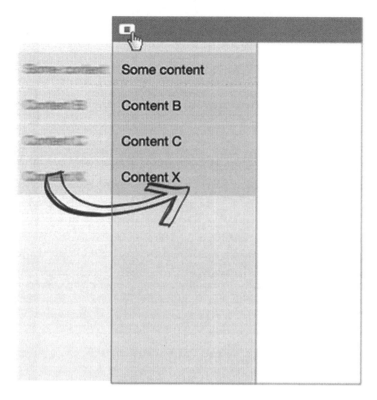

Figure 4-2. *Project with sidebar opened on button click*

You will start with a CSS class that defines the basic sidebar styling:

```
/* Sidebar default style */
.sidebar{
  background-color:#eee;
  box-shadow: 1px 0 3px #888888;
  position:absolute;
  width: 15rem;
  height: 100%;
}
```

Next, let's create two classes with the same properties and different values. While the first class (`.sidebar-transition`) sets the sidebar opacity to 0 (transparent) and positions it off the screen boundaries, the `.sidebar-transition-active` sets the opacity to 1 (visible) and positions the sidebar inside the screen bounds. Notice that the `sidebar-transition-active` class also defines the `transition` property for an animated transition of 0.5 seconds.

```
.sidebar-transition{
  opacity: 0;
  left: -15rem;
}
```

```
.sidebar-transition-active{
  opacity: 1;
  left: 0;
  transition: ease-in-out 0.5s;
}
```

In the HTML code, the sidebar is declared only with the `.sidebar-transition` class, not the `.sidebar-transition-active` one (so it starts off as hidden):

```
<div class='sidebar sidebar-transition'>
  <ul>
    <li>Some content</li>
    <li>Content B</li>
          ...
    <li>Concent X</li>
  </ul>
</div>
```

You won't use React or any other library here. To trigger this bare-bones example, you will use an inline JavaScript code hacked together with HTML, which is not exactly an example of good practices, but it's just a prototype to demonstrate the concept. What the JavaScript code does is add the `.sidebar-transition-active` class to the sidebar when the menu button is clicked. The sample code is shown in Listing 4-2.

Listing 4-2. Dynamicly Adding a CSS Class to Trigger a CSS Transition

```
<!DOCTYPE html>
<html>
  <head>
    <meta charset="utf-8">
    <title>Hacked together sidebar Transition</title>
    <style media="screen">
    /* the sidebar will have a list of contents. Let's style them too */
    ul {
      list-style-type: none;
      padding: 0;
    }
    li{
      padding: 15px;
      border-bottom: solid 1px #eee;
      background-color: #ddd;
    }
    .sidebar{
      background-color:#eee;
      box-shadow: 1px 0 3px #888888;
      position:absolute;
      width: 15rem;
      height: 100%;
    }
    .sidebar-transition{
      opacity: 0;
      left: -15rem;
    }
```

```
.sidebar-transition-active{
  opacity: 1;
  left: 0;
  transition: 0.5s;
}
</style>
</head>
<body>
  <header>
    <button onclick="
        document.querySelector('.sidebar').classList.add('sidebar-transition-active');
    "> &#9776; </button>
    <!-- &#9776; is the HTML Entity for the ☰ utf-8 symbol (aka "Hamburger Menu")  -->
  </header>
  <div class='sidebar sidebar-transition'>
    <ul>
      ...
    </ul>
  </div>
</body>
</html>
```

React CSSTransitionGroup

ReactCSSTransitionGroup is a simple element that wraps all of the components you are interested in animating, and triggers CSS animations and transitions at specific moments related to the component's lifecycle, such as mounting and unmounting. It is provided as an add-on, so be sure to install it using npm install --save react-addons-css-transition-group.

React Animation Example: Shopping List

As an example, let's create a basic animated shopping list where you can add and remove items.

Basic Application Setup

To begin, create a new React project (you can use this book's app boilerplate, found at https://github.com/pro-react/react-app-boilerplate) and edit the main JavaScript file to create the AnimatedShoppingList base structure, as shown in Listing 4-3.

Listing 4-3. AnimatedShoppingList Component

```
import React, { Component } from 'react';
import { render } from 'react-dom';
import ReactCSSTransitionGroup from 'react-addons-css-transition-group';

class AnimatedShoppingList extends Component {
  constructor(){
    super(...arguments);
```

```
    // Create an "items" state pre-populated with some shopping items
    this.state={
      items: [
        {id:1, name: 'Milk'},
        {id:2, name: 'Yogurt'},
        {id:3, name: 'Orange Juice'},
      ]
    }
  }

  // Called when the user changes the input field
  handleChange(evt) {
    if(evt.key === 'Enter'){
      // Create a new item and set the current time as it's id
      let newItem = {id:Date.now(), name:evt.target.value}
      // Create a new array with the previous items plus the value the user typed
      let newItems = this.state.items.concat(newItem);
      // Clear the text field
      evt.target.value='';
      // Set the new state
      this.setState({items: newItems});
    }

  }

  // Called when the user Clicks on a shopping item
  handleRemove(i) {
    // Create a new array without the clicked item
    var newItems = this.state.items;
    newItems.splice(i, 1);
    // Set the new state
    this.setState({items: newItems});
  }

  render(){
    let shoppingItems = this.state.items.map((item, i) => (
      <div key={item.id}
          className="item"
          onClick={this.handleRemove.bind(this, i)}>
        {item.name}
      </div>
    ));

    return(
      <div>
        {shoppingItems}
        <input type="text" value={this.state.newItem} onKeyDown={this.handleChange.bind(this)}/>
      </div>
    );
  }
};

render(<AnimatedShoppingList />, document.getElementById('root'));
```

Some things to notice in this component are

- Clicking on a shopping list item will remove that item.

- The user can create new items by typing in the text field and pressing the Enter key.

- Each shopping item has an ID (you're even generating a new ID for every new item based on a timestamp). IDs are used as item keys. You must provide the key attribute for all children of ReactCSSTransitionGroup, even when only rendering a single item because this is how React will determine which children have entered, left, or stayed.

Let's throw in some CSS rules for basic styling. For now, this CSS won't contain any transition rules, but they will be added in the next step.

```
input {
  padding: 5px;
  width: 120px;
  margin-top:10px;
}

.item {
  background-color: #efefef;
  cursor: pointer;
  display: block;
  margin-bottom: 1px;
  padding: 8px 12px;
  width: 120px;
}
```

Adding the ReactCSSTransitionGroup Element

The component is already working, and it's possible to add and remove shopping items. Now let's animate the entering and leaving of items.

The ReactCSSTransitionGroup element must be inserted around the children elements that you want to animate. It accepts three props: transitionName (which will be mapped to CSS class names containing the actual animation definition), transitionEnterTimeout, and transitionLeaveTimeout (with the animation's duration in milliseconds).

In your Shopping List example, you will insert the ReactCSSTransitionGroup around the shoppingItems variable in the render method. You will call the transition name "Example" and set an enter and leave duration of 300 ms:

```
return(
  <div>
    <ReactCSSTransitionGroup transitionName="example"
                             transitionEnterTimeout={300}
                             transitionLeaveTimeout={300}>
      {shoppingItems}
    </ReactCSSTransitionGroup>
    <input type="text" value={this.state.newItem} onKeyDown={this.handleChange.bind(this)}/>
  </div>
);
```

From this point on, every time a new item is added to the state, React will render the item with the additional className of example-enter. Immediately after, in the next browser tick, React will also attach the className example-enter-active: because of the nature of CSS transitions; it needs a starting class with the default style properties, and the animation is triggered when a second class with different properties and a transition rule is added to the element. Finally, after the time defined in transitionEnterTimeout prop expires, both classes will be removed.

Let's add both example-enter and example-enter-active classes to your CSS. For this project, you will transition the translateX property (making the item come from the left side of the screen):

```
.example-enter {
  opacity: 0;
  transform: translateX(-250px);
}
.example-enter.example-enter-active {
  opacity: 1;
  transform:   translateX(0);
  transition: 0.3s;
}
```

Figure 4-3 illustrates the new item's animation.

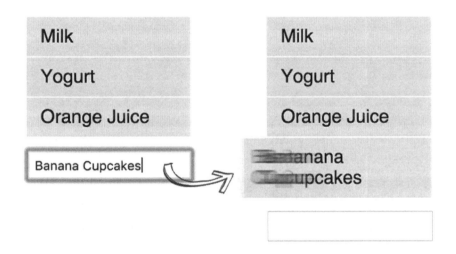

Figure 4-3. *Animating the new item*

The same mechanism applies for removing elements from the DOM. Before removing a shopping item, React will add an example-leave className followed by example-leave-active. When the defined LeaveTimeout expires, React will finally remove the element from the DOM. To complete your example, try adding this CSS:

```
.example-leave {
  opacity: 1;
  transform: translateX(0);
}
```

```css
.example-leave.example-leave-active {
  opacity: 0;
  transform: translateX(250px);
  transition: 0.3s;
}
```

Animate Initial Mounting

When testing this sample code, you may realize that the animation is performed for adding and removing elements, but the initial hard-coded items don't appear with a transition in the beginning. ReactCSSTransitionGroup provides the optional prop transitionAppear to add an extra transition phase at the initial mount of the component. There is generally no transition phase at the initial mount because the default value of transitionAppear is false. The following is an example that passes the prop transitionAppear with the value true:

```jsx
<ReactCSSTransitionGroup transitionName="example"
                         transitionEnterTimeout={300}
                         transitionLeaveTimeout={300}
                         transitionAppear={true}
                         transitionAppearTimeout={300}>
  {shoppingItems}
</ReactCSSTransitionGroup>
```

You also need to provide extra CSS classes to control the appearing transitions:

```css
.example-appear {
  opacity: 0;
  transform: translateX(-250px);
}
.example-appear.example-appear-active {
  opacity: 1;
  transform:   translateX(0);
  transition: .5s;
}
```

Now your application starts transitioning the initial elements. Listing 4-4 shows the final source code for the animated shopping list application.

Listing 4-4. The Final Source Code for the AnimatedShoppingList App

```jsx
import React, { Component } from 'react';
import { render } from 'react-dom';
import ReactCSSTransitionGroup from 'react-addons-css-transition-group';

class AnimatedShoppingList extends Component {
  constructor(){
    super(...arguments);
```

```
  // Create an "items" state pre-populated with some shopping items
  this.state={
    items: [
      {id:1, name: 'Milk'},
      {id:2, name: 'Yogurt'},
      {id:3, name: 'Orange Juice'},
    ]
  }
}

// Called when the user changes the input field
handleChange(evt) {
  if(evt.key === 'Enter'){
    // Create a new item and set the current time as it's id
    let newItem = {id:Date.now(), name:evt.target.value}
    // Create a new array with the previous items plus the value the user typed
    let newItems = this.state.items.concat(newItem);
    // Clear the text field
    evt.target.value='';
    // Set the new state
    this.setState({items: newItems});
  }

}

// Called when the user Clicks on a shopping item
handleRemove(i) {
  // Create a new array without the clicked item
  var newItems = this.state.items;
  newItems.splice(i, 1);
  // Set the new state
  this.setState({items: newItems});
}

render(){
  let shoppingItems = this.state.items.map((item, i) => (
    <div key={item.id} className="item"
         onClick={this.handleRemove.bind(this, i)}>
      {item.name}
    </div>
  ));

  return(
    <div>
      <ReactCSSTransitionGroup transitionName="example"
                               transitionEnterTimeout={300}
                               transitionLeaveTimeout={300}
                               transitionAppear={true}
                               transitionAppearTimeout={300}>
        {shoppingItems}
      </ReactCSSTransitionGroup>
```

```
      <input type="text" value={this.state.newItem} onKeyDown={this.handleChange.
      bind(this)}/>
    </div>
  );
  }
};

render(<AnimatedShoppingList />, document.getElementById('root'));
```

Drag and Drop

Drag-and-drop is a very common feature in sophisticated user interfaces. It is when you "grab" an object and drag it to a different location. Developing drag-and-drop interactions can be tricky. Until very recently there wasn't a standard API on browsers. Even in modern browsers (where a standard HTML5 drag-and-drop API is available), the API has inconsistencies across vendors and doesn't work on mobile devices. For these reasons, you will use React DnD, a drag-and-drop library that lets us work in a "React way" (not touching the DOM, embracing unidirectional data flow, defining source and drop target logic as pure data, among other benefits). Under the hood, React DnD plugs into the available API (such as the default HTML5 API for desktop browsers), and manages inconsistencies, quirks, and hides implementation details.

■ **Note**   Being an external library, to use React DnD you need to install and declare it as a dependency with npm. The examples in this book use React DND 2 with an HTML5 backend, installed via `npm install --save react-dnd@2.x.x react-dnd-html5-backend@1.x.x`.

React DnD Implementation Overview

The implementation of drag-and-drop behavior in your React application through the React DnD library is done using higher-order components. Higher-order components are JavaScript functions that accept a component as a parameter and return an enhanced version of that component, with added functionality.

The React DnD library provides three higher-order components that must be used on different components of your application: `DragSource`, `DropTarget`, and `DragDropContext`.

The `DragSource` returns an enhanced version of the given component with the added behavior of being a "draggable" element; the `DropTarget` returns an enhanced component with the ability to handle elements being dragged into it; and `DragDropContext` wraps the parent component where the drag-and-drop interaction occurs, setting up the shared DnD state behind the scenes (it is also is the simplest to implement).

The React DnD library also supports the use of JavaScript decorators as an alternative to higher-order components. JavaScript decorators are still in the experimental stage and are not part of ES 2015 specifications, so the examples in this book use higher-order components.

A React DnD Sample Implementation

Let's work on an example to see how all these parts connect together. In this example, you'll make a snack shop-themed app, with a lot of different circles representing the snacks that can be dragged into the shopping cart area. Figure 4-4 shows the end result.

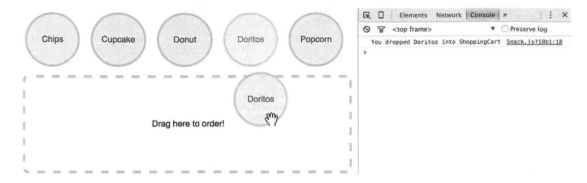

Figure 4-4. The Snack Drag'nDrop

The app will be composed of three components besides the main App component: a draggable Snack (which will be enhanced by the DragSource higher-order component), ShoppingCard (which will be enhanced by the DropTarget higher-order component), and a Container component, which will contain both the ShoppingCart and various Snacks and will be enhanced by the DragDropContext higher-order component to orchestrate the drag-and-drop workings between Snacks and the Shopping Cart.

Since the DragDropContext is the easiest part of React DnD to implement, let's start your application top-down, beginning with the App component, followed by the Container, Snack, and ShoppingCart.

The App component is straightforward: it just imports and renders the container's HOC. Listing 4-5 shows the source code.

Listing 4-5. The Main App Component

```
import React, { Component } from 'react';
import {render} from 'react-dom';
import Container from './Container'

class App extends Component {
  render(){
    return (
      <Container />
    );
  }
}

render(<App />, document.getElementById('root'));
```

The Container

Next, let's create the Container component, where all the drag-and-drop interaction will happen. You are going to render some Snack components with different name props and a ShoppingCart component below them. Listing 4-6 shows the source code.

Listing 4-6. The Container.js File

```
import React, { Component } from 'react';
import ShoppingCart from './ShoppingCart';
import Snack from './Snack';
import { DragDropContext } from 'react-dnd';
import HTML5Backend from 'react-dnd-html5-backend';

class Container extends Component {
  render() {
    return (
      <div>
        <Snack name='Chips'/>
        <Snack name='Cupcake'/>
        <Snack name='Donut'/>
        <Snack name='Doritos'/>
        <Snack name='Popcorn'/>
        <ShoppingCart/>
      </div>
    );
  }
}
export default DragDropContext(HTML5Backend)(Container);
```

Pay special attention to the fact that the module isn't exporting your Container component but a higher-order component based on the Container with all the drag-and-drop state and functions injected into it. Also notice that you imported and used the HTML5 back end to React DnD. As mentioned, the React Drag'nDrop supports different back ends.

DragSource and DropTarget Higher Order Components

Next, you create the Snack and ShoppingCart components, which are enhanced by the dragSource and the dropTarget wrappers, respectively. Both dragSource and dropTarget require some boilerplate setup that needs further explanation. To create higher-order components using any of them, you need to provide three parameters: a type, a spec, and a collecting function.

Type

It's the name of the component. In a complex UI, it is possible to have multiple types of drag sources interacting with multiple types of drop targets, so it is important that each one of them is uniquely identified.

Spec Object

The spec object describes how the enhanced component "reacts" to the drag and drop events. A spec is a plain JavaScript object with functions that are called when a drag-and-drop interaction occurs, such as beginDrag and endDrag (in the case of a DragSource) and canDrag and onDrop (in the case of a DropTarget component).

Collecting Function

The collecting function certainly looks complicated, but it is actually simple. To get some context, in Chapter 3 you learned that React components pass information to each other through props. The same happens with React DnD: both dragSource and dropTarget wrappers will inject props into the given component.

Instead of directly injecting all possible props into your component, though, reactDnD uses the collecting function to give you the control over how and which props will get injected. This gives you a lot of power, including the ability to preprocess the props before they get injected, change their names, and so on.

When a drag-and-drop interaction occurs, the React DnD library will invoke the collecting function defined in your component, passing two parameters: a connector and a monitor.

The connector must be mapped to a prop that will be used in the render function of your component to delimit a part of your component's DOM. For dragSource components, this part of the DOM will be used to represent your component while it's being dragged. For dropTarget components, this delimited part of the DOM will be used as a drop area.

The monitor lets you map props to the Drag'nDrop state. Bear with me; a drag-and-drop is inherently a stateful operation. (It can be in progress or idle. If it is in progress, there is a current type and a current item. If the user is dragging, it could possibly be over a drop target, etc.) Using the monitor you can create props such as isDragging or canDrop, for example, which are useful for rendering different things based on their value (such as rendering the element with a different text or CSS attribute when it's being dragged.)

ShoppingCart Component

Let's see how this works in practice. Start with the basic skeleton for the ShoppingCart component, without the dropTarget wrapper. Listing 4-7 shows the source code.

Listing 4-7. The Basic Skeleton for the ShoppingCart Component

```
import React, { PropTypes, Component } from 'react';
import { DropTarget } from 'react-dnd';

class ShoppingCart extends Component {
  render() {

    const style = {
      backgroundColor: '#FFFFFF'
    };

    return (
      <div className='shopping-cart' style={style}>
        Drag here to order!
      </div>
    );

  }
}
```

As you can see, it's basically a render function that returns a div. It also contains an inline CSS style with the backgroundColor attribute set to white.

In the sequence, let's implement a spec object. Remember, the spec object describes how the drop target reacts to drag and drop events. You will only respond to the drop event (called when a dragSource is dropped). Listing 4-8 shows the updated component, with some code omitted for brevity.

Listing 4-8. Spec Object Implementation on the ShoppingCart Component

```
import React, { PropTypes, Component } from 'react';
import { DropTarget } from 'react-dnd';

// ShoppingCart DND Spec
//    "A plain object implementing the drop target specification"
//
//  - DropTarget Methods (All optional)
//     - drop: Called when a compatible item is dropped.
//     - hover: Called when an item is hovered over the component.
//     - canDrop: Use it to specify whether the drop target is able to accept
//               the item.
const ShoppingCartSpec = {
  drop() {
    return { name: 'ShoppingCart' };
  }
};

class ShoppingCart extends Component {
  render() {...}
}
```

In this example, you're just returning a string when the drop event happens. This returned text will be used later, in the Snack component.

Next, you will implement the `collect` function, which lets you map the React DnD connector and state to the component's props. You will inject three props into your component: `connectDropTarget` (the required connector), `isOver`, and `canDrop`.

The `collect` function alone will look like this:

```
// ShoppingCart DropTarget - collect
//
//  - connect: An instance of DropTargetConnector.
//             You use it to assign the drop target role to a DOM node.
//
//  - monitor: An instance of DropTargetMonitor.
//     You use it to connect state from the React DnD to props.
//     Available functions to get state include canDrop(), isOver() and didDrop()

let collect = (connect, monitor) => {
  return {
    connectDropTarget: connect.dropTarget(),
    isOver: monitor.isOver(),
    canDrop: monitor.canDrop()
  };
}
```

Notice that the prop names you've created happen to have the same or similar names as the methods from `connect` and `monitor`, but they could really be anything (e.g `draggingSomethingOverMe:` `monitor.isOver()`)

All these props will be used in the render function. The `connectDropTarget` prop should return which part of this component's DOM is the target area for draggable objects. To make things simple, you will make the whole `div` target.

The `isOver` and `canDrop` props are used to display a different text and a different background color when the user is dragging an element over the shopping cart. The updated render function looks like this:

```
render() {
  const { canDrop, isOver, connectDropTarget } = this.props;
  const isActive = canDrop && isOver;

  let backgroundColor = '#FFFFFF';
  if (isActive) {
    backgroundColor = '#F7F7BD';
  } else if (canDrop) {
    backgroundColor = '#F7F7F7';
  }

  const style = {
    backgroundColor: backgroundColor
  };

  return connectDropTarget(
    <div className='shopping-cart' style={style}>
      {isActive ?
        'Hummmm, snack!' :
        'Drag here to order!'
      }
    </div>
  );
}
```

A few things to notice in the updated render method:

- You are using destructuring assignment as a shortcut to `canDrop`, `isOver`, and `connectDropTarget` props (so you can later type only `canDrop` instead of `this.props.canDrop`).

- The background color varies based on whether the user is dragging something and if it's dragging it over the Shopping Cart.

- The text also varies; by default it displays "'Drag here to order!", but when the user drags an item over the Shopping cart, it will display "Hummmm, snack!".

- Instead of returning the `div` as before, you're wrapping the `div` in `connectDropTarget`.

To finish, all you have left to do is export the higher-order component using the `DropTarget` wrapper. Also, since you're injecting props in the component, let's take the opportunity to declare propTypes. Listing 4-9 shows the complete source code for the ShoppingCart component.

Listing 4-9. The Complete Source Code for the Shopping Card Higher-Order Drop Target Component

```
import React, { PropTypes, Component } from 'react';
import { DropTarget } from 'react-dnd';

// ShoppingCart DND Spec
//    "A plain object implementing the drop target specification"
//
//  - DropTarget Methods (All optional)
//    - drop: Called when a compatible item is dropped.
//    - hover: Called when an item is hovered over the component.
//    - canDrop: Use it to specify whether the drop target is able to accept
//               the item.
const ShoppingCartSpec = {
  drop() {
    return { name: 'ShoppingCart' };
  }
};

// ShoppingCart DropTarget - collect
//   "The collecting function.
//
//  - connect: An instance of DropTargetConnector.
//             You use it to assign the drop target role to a DOM node.
//
//  - monitor: An instance of DropTargetMonitor.
//     You use it to connect state from the React DnD to props.
//     Available functions to get state include canDrop(), isOver() and didDrop()
let collect = (connect, monitor) => {
  return {
    connectDropTarget: connect.dropTarget(),
    isOver: monitor.isOver(),
    canDrop: monitor.canDrop()
  };
}

class ShoppingCart extends Component {
  render() {
    const { canDrop, isOver, connectDropTarget } = this.props;
    const isActive = canDrop && isOver;

    let backgroundColor = '#FFFFFF';
    if (isActive) {
      backgroundColor = '#F7F7BD';
    } else if (canDrop) {
      backgroundColor = '#F7F7F7';
    }

    const style = {
      backgroundColor: backgroundColor
    };
```

```
    return connectDropTarget(
      <div className='shopping-cart' style={style}>
        {isActive ?
          'Hummmm, snack!' :
          'Drag here to order!'
        }
      </div>
    );
  }
}

ShoppingCart.propTypes = {
  connectDropTarget: PropTypes.func.isRequired,
  isOver: PropTypes.bool.isRequired,
  canDrop: PropTypes.bool.isRequired
}

export default DropTarget("snack", ShoppingCartSpec, collect)(ShoppingCart);
```

Notice that that the type parameter for the DropTarget higher-order wrapper refers to the type of drag sources that can be dragged to this component (in your case, 'snack').

Snack Component

Next, let's implement the Snack component. The process is similar to what you've done to the ShoppingCart component. Listing 4-10 shows the basic component skeleton.

Listing 4-10. The Basic Structure of the Snack Component

```
import React, { Component, PropTypes } from 'react';
import { DragSource } from 'react-dnd';

class Snack extends Component {
  render() {
    const { name } = this.props;

    const style = {
      opacity: 1
    };

    return (
      <div className='snack' style={style}>
        {name}
      </div>
    )
  }
}
Snack.propTypes = {
  name: PropTypes.string.isRequired
};
```

At its basic form, the Snack component accepts a name prop and renders it inside a div tag. It also contains an inline style that currently sets the opacity to 1.

Next, let's implement the spec object. You respond to the beginDrag and endDrag events. In beginDrag you return a string (just like you did in the ShoppingCart drop event). In endDrag, you finally do something about both returned values. You take the returned string from the element you dragged, the returned string from the element where you dropped, and log both to the console. Listing 4-11 shows the updated Snack component with the spec object.

Listing 4-11. Spec Object Implementation on the Snack Component

```
import React, { Component, PropTypes } from 'react';
import { DragSource } from 'react-dnd';

//  snack Drag'nDrop spec
//
//     - Required: beginDrag
//     - Optional: endDrag
//     - Optional: canDrag
//     - Optional: isDragging
const snackSpec = {
  beginDrag(props) {
    return {
      name: props.name
    };
  },

  endDrag(props, monitor) {
    const dragItem = monitor.getItem();
    const dropResult = monitor.getDropResult();

    if (dropResult) {
      console.log(`You dropped ${dragItem.name} into ${dropResult.name}`);
    }
  }
};

class Snack extends Component {
  render() {...}
}
Snack.propTypes = {...}
```

For the last step in the Snack component, let's implement the collecting function, where you will connect the DOM node to be dragged and map the DnD state to component's props. And since you're connecting DnD state with your component's props, you will take the opportunity to do two other things: declare the additional propTypes and use the prop isDragging inside an inline style rule to make the element opacity change when it's being dragged. To finish, you will export the higher-order component using the dragSource wrapper. Listing 4-12 shows the complete source code.

Listing 4-12. The Complete Source Code for the Snack Component

```
import React, { Component, PropTypes } from 'react';
import { DragSource } from 'react-dnd';

//   snack Drag'nDrop spec
//
//     - Required: beginDrag
//     - Optional: endDrag
//     - Optional: canDrag
//     - Optional: isDragging
const snackSpec = {
  beginDrag(props) {
    return {
      name: props.name
    };
  },

  endDrag(props, monitor) {
    const dragItem = monitor.getItem();
    const dropResult = monitor.getDropResult();

    if (dropResult) {
      console.log(`You dropped ${dragItem.name} into ${dropResult.name}`);
    }
  }
};

// Snack DragSource collect collecting function.
//   - connect: An instance of DragSourceConnector.
//             You use it to assign the drag source role to a DOM node.
//
//   - monitor: An instance of DragSourceMonitor.
//       You use it to connect state from the React DnD to your component's properties.
//       Available functions to get state include canDrag(), isDragging(), getItemType(),
//       getItem(), didDrop() etc.
let collect = (connect, monitor) => {
  return {
    connectDragSource: connect.dragSource(),
    isDragging: monitor.isDragging()
  };
}

class Snack extends Component {
  render() {
    const { name, isDragging, connectDragSource } = this.props;
    const opacity = isDragging ? 0.4 : 1;

    const style = {
      opacity: opacity
    };
```

```
    return (
      connectDragSource(
        <div className='snack' style={style}>
          {name}
        </div>
      )
    );
  }
}

Snack.propTypes = {
  connectDragSource: PropTypes.func.isRequired,
  isDragging: PropTypes.bool.isRequired,
  name: PropTypes.string.isRequired
};

export default DragSource('snack', snackSpec, collect)(Snack);
```

Styling

To conclude, all you need to do is throw in some styling, as shown in Listing 4-13.

Listing 4-13. The Project's Stylesheet

```
body {
  font: 16px/1 sans-serif;
}
#root {
  height: 100%;
}
h1 {
  font-weight: 200;
  color: #3b414c;
  font-size: 20px;
}
.app {
  white-space: nowrap;
  height: 100%;
}

.snack {
  display: inline-block;
  padding: .5em;
  margin: 0 1em 1em 0.25em;
  border: 4px solid #d9d9d9;
  background: #f7f7f7;
  height: 5rem;
  width: 5rem;
  border-radius: 5rem;
  cursor: pointer;
```

```css
  line-height: 5em;
  text-align: center;
  color: #333;
}
.shopping-cart {
  border: 5px dashed #d9d9d9;
  border-radius: 10px;
  padding: 5rem 2rem;
  text-align: center;
}
```

If you test on the browser, you'll see that your sample code is already working and it's possible to drag snacks to the shopping cart. As always, the complete source code for this sample implementation is available from the www.apress.com site as well as from this book's github page (https://github.com/pro-react).

Refactor: Using Constants

Despite already working on the browser, there is one necessary adjustment before considering the example concluded: both dragSource and dropTarget require a type parameter that is used to uniquely identify the draggable component. So far, you've simply typed the same string ("snack") on both the Snack and ShoppingCart components, but manually typing an identifier across different files when it absolutely needs to be the same exact string is an error-prone task.

The best approach in cases like this is to create a separate JavaScript file for defining constant, read-only values that can be referenced anywhere in the application. This is a good practice not only for React DnD, but for any case where you need a unique identifier that can be used in different JavaScript modules and components across your application.

So, let's create a constants.js file. It will be a JavaScript module that exports an object with the SNACK constant. Listing 4-14 shows the source code.

Listing 4-14. The Contants JavaScript File

```javascript
export default {
  SNACK: 'snack'
};
```

In the sequence, let's edit the Snack and ShoppingCart components to import and reference this constant instead of having a hard-coded "snack" string. Listing 4-15 shows the updated ShoppingCart component. Listing 4-16 shows the updated Snack component.

Listing 4-15. The Updated ShoppingCart Component Passing a Constant as DropTarget's Type

```javascript
import React, { PropTypes, Component } from 'react';
import { DropTarget } from 'react-dnd';
import constants from './constants';

const ShoppingCartSpec = {...};
let collect = (connect, monitor) => {...};
class ShoppingCart extends Component {...};
ShoppingCart.propTypes = {...};

export default DropTarget(constants.SNACK, ShoppingCartSpec, collect)(ShoppingCart);
```

Listing 4-16. The Updated Snack Component Passing a Constant as DragSource's Type

```
import React, { Component, PropTypes } from 'react';
import { DragSource } from 'react-dnd';
import constants from './constants';

const snackSpec = {...};
let collect = (connect, monitor) => {...};
class Snack extends Component {...};
Snack.propTypes = {...};

export default DragSource(constants.SNACK, snackSpec, collect)(Snack);
```

Kanban App: Animations and Drag-and-Drop Support

Let's go back to the Kanban app you've been developing throughout the book to add animations and drag-and-drop capability. You will add a simple transition for opening and closing cards, and the ability to move a card between lists by dragging and dropping it.

Card Toggle Animation

To animate the card toggling when showing/hiding details, you will use the React CssTransitionGroup add-on, so let's begin by installing it on the Kanban project via npm `install --save react-addons-css-transition-group`.

Next, in the card component, you will import ReactCSSTransitionGroup and add the wrapper around the cardDetails. In the stylesheet, you'll create a CSS transition to change the max-height property. Listing 4-17 shows the Card components (with the changes highlighted). Listing 4-18 shows the added CSS styles.

Listing 4-17. The Card Component with a CSSTransitionGroup for Details

```
import React, { Component, PropTypes } from 'react';
import ReactCSSTransitionGroup from 'react-addons-css-transition-group';
import marked from 'marked'
import CheckList from './CheckList';

let titlePropType = (props, propName, componentName) => {
  if (props[propName]) {
    let value = props[propName];
    if (typeof value !== 'string' || value.length > 80) {
      return new Error(
        `${propName} in ${componentName}  is longer than 80 characters`
      );
    }
  }
}

class Card extends Component {
  constructor() {
    super(...arguments);
    this.state = {
      showDetails: false
    };
  }
```

```
  toggleDetails() {
    this.setState({showDetails: !this.state.showDetails});
  }

  render() {
    let cardDetails;
    if (this.state.showDetails) {
      cardDetails = (
        <div className="card__details">
          <span dangerouslySetInnerHTML={{__html:marked(this.props.description)}} />
          <CheckList taskCallbacks={this.props.taskCallbacks}
                     tasks={this.props.tasks} cardId={this.props.id} />
        </div>
      );
    }

    let sideColor = {
      position: 'absolute',
      zIndex: -1,
      top: 0,
      bottom: 0,
      left: 0,
      width: 7,
      backgroundColor: this.props.color
    };

    return (

      <div className="card">

        <div style={sideColor}/>
        <div className={
          this.state.showDetails? "card__title card__title--is-open" : "card__title"
          } onClick={this.toggleDetails.bind(this)}>

          {this.props.title}
        </div>
        <ReactCSSTransitionGroup transitionName="toggle"
                                 transitionEnterTimeout={250}
                                 transitionLeaveTimeout={250} >
        {cardDetails}
        </ ReactCSSTransitionGroup>
      </div>

    );
  }
}
```

```
Card.propTypes = {
  id: PropTypes.number,
  title: titlePropType,
  description: PropTypes.string,
  color: PropTypes.string,
  tasks: PropTypes.array,
  taskCallbacks: PropTypes.object,
}
```

export default Card;

Listing 4-18. The Added CSS Styles for Transitioning the max-height Property

```
.toggle-enter {
  max-height: 0;
  overflow: hidden;
}

.toggle-enter.toggle-enter-active {
  max-height: 300px;
  overflow: hidden;
  transition: max-height .25s ease-in;
}

.toggle-leave {
  max-height: 300px;
  overflow: hidden;
}

.toggle-leave.toggle-leave-active {
  max-height: 0;
  overflow: hidden;
  transition: max-height .25s ease-out;
}
```

Card Dragging

Finally, you will implement the card drag-and-drop, but differently from what you've done so far. Here you're also going to make the cards sortable, so not only will you be able to drag a card across lists, but you'll also be able to switch the card position with the other cards. You start by installing React DND 2 and its HTML5 back end:

```
npm install --save react-dnd@2.x.x react-dnd-html5-backend@1.x.x
```

Next, you create two new methods inside the KanbanAppContainer component, one to update the Card status (the list in which the Card is in) and another one to update the Card position. Both methods are along the lines of the task methods and callbacks you did before: receive the Card Id; find the Card's index; use the immutability helpers to update the state information, and, finally, set the state (you won't persist anything on the server yet). Listing 4-19 shows updated KanbanBoardContainer.

Listing 4-19. The Updated KanbanBoardContainer Component, with the Added updateCardStatus and updateCardPosition Methods

```
import React, { Component } from 'react';
import KanbanBoard from './KanbanBoard';
import update from 'react-addons-update';
// Polyfills
import 'whatwg-fetch';
import 'babel-polyfill';
const API_URL...
const API_HEADERS...

class KanbanBoardContainer extends Component {
  constructor(){...}
  componentDidMount(){...}

  addTask(cardId, taskName){...}
  deleteTask(cardId, taskId, taskIndex){...}
  toggleTask(cardId, taskId, taskIndex){...}

  updateCardStatus(cardId, listId){
    // Find the index of the card
    let cardIndex = this.state.cards.findIndex((card)=>card.id == cardId);
    // Get the current card
    let card = this.state.cards[cardIndex]
    // Only proceed if hovering over a different list
    if(card.status !== listId){
      // set the component state to the mutated object
      this.setState(update(this.state, {
          cards: {
            [cardIndex]: {
              status: { $set: listId }
            }
          }
      }));
    }
  }

  updateCardPosition (cardId , afterId) {
    // Only proceed if hovering over a different card
    if(cardId !== afterId) {
      // Find the index of the card
      let cardIndex = this.state.cards.findIndex((card)=>card.id == cardId);
      // Get the current card
      let card = this.state.cards[cardIndex]
      // Find the index of the card the user is hovering over
      let afterIndex = this.state.cards.findIndex((card)=>card.id == afterId);
      // Use splice to remove the card and reinsert it a the new index
```

```
        this.setState(update(this.state, {
          cards: {
            $splice: [
              [cardIndex, 1],
              [afterIndex, 0, card]
            ]
          }
        }));
      }
    }

    render() {
      return (
        <KanbanBoard cards={this.state.cards}
          taskCallbacks={{
            toggle: this.toggleTask.bind(this),
            delete: this.deleteTask.bind(this),
            add: this.addTask.bind(this)
          }}
          cardCallbacks={{
            updateStatus: this.updateCardStatus.bind(this),
            updatePosition: this.updateCardPosition.bind(this)
          }}
        />
      )
    }
  }
}
export default KanbanBoardContainer;
```

Also notice in this code that an object cardCallbacks with references to the new methods is being passed to the KanbanBoard component. The new cardCallbacks function is invoked by both the list component (when you drag the card to a different list) and by the Card itself (when you make the sorting functionality later), so you must edit all the components in the middle of the hierarchy to receive and pass along this prop. These components are the KanbanBoard and the List. Listings 4-20 and 4-21 show the updated code for each.

Listing 4-20. The Kanban Component Receiving the cardCallbacks Props and Passing It to List

```
class KanbanBoard extends Component {
  render() {
    return (
      <div className="app">

        <List id='todo' title="To Do" taskCallbacks={this.props.taskCallbacks}
          cardCallbacks={this.props.cardCallbacks}
          cards={ this.props.cards.filter((card) => card.status === "todo") }
        />

        <List id='in-progress' title="In Progress" taskCallbacks={this.props.taskCallbacks}
          cardCallbacks={this.props.cardCallbacks}
          cards={ this.props.cards.filter((card) => card.status == "in-progress") }
        />
```

```
            <List id='done' title='Done' taskCallbacks={this.props.taskCallbacks}
                cardCallbacks={this.props.cardCallbacks}
                cards={ this.props.cards.filter((card) => card.status == "done") }
            />
        </div>
    );
  }
}
KanbanBoard.propTypes = {
  cards: PropTypes.arrayOf(PropTypes.object),
  taskCallbacks: PropTypes.object,
  cardCallbacks: PropTypes.object
};

export default KanbanBoard;
```

Listing 4-21. The List Component Receiving the cardCallbacks Props and Passing It to Card

```
class List extends Component {
  render() {
    let cards = this.props.cards.map((card) => {
      return <Card key={card.id}
                taskCallbacks={this.props.taskCallbacks}
                cardCallbacks={this.props.cardCallbacks} {...card} />
    });

    return (...);
  }
}
List.propTypes = {
  id: PropTypes.string.isRequired,
  title: PropTypes.string.isRequired,
  cards: PropTypes.arrayOf(React.PropTypes.object),
  taskCallbacks: PropTypes.object,
  cardCallbacks: PropTypes.object
};
```

export default List;

To finish all the preparations for the drag-and-drop, let's create a constants.js file and declare the CARD type, as shown in Listing 4-22.

Listing 4-22. A Constants File to Hold the Type of CARD

```
export default {
  CARD: 'card'
};
```

Dragging Across Lists

Now you need to use React DnD's higher-order components to set up a drag source, a drop target, and a drag-and-drop context. The DragSource will be the card component, the DropTarget will be the List, and the context will be the KanbanBoard.

Starting with the Card component, you will set it as a DragSource. It will be very similar to the sample drag-and-drop implementation you did earlier on this chapter, but you won't implement the endDrag method in the cardSpec because you want the card to be able to change lists while you are still dragging, just by hovering over a new list. Listing 4-23 shows the code.

Listing 4-23. The Card Component as a DragSource, Only Implementing the Require beginDrag Method on the Spec

```
import React, { Component, PropTypes } from 'react';
import ReactCSSTransitionGroup from 'react-addons-css-transition-group';
import marked from 'marked';
import CheckList from './CheckList';
import { DragSource } from 'react-dnd';
import constants from './constants';

let titlePropType = (props, propName, componentName) => {...}

const cardDragSpec = {
  beginDrag(props) {
    return {
      id: props.id
    };
  }
}

let collectDrag = (connect, monitor) => {
  return {
    connectDragSource: connect.dragSource()
  };
}

class Card extends Component {
  constructor() {...}
  toggleDetails() {...}

  render() {
    const { connectDragSource } = this.props;

    let cardDetails;
    if (this.state.showDetails) {...}

    let sideColor = {...}

    return connectDragSource(
      <div className="card">
        <div style={sideColor}/>
        <div className={...} onClick={this.toggleDetails.bind(this)}>
          {this.props.title}
        </div>
```

```
      <ReactCSSTransitionGroup transitionName="toggle">
      {cardDetails}
      </ ReactCSSTransitionGroup>
    </div>
  );
  }
}
Card.propTypes = {
  id: PropTypes.number,
  title: titlePropType,
  description: PropTypes.string,
  color: PropTypes.string,
  tasks: PropTypes.array,
  taskCallbacks: PropTypes.object,
  cardCallbacks: PropTypes.object,
  connectDragSource: PropTypes.func.isRequired
};

export default DragSource(constants.CARD, cardDragSpec, collectDrag)(Card);
```

Next, let's make the List a DropTarget. You will use a hover method on the list spec to call the card callback to update its status as soon as it is hovering over the list; the feedback to the user will be immediate. Listing 4-24 shows the implementation.

Listing 4-24. The List Component as a DropTarget

```
import React, { Component, PropTypes } from 'react';
import { DropTarget } from 'react-dnd';
import Card from './Card';
import constants from './constants';

const listTargetSpec = {
  hover(props, monitor) {
    const draggedId = monitor.getItem().id;
    props.cardCallbacks.updateStatus(draggedId, props.id)
  }
};

function collect(connect, monitor) {
  return {
    connectDropTarget: connect.dropTarget()
  };
}

class List extends Component {
  render() {
    const { connectDropTarget } = this.props;

    let cards = this.props.cards.map((card) => {
      return <Card key={card.id} taskCallbacks={this.props.taskCallbacks}
                   cardCallbacks={this.props.cardCallbacks} {...card} />
    });
```

```
    return connectDropTarget(
      <div className="list">
        <h1>{this.props.title}</h1>
        {cards}
      </div>
    );
  }
}
List.propTypes = {
  id: PropTypes.string.isRequired,
  title: PropTypes.string.isRequired,
  cards: PropTypes.arrayOf(React.PropTypes.object),
  taskCallbacks: PropTypes.object,
  cardCallbacks: PropTypes.object,
  connectDropTarget: PropTypes.func.isRequired
}
```

```
export default DropTarget(constants.CARD, listTargetSpec, collect)(List);
```

The last piece missing is to get a common parent component of both Card and List to use as the drag-and-drop context. You will use the KanbanBoard component, as shown in Listing 4-25.

Listing 4-25. Setting the KanbanBoard Component as the Drag-and-Drop Context

```
import React, { Component, PropTypes } from 'react';
import { DragDropContext } from 'react-dnd';
import HTML5Backend from 'react-dnd-html5-backend';
import List from './List';

class KanbanBoard extends Component {
  render() {
    return (...)
  }
}
KanbanBoard.propTypes = {...}
```

```
export default DragDropContext(HTML5Backend)(KanbanBoard);
```

If you test now, you can drag a card across the lists and it gets updated immediately. Let's move on to implement the sorting.

Card Sorting

The key to implement item sorting using React DnD is to make the element both a DragSource and a DropTarget. This way, when the user starts dragging one element, you can use the hover handler to detect over which other element he is hovering and change positions with it.

Your Card component is already a DragSource. Let's turn it into a DropTarget as well by adding different spec property and collect function for when it's acting like a drop target. In the Card's dropSpec, you will use the hover function (just like you did on the List) to detect when another card is hovering over. In this case, you will invoke the updatePosition callback to switch the position between the two cards. Finally, you will also use the DropTarget higher order component to export the Card as a DropTarget appropriately.

123

Listing 4-26 shows the updated Card component. Notice the addition of a `cardDropSpec`, a `CollectDrop` function, the call to `connectDropTarget` and the exporting with the DropTarget higher order function.

Listing 4-26. The Card Component as a DropTarget

```
import React, { Component, PropTypes } from 'react';
import ReactCSSTransitionGroup from 'react-addons-css-transition-group';
import marked from 'marked';
import { DragSource, DropTarget } from 'react-dnd';
import constants from './constants';
import CheckList from './CheckList';

let titlePropType = (props, propName, componentName) => {...}

const cardDragSpec = {
  beginDrag(props) {
    return {
      id: props.id
    };
  },
};

const cardDropSpec = {
  hover(props, monitor) {
    const draggedId = monitor.getItem().id;
    props.cardCallbacks.updatePosition(draggedId, props.id);
  }
}

let collectDrag = (connect, monitor) => {
  return {
    connectDragSource: connect.dragSource()
  };
}

let collectDrop = (connect, monitor) => {
  return {
    connectDropTarget: connect.dropTarget(),
  };
}

class Card extends Component {
  constructor() {...}
  toggleDetails() {...}

  render() {
    const { connectDragSource, connectDropTarget } = this.props;

    let cardDetails;
    if (this.state.showDetails) {...}

    let sideColor = {...}
```

```
      return connectDropTarget(connectDragSource(
        <div className='card'>
          <div style={sideColor}/>
          <div className="card__edit"></div>
          <div className={...} onClick-{this.toggleDetails.bind(this)}>
            {this.props.title}
          </div>
          <ReactCSSTransitionGroup transitionName="toggle">
          {cardDetails}
          </ ReactCSSTransitionGroup>
        </div>
      ));
    }
}
Card.propTypes = {
  id: PropTypes.number,
  title: titlePropType,
  description: PropTypes.string,
  color: PropTypes.string,
  tasks: PropTypes.array,
  taskCallbacks: PropTypes.object,
  cardCallbacks: PropTypes.object,
  connectDragSource: PropTypes.func.isRequired,
  connectDropTarget: PropTypes.func.isRequired
};

const dragHighOrderCard = DragSource(constants.CARD, cardDragSpec, collectDrag)(Card);
const dragDropHighOrderCard = DropTarget(constants.CARD, cardDropSpec, ↵
                                         collectDrop)(dragHighOrderCard);
export default dragDropHighOrderCard
```

Voila! You can now drag a card across lists and move between other cards. The only thing you didn't do is persist the changes to the server. If you try moving cards around and refreshing, it will revert back to the original positions.

Throttle Callbacks

There are a lot of callbacks being fired as the user drags a card. Hovering the card on top of other cards successively invokes updatePosition callback, while hovering different lists successively invokes updateStatus.

Calling the card callbacks dozens of times per second like this has the potential to be a drag on performance, and for this reason you need to implement a throttling function. A throttling function receives two parameters, the original function you want to have throttled and wait. It returns a throttled version of the passed function that, when invoked repeatedly, will only actually call the original function at most once per every wait milliseconds. The throttling function you will implement is also smart enough to invoke the original function immediately if the calling arguments change.

To keep your project organized, you create the throttling function in a new JavaScript file called utils.js, shown in Listing 4-27.

Listing 4-27. The Throttling Function Inside utils.js JavaScript Module

```javascript
export const throttle = (func, wait) => {
  let context, args, prevArgs, argsChanged, result;
  let previous = 0;
  return function() {
    let now, remaining;
    if(wait){
      now = Date.now();
      remaining = wait - (now - previous);
    }
    context = this;
    args = arguments;
    argsChanged = JSON.stringify(args) != JSON.stringify(prevArgs);
    prevArgs = {...args};
    if (argsChanged || wait && (remaining <= 0 || remaining > wait)) {
      if(wait){
        previous = now;
      }
      result = func.apply(context, args);
      context = args = null;
    }
    return result;
  };
};
```

Next, let's edit the KanbanBoardContainer to create throttled versions of both updateCardPosition and updateCardStatus. First, import the throttle utility function, AND then use it in the KanbanBoardContainer's constructor to create throttled versions of updateCardPosition and updateCardStatus. Finally, update the cardCallbacks object in the render method to hand the throttled versions to the Kanban component. Listing 4-28 shows the updated KanbanBoardContainer source code.

Listing 4-28. Throttling the updateCartStatus and updateCardPosition Methods

```javascript
import React, { Component } from 'react';
import update from 'react-addons-update';
import {throttle} from './utils';
import KanbanBoard from './KanbanBoard';
// Polyfills
import 'whatwg-fetch';
import 'babel-polyfill';

const API_URL = '...';
const API_HEADERS = {...};

class KanbanBoardContainer extends Component {
  constructor(){
    super(...arguments);
    this.state = {
      cards:[],
    };
```

```
      // Only call updateCardStatus when arguments change
      this.updateCardStatus = throttle(this.updateCardStatus.bind(this));
      // Call updateCardPosition at max every 500ms (or when arguments change)
      this.updateCardPosition = throttle(this.updateCardPosition.bind(this),500);
    }

    componentDidMount(){...}
    addTask(cardId, taskName){...}
    deleteTask(cardId, taskId, taskIndex){...}
    toggleTask(cardId, taskId, taskIndex){...}
    updateCardStatus(cardId, listId) {...}
    updateCardPosition(cardId , afterId){...}

    render() { return (
      <KanbanBoard cards={this.state.cards}
                  taskCallbacks={{
                     toggle: this.toggleTask.bind(this),
                     delete: this.deleteTask.bind(this),
                     add: this.addTask.bind(this) }}
                  cardCallbacks={{
                     updateStatus: this.updateCardStatus,
                     updatePosition: this.updateCardPosition
        }} />
      )
    }
}

export default KanbanBoardContainer;
```

If you try again, everything should be working as before, except that now you have prevented some performance issues from occurring.

In the next topic, you will persist the card updates on the server.

Persist the New Card's Positions and Status

The first thing that might come to mind when thinking about persisting the new Card's state is to do it inside the updateCardStatus and updateCardPosition methods in the KanbanBoardContainer component. The problem here is that while the user is still dragging the Card, it may hover over a lot of different other cards and lists before settling on a final destination. If you try to persist on these methods, you will keep calling the server repeatedly during this process, which is bad not only for the obvious performance reasons, but also because it makes difficult to perform a rollback on the interface in case of a server error.

What you'll do instead is register the original card id and status when the user starts dragging it, and then only call the server when the user stops dragging. If the operation fails, you can revert back to the original card status you saved.

To do this, in the KanbanBoardContainer component you create a new method called persistCardDrag. In this new method you use the fetch function to call the Kanban API with both the new status and position of the card. If the fetch fails, you revert the UI back to the original card status. You also make the persistCardDrag method available inside the cardCallbacks object (so it can be called from the Card component). Listing 4-29 shows the updated KanbanBoardContainer.

Listing 4-29. KanbanBoardContainer with the prepareCardMove and persistCardMove Methods

```
import React, { Component } from 'react';
import update from 'react-addons-update';
import {throttle} from './utils';
import KanbanBoard from './KanbanBoard';
// Polyfills
import 'whatwg-fetch';
import 'babel-polyfill';

const API_URL...
const API_HEADERS...

class KanbanBoardContainer extends Component {
  constructor(){...}

  componentDidMount(){...}

  addTask(cardId, taskName){...}
  deleteTask(cardId, taskId, taskIndex){...}
  toggleTask(cardId, taskId, taskIndex){...}

  updateCardPosition (cardId , afterId) {...}
  updateCardStatus(cardId, listId){...}

  persistCardDrag (cardId, status) {
    // Find the index of the card
    let cardIndex = this.state.cards.findIndex((card)=>card.id == cardId);
    // Get the current card
    let card = this.state.cards[cardIndex]

    fetch(`${API_URL}/cards/${cardId}`, {
      method: 'put',
      headers: API_HEADERS,
      body: JSON.stringify({status: card.status, row_order_position: cardIndex})
    })
    .then((response) => {
      if(!response.ok){
        // Throw an error if server response wasn't 'ok'
        // so you can revert back the optimistic changes
        // made to the UI.
        throw new Error("Server response wasn't OK")
      }
    })
    .catch((error) => {
      console.error("Fetch error:",error);
      this.setState(
        update(this.state, {
```

```
          cards: {
            [cardIndex]: {
              status: { $set: status }
            }
          }
        })
      );
    });
  }

  render() {
    return (
      <KanbanBoard cards={this.state.cards}
          taskCallbacks={{
            toggle: this.toggleTask.bind(this),
            delete: this.deleteTask.bind(this),
            add: this.addTask.bind(this)
          }}
          cardCallbacks={{
            updateStatus: this.updateCardStatus,
            updatePosition: this.updateCardPosition,
            persistCardDrag: this.persistCardDrag.bind(this)
          }}
        />
      )
    }
  }
}

export default KanbanBoardContainer;
```

Next, all you have to do is use the Card's cardDragSpec to call the persistDrag callback when the user stops dragging. Listing 4-30 shows the updated Card component.

Listing 4-30. The Updated Card Component Calling prepareMove and persistMove

```
import React, { Component, PropTypes } from 'react';
import ReactCSSTransitionGroup from 'react-addons-css-transition-group';
import marked from 'marked';
import { DragSource, DropTarget } from 'react-dnd';
import constants from './constants';
import CheckList from './CheckList';

let titlePropType = (props, propName, componentName) => {...}

const cardDragSpec = {
  beginDrag(props) {
    return {
      id: props.id,
      status: props.status
    };
  },
```

```
  endDrag(props) {
    props.cardCallbacks.persistCardDrag(props.id, props.status);
  }
}

const cardDropSpec = {...}

let collectDrag = (connect, monitor) => {...}

let collectDrop = (connect, monitor) => {...}

class Card extends Component {
  constructor() {...}
  toggleDetails() {...}
  render() {...}
}
Card.propTypes = {...}

let dragHighOrderCard = DragSource(constants.CARD, cardDragSpec, collectDrag)(Card);
let dragDropHighOrderCard = DropTarget(constants.CARD, cardDropSpec, collectDrop)
(dragHighOrderCard);
export default dragDropHighOrderCard
```

Summary

In this chapter, you saw how to implement a modern, smooth, and sophisticated user interface using CSS animations (with the help of React's add-on CSSTransitionGroup) as well as drag and drop using an external library called React DnD.

CHAPTER 5

Routing

The URL is an important strength that the Web has over native apps. It was born as simple pointer to a document on a server, but in web applications the best way to think of it is as the representation of the application's current state. By looking at the URL the user can understand the part of the application where he currently is, but he can also copy it for later use or pass it along.

Implementing Routing the "Naive" Way

To understand how basic routing works as well as the complications that quickly arise in scenarios a little bigger than basic, non-nested navigation, let's begin by implementing a simple component that, depending on the current URL, renders a different child component. You'll create an application that will use the GitHub API to return the list of repositories for the pro React user. Besides this "repositories" section, the application will also have a home page and an About section. Let's focus on the main component and the routing code, shown in Listing 5-1.

Listing 5-1. A Component That Renders Child Components Based on the URL

```
import React, { Component } from 'react';
import { render } from 'react-dom';

import About from './About';
import Home from './Home';
import Repos from './Repos';

class App extends Component {
  constructor(){
    super(...arguments);
    this.state= {
      route: window.location.hash.substr(1)
    };
  }
```

```
componentDidMount() {
  window.addEventListener('hashchange', () => {
    this.setState({
      route: window.location.hash.substr(1)
    });
  });
}


render() {...}
}

render(<App />, document.getElementById('root'));
```

The code is pretty straightforward. On the component constructor, you get the current hash location of the URL and assign it to the route state. For simplicity purposes, you will not be dealing with HTML5 URL History API for now. Then, when the component mounts, you add an event listener, so every time the URL changes the route state will be updated and the component will render again. Speaking of rendering, all you need to do in the render method is use the appropriate component based on the current route, as shown in Listing 5-2.

Listing 5-2. The render Method Rendering Different Components Based on the Current Route State

```
render() {
  var Child;
  switch (this.state.route) {
    case '/about': Child = About; break;
    case '/repos': Child = Repos; break;
    default:       Child = Home;
  }

  return (
    <div>
      <header>App</header>
      <menu>
        <ul>
          <li><a href="#/about">About</a></li>
          <li><a href="#/repos">Repos</a></li>
        </ul>
      </menu>
      <Child/>
    </div>
  )
}
```

In this simple example, all child components that represent internal navigation pages have this same structure (but with different headings), as shown in Listings 5-3 through 5-5.

Listing 5-3. The Home Component

```
import React, { Component } from 'react';

class Home extends Component {
  render() {
    return (
      <h1>HOME</h1>
    );
  }
}

export default Home;
```

Listing 5-4. The About Component

```
import React, { Component } from 'react';

class About extends Component {
  render() {
    return (
      <h1>ABOUT</h1>
    );
  }
}

export default About;
```

Listing 5-5. The Repos Component

```
import React, { Component } from 'react';

class Repos extends Component {
  render() {
    return (
      <h1>Github Repos</h1>
    );
  }
}

export default Repos;
```

The routing system already works, and if you throw in some styling, it can look like Figure 5-1. The sample CSS used in this case is shown in Listing 5-6.

Figure 5-1. *Sample routing*

Listing 5-6. CSS for the Example Routing

```css
body {
  margin: 0;
  font: 16px/1 sans-serif;
}
menu ul{
  margin: 0;
  padding: 0;
}
menu li {
  display: inline-block;
  padding: 5px;
}
a.active {
  color: #444;
  font-weight: bold;
  text-decoration: none;
}
header {
  padding: 10px;
  background-color: #333;
  color: #ccc;
  font-size: 20px;
  font-weight: bold;
}
menu {
  background-color: #ccc;
  padding: 5px;
  margin-top: 0;
  margin-bottom: 10px;
}
```

Although it works for this sample scenario case, there are at least two concerns with this approach, one more conceptual and one more practical:

- In this sample implementation, URL maintenance has taken center stage: instead of automatically updating the URL while the application state flows programmatically, you're directly listening and manipulating the URL to get the app to a different state.

- The routing code can grow exponentially in complexity in non-trivial scenarios. Imagine for example that inside the Repos page you can see a list of repos for the pro React user on GitHub, with internal routes for repository details, something like /repos/repo_id (as illustrated in Figure 5-2).

Figure 5-2. *Illustrating nested routes*

- You'd have to make your URL parsing a lot more intelligently, and end up with a lot of code to figure out which branch of nested components to be rendered at any given URL.

For scenarios more complex than a single-level, basic routing, the recommended approach is to use the React Router library. Nested URLs and nested component hierarchy are at the heart of React Router's declarative API, and despite not being part of the React core, it's well regarded by the React community as the standard library for the matter.

React Router

React Router is the most popular solution for adding routing to a React application. It keeps the UI in sync with the URL by having components associated with routes (at any nesting level). When the user changes the URL, components get unmounted and mounted automatically. Another advantage of the React Router library is that it provides mechanisms so that you can control the flow of your application without different entry points depending whether the user entered a state programmatically or by hitting a new URL: the code that runs in any case is the same.

Since React Router is an external library, it must be installed with npm (along with the History library, which is a React Router peer dependency). To install version 1 of both libraries, use `npm install --save react-router@1.x.x history@1.x.x`.

React Router provides three components to get started:

- Router and Route: Used to declaratively map routes to your application's screen hierarchy.

- Link: Used to create a fully accessible anchor tag with the proper href. Of course this isn't the only way to navigate the project, but usually it's the main form the end user will interact with.

Let's change the first example from a "naive" implementation to using React Router. Once installed, begin by making the appropriate imports on your App component, as show in Listing 5-7.

Listing 5-7. Importing the React Router Components

```
import React, { Component } from 'react';
import { render } from 'react-dom';

// first we import some components
import { Router, Route, Link } from 'react-router';

import About from './About';
import Home from './Home';
import Repos from './Repos';

class App extends Component {...}
```

Inside the class, you can get rid of the constructor and componentDidMount methods that you used to manage URL parsing and event listening; this will be automatically taken of care now. Inside the render method, you can also get rid of the switch statement; the React Router will automatically set the children props to whichever is the appropriate component based on the current route. Notice, also, that you need to replace <a> tags for <Link> components to generate the suitable navigation links. Listing 5-8 shows the updated App component's class.

Listing 5-8. Updated App Component Class

```
class App extends Component {
  render() {
    return (
      <div>
        <header>App</header>
        <menu>
          <ul>
            <li><Link to="/about">About</Link></li>
            <li><Link to="/repos">Repos</Link></li>
          </ul>
        </menu>
        {this.props.children}
      </div>
    );
  }
}
```

Finally, you need to declare your routes. You do this at the end of the file. Instead of rendering the App component to the DOM, you pass the Router component with some routes to React DOM render method, as shown in Listing 5-9.

Listing 5-9. The Updated Render

```
render((
  <Router>
    <Route path="/" component={App}>
      <Route path="about" component={About}/>
      <Route path="repos" component={Repos}/>
    </Route>
  </Router>
), document.getElementById('root'));
```

The complete code for the App.js file is shown in Listing 5-10.

Listing 5-10. The Complete Code with React Router

```
import React, { Component } from 'react';
import { render } from 'react-dom';

import { Router, Route, Link } from 'react-router';

import About from './About';
import Repos from './Repos';
import Home from './Home';

class App extends Component {
  render() {
    return (
      <div>
        <header>App</header>
        <menu>
          <ul>
            <li><Link to="/about">About</Link></li>
            <li><Link to="/repos">Repos</Link></li>
          </ul>
        </menu>
        {this.props.children}
      </div>
    );
  }
}

render((
  <Router>
    <Route path="/" component={App}>
      <Route path="about" component={About}/>
      <Route path="repos" component={Repos}/>
    </Route>
  </Router>
), document.getElementById('root'));
```

■ **Tip**   Named Components: Usually a route has a single component, which is made available through this.props. children on the parent component. It's also possible to declare one or more named components when setting the route. In this case, the components will be made available to their parent by name on props.children. Example:

```
React.render((
 <Router>
  <Route path="/" component={App}>
   <Route path="groups" components={{content: Groups, sidebar: GroupsSidebar}}/>
   <Route path="users" components={{content: Users, sidebar: UsersSidebar}}/>
  </Route>
 </Router>
), element);
```

Then, in the component:

```
render() {
 return (
  <div>
   {this.props.children.sidebar}-{this.props.children.content}
  </div>
 );
}
```

Index Route

If you test right now, you will see that everything works as expected. But there is a difference from the original implementation. You're not showing the Home component in any route anymore. If you hit the server on the "/" route, it renders the App component without any children, as shown in Figure 5-3.

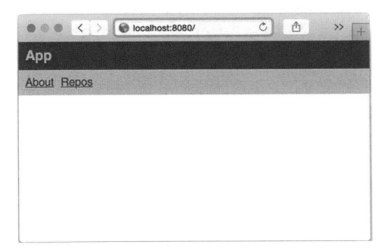

Figure 5-3. *Home route renders the App component with no children*

The first thing that may come to mind is to simply add a new Home route the router, but which path are you going to use?

```
<Router>
  <Route path="/" component={App}>
    <Route path="???" component={Home}/>
    <Route path="about" component={About}/>
    <Route path="repos" component={Repos}/>
  </Route>
</Router>
```

Instead, you can use an <IndexRoute> for this. Just import the additional component and use it to configure the index route, as shown here and in Figure 5-4.

```
import React, { Component } from 'react';
import { render } from 'react-dom';

import { Router, Route, IndexRoute, Link } from 'react-router';

import About from './About';
import Repos from './Repos';
import Home from './Home';

class App extends Component {...}

render((
  <Router>
    <Route path="/" component={App}>
      <IndexRoute component={Home}/>
      <Route path="about" component={About} />
      <Route path="repos" component={Repos} />
    </Route>
  </Router>
), document.getElementById('root'));
```

Figure 5-4. *If no route is provided, the home component is rendered*

Routes with Parameters

Now that you have an implementation on par with your original "naive" routing, let's expand on it to actually fetch data from the GitHub API in the Repos component. You won't do anything new here: you will create a local state for the repositories and fetch the API from the componentDidMount lifecycle method, as you did in earlier examples. Listing 5-11 shows the Repo component with the additional fetching.

■ **Note**   In this sample code, you use the new window.fetch function, as you did in earlier examples of this book. Since older browsers don't have support for the new standard, make sure to install and require the whatwg-fetch polyfill from npm.

```
npm install --save whatwg-fetch
```

Listing 5-11. Repos Component Fetching from the GitHub API

```jsx
import React, { Component } from 'react';

import 'whatwg-fetch';

class Repos extends Component {
  constructor(){
    super(...arguments);
    this.state = {
      repositories: []
    };
  }

  componentDidMount(){
    fetch('https://api.github.com/users/pro-react/repos')
    .then((response) => response.json())
    .then((responseData) => {
      this.setState({repositories:responseData});
    });
  }

  render() {
    let repos = this.state.repositories.map((repo) => (
      <li key={repo.id}>{repo.name}</li>
    ));
    return (
      <div>
        <h1>Github Repos</h1>
        <ul>
          {repos}
        </ul>
      </div>
    );
  }
}

export default Repos;
```

■ **Note**   The GitHub API is limited to 60 requests per hour for unregistered users. To learn more about GitHub API, visit `https://developer.github.com/v3/`.

If you test the application, you will see a list of repositories when navigating to the Repo component. Next, you will create a new route where you can show specific repository details. The idea is to get the URL to look something like /repos/details/repo_name.

You need to create a new RepoDetails component and update the routes in the App.js file, but before you do all that, let's edit the Repos component to add links to repositories list and to load the RepoDetails as a nested child. The updated code is shown in Listing 5-12 (code parts that didn't change were omitted for brevity).

Listing 5-12. Adding Link Components for Repositories List and Rendering the Nested RepoDetails Component

```
import React, { Component } from 'react';
import 'whatwg-fetch';
import { Link } from 'react-router';

class Repos extends Component {
  constructor(){...}

  componentDidMount(){...}

  render() {
    let repos = this.state.repositories.map((repo) => (
      <li key={repo.id}>
        <Link to={"/repos/details/"+repo.name}>{repo.name}</Link>
      </li>
    ));
    return (
      <div>
      <h1>Github Repos</h1>
      <ul>
        {repos}
      </ul>
      {this.props.children}
      </div>
    );
  }
}

export default Repos;
```

In the sequence, let's create the RepoDetails component. There are two things to notice in this code:

- The React Router will inject the repo_name parameter in the component's properties. You can use this value to fetch the GitHub API and get the project's details.

- In all previous examples of this book, you always fetched data in the componentDidMount lifecycle method. In the RepoDetails case, you need to implement the fetch in an additional lifecycle method: componentWillReceiveProps. This is necessary because the component may keep receiving new parameters as the user clicks in different repositories after it is mounted. In this case, the componentDidMount won't be called again. Instead, componentWillReceiveProps will be invoked.

Listing 5-13 shows the complete code for RepoDetails component.

Listing 5-13. The RepoDetails Component

```
import React, { Component } from 'react';
import 'whatwg-fetch';

class RepoDetails extends Component {
  constructor(){
    super(...arguments);
    this.state={
      repository:{}
    };
  }

  fetchData(repo_name){
    fetch('https://api.github.com/repos/pro-react/'+repo_name)
    .then((response) => response.json())
    .then((responseData) => {
      this.setState({repository:responseData});
    });
  }

  componentDidMount(){
    // The Router injects the key "repo_name" inside the params prop
    let repo_name = this.props.params.repo_name;
    this.fetchData(repo_name)
  }

  componentWillReceiveProps(nextProps){
    // The Router injects the key "repo_name" inside the params prop
    let repo_name = nextProps.params.repo_name;
    this.fetchData(repo_name)
  }

  render() {
    let stars = [];
    for (var i = 0; i < this.state.repository.stargazers_count; i++) {
      stars.push('*');
    }
```

```
    return (
      <div>
        <h2>{this.state.repository.name}</h2>
        <p>{this.state.repository.description}</p>
        <span>{stars}</span>
      </div>
    );
  }
}
```

```
export default RepoDetails;
```

To finish your implementation of the nested Repo details route, you need to update the main App.js file. You import the new component and update the Router component implementing the details route as a child of the repos route, declaring the named parameter of repo_name, as shown in Listing 5-14.

Listing 5-14. The Updated App.js

```
import React, { Component } from 'react';
import { render } from 'react-dom';
import { Router, Route, IndexRoute, Link } from 'react-router';
import Home from './Home';
import About from './About';
import Repos from './Repos';
import RepoDetails from './RepoDetails';

class App extends Component {...}

render((
  <Router>
    <Route path="/" component={App}>
      <IndexRoute component={Home}/>
      <Route path="about" component={About}/>
      <Route path="repos" component={Repos}>
        {/* Add the route, nested where we want the UI to nest */}
        <Route path="details/:repo_name" component={RepoDetails} />
      </Route>
    </Route>
  </Router>
), document.getElementById('root'));
```

When declaring a dynamic segment inside a route (such as :repo_name), React Router will inject any data that is in that part of the URL into a parameter attribute inside the component props.

If you followed along, you should be seeing something like Figure 5-5.

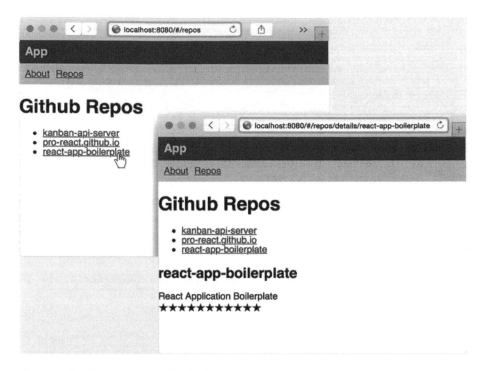

Figure 5-5. *Nested routes inside the Repos component*

Setting Active Links

The Link component has nice additional touch: it accepts an optional prop called activeClassName. If this prop is set, it will automatically add this class name to active links. Let's add this prop to your App component, as shown in Listing 5-15.

Listing 5-15. The App Component's Links with activeClassName

```
class App extends Component {
  render() {
    return (
      <div>
        <header>App</header>
        <menu>
          <ul>
            <li><Link to="/about" activeClassName="active">About</Link></li>
            <li><Link to="/repos" activeClassName="active">Repos</Link></li>
          </ul>
        </menu>
```

```
        {this.props.children}
      </div>
    );
  }
}
```

Passing Props

There's a big problem with your implementation so far: you doing an unnecessary fetch. The GitHub API already provides all the repositories details when you first fetch `https://api.github.com/users/pro-react/repos`. You could pass all the data about the repositories down as props to render on the repoDetails component. There are two ways of passing props in React Router: by specifying props on the route configuration object or by injecting props on a clone of the children. The first one is more idiomatic, but it won't solve all problems. The further looks a little "hacky" but does allow for more flexibility.

Props on the Route Configuration

The `<Route>` component is just a declarative way to configure a route; it is not rendered as a regular React component. When active, it renders the specified component instead. The `<Route path="about" component={About} />` element, for example, renders the About component when the route is active. What's interesting to notice is that besides rendering the specified component, the React Router injects all the Route properties inside the component's props, which means that any additional props you define in the route will be accessible by the component.

To illustrate, let's make the About component receive its title as props from the route. First, you add an arbitrary "title" prop to the about route:

```
React.render((
  <Router>
    <Route path="/" component={App}>
      <IndexRoute component={Home}/>
      <Route path="about" component={About} title="About Us" />
      <Route path="repos" component={Repos}>
        <Route path="details/:repo_name" component={RepoDetails} />
      </Route>
    </Route>
  </Router>
), document.getElementById('root'));
```

Next, in the About component, you access the route configuration from `this.props.route`:

```
import React, { Component } from 'react';

class About extends Component {
  render() {
    return (
      <h1>{this.props.route.title}</h1>
    );
  }
}

export default About;
```

Cloning and Injecting Props on Children

Another approach, especially useful for dynamic props, is to clone the `child` component that gets injected as props by React Router, which gives you the opportunity to pass additional props in the process.

That's exactly the case for the GitHub Repos project you've been building. You want to pass the repositories' data you fetched in the Repo component to the RepoDetails component, but as you already know, the React Router will automatically create the RepoDetails component and inject it into the Repo's props.children, which doesn't give you any chance to manipulate its props.

Inside the Repo component, instead of simply rendering this.props.children provided by the router, you clone it and inject additional props (the list of repositories), as shown in Listing 5-16.

Listing 5-16. The Updated Repos Component Using React.cloneElement to Pass Additional Props to the Children Provided by the Router

```
class Repos extends Component {
  constructor(){...}
  componentDidMount(){...}

  render() {
    let repos = this.state.repositories.map((repo) => (
      <li key={repo.id}>
        <Link to={"/repos/details/"+repo.name}>{repo.name}</Link>
      </li>
    ));

    let child = this.props.children && React.cloneElement(this.props.children,
      { repositories: this.state.repositories }
    );

    return (
      <div>
      <h1>Github Repos</h1>
      <ul>
        {repos}
      </ul>
        {child}
      </div>
    );
  }
}
```

Now the RepoDetails will be treated as a pure component. It won't have internal state, it'll just receive and display props. You remove the `constructor`, `componentWillReceiveProps`, `componentDidMount`, and `fetchData` methods, and change the `render` method to find the repository based on the URL parameter. Listing 5-17 shows the updated `RepoDetails.js`.

■ **Note**   As mentioned, `Array.prototype.find` is a new method not supported on older browsers. Make sure to install the polyfills from Babel with `npm install --save babel-polyfill` and import it on the JavaScript module with `import 'babel-polyfill'`.

Listing 5-17. The Updated RepoDetails.js File

```
import React, { Component } from 'react';
import 'babel-polyfill';

class RepoDetails extends Component {

  renderRepository() {
    let repository = this.props.repositories.find((repo)=>repo.name === this.props.params.
    repo_name);
    let stars = [];
    for (var i = 0; i < repository.stargazers_count; i++) {
      stars.push('*');
    }
    return(
      <div>
        <h2>{repository.name}</h2>
        <p>{repository.description}</p>
        <span>{stars}</span>
      </div>
    );
  }

  render() {
    if(this.props.repositories.length > 0 ){
      return this.renderRepository();
    } else {
      return <h4>Loading...</h4>;
    }
  }
}

export default RepoDetails;
```

Decoupling the UI from the URL

While the details route works pretty well, you ended up with a URL segment that is a bit too long: `/repos/details/:repo_name`. It would be nice if you could change the URL segment to the smaller and singular form of `/repo/:repo_name`, but still render the RepoDetails component nested inside App ⌐ Repos. In React Router, it is possible to do this kind of setup using an absolute path in the route definition.

So, instead of

```
render((
  <Router>
    <Route path="/" component={App}>
      <IndexRoute component={Home}/>
      <Route path="about" component={About} />
      <Route path="repos" component={Repos}>
        <Route path="details/:repo_name" component={RepoDetails} />
      </Route>
    </Route>
  </Router>
), document.getElementById('root'));
```

you use an absolute path, like

```
render((
  <Router>
    <Route path="/" component={App}>
      <IndexRoute component={Home}/>
      <Route path="about" component={About} />
      <Route path="repos" component={Repos}>
        <Route path="/repo/:repo_name" component={RepoDetails} />
      </Route>
    </Route>
  </Router>
), document.getElementById('root'));
```

Of course, you also need to update the links on the Repo component to reflect the new URL, as show in Listing 5-18.

Listing 5-18. The Updated Link on the Repo Component

```
class Repos extends Component {
  constructor(){...}
  componentDidMount(){...}

  render() {
    let repos = this.state.repositories.map((repo) => (
      <li key={repo.id}><Link to={"/repo/"+repo.name}>{repo.name}</Link></li>
    ));

    let child = this.props.children && React.cloneElement(...);

    return (...);
  }
}

export default Repos;
```

The new URLs are shown in Figure 5-6.

Figure 5-6. *The UI keeps nested hierarchy, but with custom decoupled routes*

Changing Routes Programmatically

The Link component you used earlier provides a nice way for the end user to transition between routes, but sometimes you need to be able to do it programmatically from inside your components. You might want to automatically go back or redirect the user to a different route under certain circumstances.

For this purpose, React Router automatically injects its history object into all components that it mounts. The history object is responsible for managing the browser's history stack, and provides the methods for navigation shown in Table 5-1.

Table 5-1. *History Methods*

Method	Description

pushState	The basic history navigation method transitions to a new URL. You can optionally pass a parameters object. Example:
	
	`history.pushState(null, '/users/123')`
	`history.pushState({showGrades: true}, '/users/123')`

replaceState	Has the same syntax as pushState, but it replaces the current URL with a new one. It's analogous to a redirect, because it replaces the URL without affecting the length of the history.
goBack	Go back one entry in the navigation history.
goForward	Go forward one entry in the navigation history.
Go	Go forward or backward in the history by n or -n
createHref	Makes a URL, using the router's config.

To illustrate, let's create a new Server Error route. From the Repos component you redirect to this new route if the `fetch` method can't connect to the API. Listings 5-19 and 5-20 show the new ServerError component and the updated routes in the App.js, respectively.

Listing 5-19. The ServerError Component with Some Inline Styling

```
import React, { Component } from 'react';

const styles={
  root:{
    textAlign:'center'
  },
  alert:{
    fontSize:80,
    fontWeight: 'bold',
    color:'#e9ab2d'
  }
};

class ServerError extends Component {
  render() {
    return (
      <div style={styles.root}>
        <div style={styles.alert}>&#9888; </div>
        {/* &#9888; is the html entity code for the warning character: ⚠ */}
        <h1>Ops, we have a problem</h1>
        <p>Sorry, we could't access the repositories. Please try again in a few moments.</p>
      </div>
    );
  }
}

export default ServerError;
```

Listing 5-20. The Updated Import and Route Definition on App.js

```
import React, { Component } from 'react';
import { render } from 'react-dom';
import { Router, Route, Link, IndexRoute } from 'react-router';

import About from './About';
import Repos from './Repos';
import RepoDetails from './RepoDetails';
import Home from './Home';
import ServerError from './ServerError';

class App extends Component {...}

render((
  <Router>
    <Route path="/" component={App}>
      <IndexRoute component={Home}/>
```

150

```
      <Route path="about" component={About} />
      <Route path="repos" component={Repos}>
        <Route path="/repo/:repo_name" component={RepoDetails} />
      </Route>
      <Route path="error" component={ServerError} />
    </Route>
  </Router>
), document.getElementById('root'));
```

Back to the Repos component, you use the pushState method inside the fetch's catch statement, as shown in Listing 5-21.

Listing 5-21. The Updated Repos Component Using pushState to Redirect to Error Page

```
import React, { Component } from 'react';
import { Link } from 'react-router';
import 'whatwg-fetch';

class Repos extends Component {
  constructor(){...}
  componentDidMount(){
    fetch('https://api.github.com/users/pro-react/repos')
    .then((response) => {
      if(response.ok){
        return response.json();
      } else {
        throw new Error("Server response wasn't OK");
      }
    })
    .then((responseData) => {
      this.setState({repositories:responseData});
    })
    .catch((error) => {
      this.props.history.pushState(null,'/error');
    });
  }

  render() {...}
}

export default Repos;
```

When trying to access the /repos route after the GitHub API limit has expired, the component changes the route to the error route, as shown in Figure 5-7.

Figure 5-7. *Route redirection from inside the component*

Of course, you don't have to exceed the GitHub's API rate limit to test this. Simply disconnect the Internet and try accessing the repos route. The fetch will retry three times and fail.

Histories

React Router is built on top of the History library (remember that when you installed the React Router using npm, you also installed History). Its purpose is to abstract URL and session management, providing a common API for manipulating the history stack and the URL across different browsers, testing environments, and platforms.

The History library has different possible setups. By default, React Router uses the hash history setup, which uses the hash (#) portion of the URL creating routes that look like example.com/#/path.

The hash history is the default setup because it works on older browsers (Internet Explorer 8 and 9) and doesn't require any server configuration. If your application doesn't need to run on legacy browsers and you have the possibility to configure your server, the ideal approach is to use the browser history setup, which creates real URLs that look like example.com/path.

■ **Note**   Server Configuration: The browser history setup can generate real looking URLs without reloading the page. But what happens if the user refreshes or bookmarks on a deep nested URL? These URLs are dynamically generated at the browser; they do not correspond to real paths on the server, and since any URL will always hit the server on the first request, it will likely return a Page Not Found error.

To work with browser history setup, you need to make rewrite configurations on your server, so when the user hits /some-path on the browser, the server will serve index page from where React Router will render the right view.

The Webpack dev server has the historyApiFallback option to always render the index page for unknown paths (and if you are using this book's boilerplate app, this configuration is already in place). Node.js and all common web servers such as Apache and Nginx have such configurations. Please refer to the React Router's documentation and your server's documentation.

To implement the browser history setup, you need to import the `createBrowserHistory` method from the History library. You can then invoke it, passing the generated browser history configuration as the history prop of the Router component. Let's implement it in your sample application, as shown in Listing 5-22.

Listing 5-22. The Updated App.js Using the BrowserHistory Setup

```
import React, { Component } from 'react';
import { render } from 'react-dom';

import { Router, Route, IndexRoute, Link } from 'react-router';
import createBrowserHistory from 'history/lib/createBrowserHistory';

import About from './About';
import Repos from './Repos';
import RepoDetails from './RepoDetails';
import Home from './Home';
import ServerError from './ServerError';

class App extends Component {...}

render((
  <Router history={createBrowserHistory()}>
    <Route path="/" component={App}>
      <IndexRoute component={Home}/>
      <Route path="about" component={About} />
      <Route path="repos" component={Repos}>
        <Route path="/repo/:repo_name" component={RepoDetails} />
      </Route>
      <Route path="error" component={ServerError} />
    </Route>
  </Router>
), document.getElementById('root'));
```

Kanban App: Routing

So far, the Kanban application has been very effective as an exercise, but it's not yet very useful on its own because you can't edit or create new cards. Let's implement these two features using routes. The /new route will show a form to create a new card, whereas the /edit/:card_id route will show a form with the card's current properties so the user can edit it. Both NewCard and EditCard will be new components, and since both share much of the same characteristics (like the complete card form), you will also create a CardForm component that will be used by both and retain all the shared UI.

Since you're going to implement code in lots of different files, let's review everything that needs to be done:

- Starting bottom up, let's create the CardForm component.

- Next, you create the NewCard and EditCard components.

- In the sequence, you edit the `App.js` to set up the new routes.

- In the `KanbanBoardContainer` class, you create methods for creating and editing cards. You pass these methods as props to the NewCard and EditCard components.

153

Before you start, make sure to install React Router and History: `npm install --save react-router@1.x.x history@1.x.x`.

CardForm Component

As mentioned, since the NewCard and EditCard components share much of the same UI, you will create the CardForm component and use it in both components. It will contain a form (that needs to be flexible enough to be used blank or pre-filled with existing card values.) and an overlay. The form will appear as a modal on top of the Kanban board, and the overlay will be used behind the modal to "darken" everything behind it. Figure 5-8 shows the desired effect.

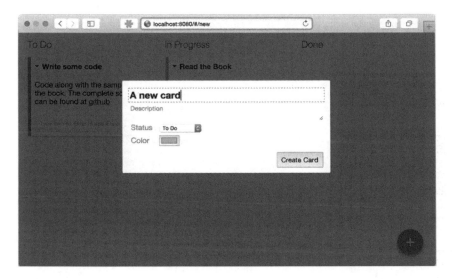

Figure 5-8. *Form and overlay*

The CardForm component will be a pure component. It won't have state. Both NewCard or EditCard components need to provide the following props to the CardForm:

- An object (let's call it a draft card) containing the card values to display on the form. In the case of EditCard, this object will contain the values of the card being edited. In the case of NewCard, this object will contain blank/default values for a new card.

- The label of the Submit button.

- Functions to handle form field change and form submit.

- A function to handle the modal closing (when the user clicks outside the modal).

Listing 5-23 shows the CardForm component source code.

Listing 5-23. The CardForm Component Source Code

```
import React, {Component, PropTypes} from 'react';

class CardForm extends Component {
```

```
handleChange(field, e){
  this.props.handleChange(field, e.target.value);
}

handleClose(e){
  e.preventDefault();
  this.props.handleClose();
}

render(){
  return (
    <div>
      <div className="card big">
        <form onSubmit={this.props.handleSubmit.bind(this)}>
          <input type='text'
                 value={this.props.draftCard.title}
                 onChange={this.handleChange.bind(this,'title')}
                 placeholder="Title"
                 required={true}
                 autoFocus={true} />
          <textarea value={this.props.draftCard.description}
                    onChange={this.handleChange.bind(this,'description')}
                    placeholder="Description"
                    required={true} />
          <label htmlFor="status">Status</label>
          <select id="status"
                  value={this.props.draftCard.status}
                  onChange={this.handleChange.bind(this,'status')}>
            <option value="todo">To Do</option>
            <option value="in-progress">In Progress</option>
            <option value="done">Done</option>
          </select>
          <br />
          <label htmlFor="color">Color</label>
          <input id="color"
                 value={this.props.draftCard.color}
                 onChange={this.handleChange.bind(this,'color')}
                 type="color"
                 defaultValue="#ff0000" />

          <div className='actions'>
            <button type="submit">{this.props.buttonLabel}</button>
          </div>
        </form>
      </div>
      <div className="overlay" onClick={this.handleClose.bind(this)}>
      </div>
    </div>
  );
}
}
```

```
CardForm.propTypes = {
  buttonLabel: PropTypes.string.isRequired,
  draftCard: PropTypes.shape({
    title: PropTypes.string,
    description: PropTypes.string,
    status: PropTypes.string,
    color: PropTypes.string
  }).isRequired,
  handleChange: PropTypes.func.isRequired,
  handleSubmit: PropTypes.func.isRequired,
  handleClose: PropTypes.func.isRequired,
}
```

export default CardForm;

Next, in order to create the results shown in Figure 5-8, you need to add some additional styling for the form and overlay. Listing 5-24 shows the additional styles.

Listing 5-24. Aditional CSS Styling

```
.overlay {
  position: absolute;
  width: 100%;
  height: 100%;
  top: 0; left: 0; bottom: 0; right: 0;
  z-index: 2;
  background-color: rgba(0, 0, 0, 0.6);
}

.card.big {
  position: absolute;
  width: 450px;
  height: 200px;
  margin: auto;
  padding: 15px;
  top: 0; left: 0; bottom: 100px; right: 0;
  z-index: 3;
}

.card.big input[type=text], textarea {
  width : 100%;
  margin: 3px 0;
  font-size: 13px;
  border: none;
}

.card.big input[type=text] {
  font-size: 20px;
  font-weight: bold;
```

```
}

.card.big input[type=text]:focus,
.card.big textarea:focus {
  outline: dashed thin #999;
  outline-offset: 2px;
}

.card.big label {
  margin: 3px 0 7px 3px;
  color: #a7a7a7;
  display: inline-block;
  width: 60px;
}

.actions {
  margin-top: 10px;
  text-align: right;
}

.card.big button {
  font-size:14px;
  padding: 8px;
}
```

NewCard and EditCard Components

Let's move on to the NewCard end EditCard components. They have a lot in common: both will hold the draft card state, render the CardForm, and provide it with callbacks to manipulate that state and persist the new/edited card.

Starting with the NewCard component, Listing 5-25 shows its source code.

Listing 5-25. The Final Code for the NewCard.js Component

```
import React,{Component, PropTypes} from 'react';
import CardForm from './CardForm'

class NewCard extends Component{

  componentWillMount(){
    this.setState({
      id: Date.now(),
      title:'',
      description:'',
      status:'todo',
      color:'#c9c9c9',
      tasks:[]
    });
  }
```

```
  handleChange(field, value){
    this.setState({[field]: value});
  }

  handleSubmit(e){
    e.preventDefault();
    this.props.cardCallbacks.addCard(this.state);
    this.props.history.pushState(null,'/');
  }

  handleClose(e){
    this.props.history.pushState(null,'/');
  }

  render(){
    return (
      <CardForm draftCard={this.state}
                buttonLabel="Create Card"
                handleChange={this.handleChange.bind(this)}
                handleSubmit={this.handleSubmit.bind(this)}
                handleClose={this.handleClose.bind(this)} />
    );
  }
}

NewCard.propTypes = {
  cardCallbacks: PropTypes.object,
};

export default NewCard;
```

There are a few things to notice in the code above:

- When the component mounts, it sets the component state to an empty draft card with some default values and a temporary ID (based on the current date). The values of this draft card will be presented in the CardForm, and for every change you update the state.

- When the user submits the form, you save the new card by invoking the cardCallbacks.addCard that came down as props from the KanbanBoardContainer.

That's all for the NewCard component. Let's move to the EditCard, which will be similar except for the fact that the EditCard expects to receive a card_id querystring parameter from the route. With the card id you can filter the card information and set the draft card in its state with the values from the card the user wants to edit, as shown in Listing 5-26.

Listing 5-26. The Complete Code for the EditCard.js Component

```
import React,{Component, PropTypes} from 'react';
import CardForm from './CardForm';

class EditCard extends Component{

  componentWillMount(){
    let card = this.props.cards.find((card)=>card.id == this.props.params.card_id);
    this.setState({...card});
  }

  handleChange(field, value){
    this.setState({[field]: value});
  }

  handleSubmit(e){
    e.preventDefault();
    this.props.cardCallbacks.updateCard(this.state);
    this.props.history.pushState(null,'/');
  }

  handleClose(e){
    this.props.history.pushState(null,'/');
  }

  render(){
    return (
      <CardForm draftCard={this.state}
                buttonLabel="Edit Card"
                handleChange={this.handleChange.bind(this)}
                handleSubmit={this.handleSubmit.bind(this)}
                handleClose={this.handleClose.bind(this)} />
    )
  }
}

EditCard.propTypes = {
  cardCallbacks: PropTypes.object,
}

export default EditCard;
```

Setting Up the Routes

Let's skip the KanbanBoardContainer for a minute to set up the routes on the App.js file. This will help you better comprehend how you will modify the KanbanBoardContainer later. You will create three routes: an index route that leads to the Kanban board, a new route associated with the NewCard component, and an edit/:card_id route associated with the EditCard component. It's also important to note that both the new and the edit routes will be nested inside the Kanban. That's so you can see the Kanban board and the cards behind the form; you don't want the form to be a completely isolated section. Listing 5-27 shows the App.js with the routing.

Listing 5-27. The Routes on App.js

```
import React from 'react';
import { render } from 'react-dom';
import { Router, Route } from 'react-router';
import createBrowserHistory from 'history/lib/createBrowserHistory';
import KanbanBoardContainer from './KanbanBoardContainer';
import KanbanBoard from './KanbanBoard';
import EditCard from './EditCard';
import NewCard from './NewCard';

render((
  <Router history={createBrowserHistory()}>
    <Route component={KanbanBoardContainer}>
      <Route path="/" component={KanbanBoard}>
        <Route path="new" component={NewCard} />
        <Route path="edit/:card_id" component={EditCard} />
      </Route>
    </Route>
  </Router>
), document.getElementById('root'));
```

Creating the Callbacks and Rendering the Children on KanbanBoardContainer

The first thing you do in the KanbanBoardContainer component is create the two methods for creating and updating cards. They will be very similar to the analogous methods for tasks. Listing 5-28 shows the addCard method and Listing 5-29 shows the updateCard.

Listing 5-28. The addCard Method Inside the KanbanBoardContainer

```
addCard(card){
  // Keep a reference to the original state prior to the mutations
  // in case we need to revert the optimistic changes in the UI
  let prevState = this.state;

  // Add a temporary ID to the card
  if(card.id===null){
    let card = Object.assign({}, card, {id:Date.now()});
  }

  // Create a new object and push the new card to the array of cards
  let nextState = update(this.state.cards, { $push: [card] });

  // set the component state to the mutated object
  this.setState({cards:nextState});

  // Call the API to add the card on the server
  fetch(`${API_URL}/cards`, {
    method: 'post',
    headers: API_HEADERS,
    body: JSON.stringify(card)
  })
```

```
    .then((response) => {
      if(response.ok){
        return response.json()
      } else {
        // Throw an error if server response wasn't 'ok'
        // so we can revert back the optimistic changes
        // made to the UI.
        throw new Error("Server response wasn't OK")
      }
    })
    .then((responseData) => {
      // When the server returns the definitive ID
      // used for the new Card on the server, update it on React
      card.id=responseData.id
      this.setState({cards:nextState});
    })
    .catch((error) => {
      this.setState(prevState);
    });
}
```

Listing 5-29. The updateCard Method Inside the KanbanBoardContainer

```
updateCard(card){
  // Keep a reference to the original state prior to the mutations
  // in case we need to revert the optimistic changes in the UI
  let prevState = this.state;

  // Find the index of the card
  let cardIndex = this.state.cards.findIndex((c)=>c.id == card.id);

  // Using the $set command, we will change the whole card
  let nextState = update(
                    this.state.cards, {
                      [cardIndex]: { $set: card }
                    });
  // set the component state to the mutated object
  this.setState({cards:nextState});

  // Call the API to update the card on the server
  fetch(`${API_URL}/cards/${card.id}`, {
      method: 'put',
      headers: API_HEADERS,
      body: JSON.stringify(card)
  })
  .then((response) => {
    if(!response.ok){
      // Throw an error if server response wasn't 'ok'
      // so we can revert back the optimistic changes
      // made to the UI.
      throw new Error("Server response wasn't OK")
    }
```

161

```
  })
  .catch((error) => {
    console.error("Fetch error:",error)
    this.setState(prevState);
  });
}
```

Finally, you need to update the render method. You don't get to render the KanbanBoard manually; it will be injected by the router. The problem is that there's no way to add new props to a component that the router passes as children, but the alternative is actually pretty simple. As you saw earlier, you will clone the props.children injected by the router and add the new props, as shown in Listing 5-30.

Listing 5-30. Cloning the Child to Insert the Cards List and Callbacks as Props

```
render() {
  let kanbanBoard = this.props.children && React.cloneElement(this.props.children, {
    cards: this.state.cards,
    taskCallbacks:{
      toggle: this.toggleTask.bind(this),
      delete: this.deleteTask.bind(this),
      add: this.addTask.bind(this)
    },
    cardCallbacks:{
      addCard: this.addCard.bind(this),
      updateCard: this.updateCard.bind(this),
      updateStatus: this.updateCardStatus.bind(this),
      updatePosition: throttle(this.updateCardPosition.bind(this),500),
      persistMove: this.persistCardMove.bind(this)
    }
  });

  return kanbanBoard;
}
```

Rendering the Card Forms in the KanbanBoard

In the routes you configured earlier in the App.js file, the NewCard and EditCard components are children of KanbanBoard. When the user points to the routes /new or /edit, the router will inject the corresponding component as a children prop in the KanbanBoard. You need now to edit the KanbanBoard to clone the children props (to insert new props such as the list of cards and card callbacks) and render it. It is pretty much the same thing you just did for the KanbanBoardContainer. Listing 5-31 shows the new render function.

Listing 5-31. Rendering NewCard and EditCard in KanbanBoard Component

```
render() {
  let cardModal=this.props.children && React.cloneElement(this.props.children, {
    cards: this.props.cards,
    cardCallbacks: this.props.cardCallbacks
  });
```

```
  return (
    <div className="app">
      <List ... />
      <List ... />
      <List ... />

      {cardModal}

    </div>
  )
}
```

Finishing Touches: Transitioning

Your application is all wired up and is already working. If you manually input the /new route or the /
edit/:card_id (with a valid card id, of course), everything will work as expected, but that's not very practical,
so let's finish by making handling transitions to the routes, starting with the new route.

You will create a new link (using the Link component) inside the KanbanBoard component, pointing to
new. See Listing 5-32.

Listing 5-32. Link to New Route on KanbanBoard Component

```
import React, { Component, PropTypes } from 'react';
import { DragDropContext } from 'react-dnd';
import HTML5Backend from 'react-dnd-html5-backend';
import List from './List';
import { Link } from 'react-router';

class KanbanBoard extends Component {
  render() {
    let cardModal=this.props.children && React.cloneElement(this.props.children, {
      cards: this.props.cards,
      cardCallbacks: this.props.cardCallbacks
    });

    return (
      <div className="app">
        <Link to='/new' className="float-button">+</Link>

        <List ... />
        <List ... />
        <List ... />

        {cardModal}

      </div>
    )
  }
}
KanbanBoard.propTypes = {...}

export default DragDropContext(HTML5Backend)(KanbanBoard);
```

163

You also add some styling on the link. It will be a round button absolutely positioned on the bottom right side of the screen, as shown in Listing 5-33 and Figure 5-9.

Listing 5-33. CSS Styling for the Button

```css
.float-button {
  position: absolute;
  height: 56px;
  width: 56px;
  z-index: 2;
  right: 20px;
  bottom: 20px;
  background: #D43A2F;
  color: white;
  border-radius: 100%;
  font-size: 34px;
  text-align: center;
  text-decoration: none;
  line-height: 50px;
  box-shadow: 0 5px 10px rgba(0, 0, 0, 0.5);
}
```

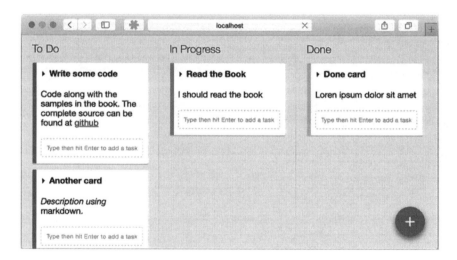

Figure 5-9. *The add card button*

Finally, let's also add a Link component to the card. Similar to the New button, you will style it so it doesn't appear as a plain link. In the case of the card, you even use some CSS tricks to only show the edit link when the user is hovering over the card. Listing 5-34 shows the code for the Card component, Listing 5-35 shows the additional styling for this element, and Figure 5-10 shows the final result.

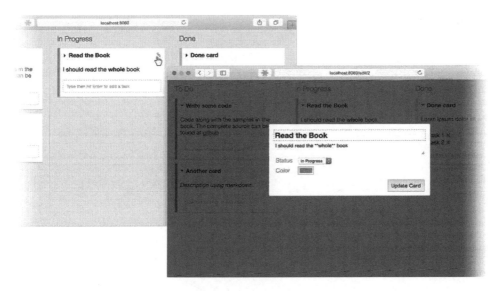

Figure 5-10. *The Edit button on the Card component*

Listing 5-34. Link Component on the Card

```
import React, { Component, PropTypes } from 'react';
import ReactCSSTransitionGroup from 'react-addons-css-transition-group';
import marked from 'marked';
import { DragSource, DropTarget } from 'react-dnd';
import constants from './constants';
import CheckList from './CheckList';
import {Link} from 'react-router';

let titlePropType = (props, propName, componentName) => {...};
const cardDragSpec = {...};
const cardDropSpec = {...};
let collectDrag = (connect, monitor) => {...};
let collectDrop = (connect, monitor) => {...};

class Card extends Component {
  constructor() {...}
  toggleDetails() {...}
  render() {
    const { connectDragSource, connectDropTarget } = this.props;

    let cardDetails;
    if (this.state.showDetails) {...};
    let sideColor = {...};

    return connectDropTarget(connectDragSource(
      <div className="card">
        <div style={sideColor}/>
        <div className="card__edit"><Link to={'/edit/'+this.props.id}>&#9998;</Link></div>
```

```
    {/* &#9998; is the HTML entity for the utf-8 pencil character (✎) */}
    <div className={...} onClick={...}>
      {this.props.title}
    </div>
    <ReactCSSTransitionGroup transitionName="toggle"
                             transitionEnterTimeout={250}
                             transitionLeaveTimeout={250} >
    {cardDetails}
    </ ReactCSSTransitionGroup>
  </div>
  ));
  }
}
Card.propTypes = {...};

const dragHighOrderCard = DragSource(constants.CARD, cardDragSpec, collectDrag)(Card);
const dragDropHighOrderCard = DropTarget(constants.CARD, cardDropSpec, collectDrop)
(dragHighOrderCard);

export default dragDropHighOrderCard
```

Listing 5-35. Additional CSS Styles for the Card Edit Link

```
.card__edit{
  position: absolute;
  top:10px;
  right: 10px;
  opacity: 0;
  transition: opacity .25s ease-in;
}
.card:hover .card__edit{
  opacity: 1;
}
.card__edit a{
  text-decoration: none;
  color: #999;
  font-size: 17px;
}
```

Summary

This chapter discussed routing. You started by manually implementing a basic routing and understanding the complexities that can arise with nested routing. Next, you learned how to use one of the most used libraries in the React community, the React Router. You saw how to set up nested routes and a default home route, how to pass parameters through the route to a component, and how to directly pass properties from a component to its children. You then learned how make transitions via code using the History object.

Your applications (specially the Kanban app) have become larger and more feature rich since their first iterations and are starting to feel growing pains. In the next chapter, you're going to study Flux, an application architecture that complements React and will help you better organize your projects.

CHAPTER 6

■ ■ ■

Architecting React Applications with Flux

As you saw earlier, one core philosophy of React is that data flows in a single direction, from parent to child components as props. When a parent component needs its children to reach back, it can pass callback functions down as props as well.

This one-way data flow leads to clear, explicit, and easy-to-follow code. You can trace a React application from start to finish and see what code is executed on changes.

But while this architectural pattern has many advantages, it also brings some challenges. React applications usually grow to have many nesting levels where top components act as containers and many pure components are like leafs on an interface tree. With state living on the top levels the hierarchy, you end up creating callbacks that needs to get passed down as props, sometimes many levels deep in a repetitive and error-prone task.

Ryan Florence, React Router co-author and prominent community member, uses an analogy to describe the act of passing data and callbacks as props many levels deep: drilling your application. If you have many nested components, you have a lot of drill work going on, and if you want to refactor (move some components around), you must do a whole lot of drilling all over again.

Let me be clear here: using nested React components is a great way to structure UIs. It reduces complexity and leads to separation of concerns, and to code that is easier to extend and maintain. And since React is built around the concept of reactive rendering, for every change on the component's state or props, React updates the DOM (using its virtual DOM implementation to calculate the minimum necessary mutations). You get a very simple mindset for developing and great performance for free.

What we're trying to address here is, given the fact that you want to have nested components, how do you bring data and, most importantly, the callbacks to manipulate that data closer to each of these components when the applications grow? That's exactly where Flux comes in.

What Is Flux?

Flux is an architectural guideline for building web applications. It was created by Facebook, and while it's not part of React, nor was it built exclusively for React, it pairs exceptionally well with the library.

The main point of Flux is to allow an uni-directional data flow in your application. It is composed of basically three pieces: actions, stores, and a dispatcher. Let's take a look at these three pieces.

Stores

As mentioned, one of the main points you are trying to address is how to bring data closer to each of the application's components. Our ideal view of the world looks like Figure 6-1. Data is completely separated from the component, but you want the component to be notified when data changes so it can re-render.

Figure 6-1. *An ideal view of the world*

That's exactly what stores do. Stores hold all the application state (including data and even UI state) and dispatch events when the state has changed. Views (React components) subscribe to the stores that contain the data they needs and when the data changes, re-render themselves, as shown in Figure 6-2.

Figure 6-2. *Views re-render themselves*

One important characteristic of stores is that they are closed black boxes; they expose public getters to access data, but nobody can insert, update, or change their data in any way, not the views nor any of the other Flux pieces. Only the store itself can mutate its own data.

If you know the MVC paradigm, stores do bear resemblance with models, but again the main difference is that stores only have getters; nobody can set a value on a store.

But if no other part of the application can change the data in a store, what in the system causes stores to update their state? The answer is Actions.

Actions

Actions are loosely defined as "things that happen in your app." They are created by almost any part of the application, basically from user interactions (such as clicking on a button, leaving a comment, requesting search results, and so on...), but also as results of AJAX requests, timers, web socket events, etc.

Every action contains a type (its unique name) and an option payload. When dispatched, actions reach the stores, and that's how a store knows it needs to update its own data. See Figure 6-3.

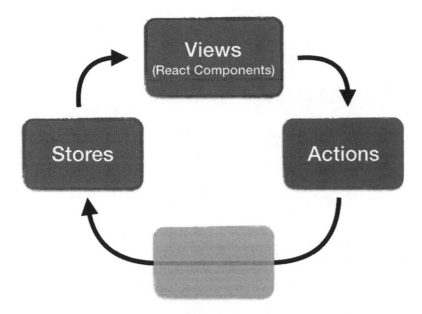

Figure 6-3. *Store updates its own data*

Actually, that's pretty much all that is to Flux: React components create actions (say, after user types a name in a text field); that action reach the stores; stores that are interested in that particular action update their own data and dispatch change events; finally, the view responds to that store's event by re-rendering with the latest data. But there's a missing piece in this diagram, the dispatcher.

Dispatcher

The dispatcher is responsible for coordinating the relaying of the actions to the stores and ensuring that the stores' action handlers are executed in the correct order. See Figure 6-4.

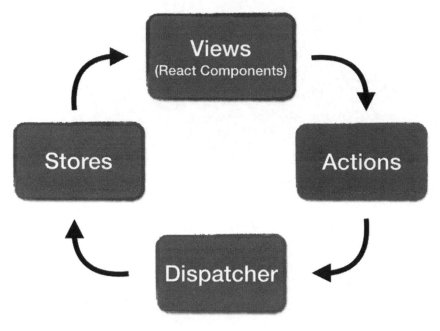

Figure 6-4. *Dispatcher workflow*

Despite being an essential piece of Flux architecture, you don't have to think too much about dispatchers. All you need to do is to create an instance to use; the rest is handled by the given dispatcher implementation.

The Unrealistic, Minimal Flux App

When used in complex applications, Flux helps keep the code easier to read, maintain, and grow. It certainly reduces complexity, and as a consequence in many cases it also reduces the number of lines of code in the project (although that's not an appropriate metric for code complexity). But no such thing will happen in your first sample project, where the use of Flux will actually increase the amount of code necessary to build it. This is because the purpose of this first example is to help you grasp all of the elements in a Flux application. Flux can be tricky to newcomers, so you will start on a very basic project, with almost no UI (or practical use, for that matter) but one that designed to make explicit and well-defined use of all of the elements in a Flux + React application. In the next section, you will move to complete, real-world examples.

The Bank Account Application

The analogy of using a bank account to describe Flux's actions and stores was first made by Jeremy Morrell in his presentation "Those who forget the past are doomed to debug it" (https://speakerdeck.com/jmorrell/jsconf-uy-flux-those-who-forget-the-past-dot-dot-dot-1), and is used here with his permission.

A bank account is defined by two things: a transaction and a balance. With every transaction, you update the balance, as shown in Tables 6-1 and 6-2.

Table 6-1. *The First Transaction Initiates the Balance*

Transaction	Amount	Balance
Create Account	$0	$0

Table 6-2. *With Every Transaction, You Update the Balance*

Transaction	Amount	Balance
Create Account	$0	$0
Deposit	$200	$200
Withdrawal	($50)	$150
Deposit	$100	$250
	$250	

These transactions are how you interact with your bank; they modify the state of your account.

You will recreate this process in a Flux application. In Flux terms, the transactions on the left are your actions, and the balance on the right is a value that you will track in a store. Your sample application structure will include

- A `constants.js` file (since all actions should have uniquely identifiable names across the app, you will store these names as constants).

- The standard `AppDispatcher.js`.

- `BankActions.js`, which will contain three action creators: `CreateAccount`, `depositIntoAccount`, and `WithdrawFromAccount`. We call the methods "action creators" because the actions are really just objects. The methods that create and dispatch these actions, for lack of a better name, are called the action creators.

- `BankBalanceStore.js`, which will keep track of the user's balance.

- Finally, the `App.js` file, which contains the single UI component you will use in this project.

Start by creating a new project and installing the Flux library with npm (`npm install --save flux`). The next sections will walk through each file in the project.

The Application's Constants

Let's get started by defining the constants file. You need three constants to uniquely identify your actions across the app for creating an account, depositing in the account, and withdrawing from the account. Listing 6-1 shows the code.

Listing 6-1. The constants.js File

```
export default {
  CREATED_ACCOUNT: 'created account',
  WITHDREW_FROM_ACCOUNT: 'withdrew from account',
  DEPOSITED_INTO_ACCOUNT: 'deposited into account'
};
```

The Dispatcher

Next, let's define your application dispatcher. As said earlier, you don't have to think too much about it. For all that matters, your AppDispatcher file could be as simple as just instantiating a Flux dispatcher.

```
import {Dispatcher} from 'flux';
export default new Dispatcher();
```

However, you do have the opportunity to extend the standard dispatcher in your application, and one thing that will help you better comprehend the dispatcher role is making it log every action that gets dispatched, as shown in Listing 6-2.

Listing 6-2. The AppDispatcher.js Extending the Standard Flux Dispatcher to Log Every Dispatch

```
import {Dispatcher} from 'flux';

class AppDispatcher extends Dispatcher{
  dispatch(action = {}) {
    console.log("Dispatched", action);
    super.dispatch(action);
  }
}

export default new AppDispatcher();
```

Action Creators

Moving on in your fake banking application, let's define some functions that will generate actions in the application. Remember, an action in the context of a Flux application is just an object that contains a type and optional data payload. For lack of a better term, we call the functions that define and dispatch actions as action creators. You create a single JavaScript file with three action creators (creating an account, depositing, and withdrawing), as shown in Listing 6-3.

Listing 6-3. The BankActions.js File

```
import AppDispatcher from './AppDispatcher';
import bankConstants from './constants';

let BankActions = {

  /**
   * Create an account with an empty value
   */
  createAccount() {
    AppDispatcher.dispatch({
      type: bankConstants.CREATED_ACCOUNT,
      ammount: 0
    });
  },
```

```
/**
 * @param   {number} ammount to whithdraw
 */
depositIntoAccount(ammount) {
  AppDispatcher.dispatch({
    type: bankConstants.DEPOSITED_INTO_ACCOUNT,
    ammount: ammount
  });
},

/**
 * @param   {number} ammount to whithdraw
 */
withdrawFromAccount(ammount) {
  AppDispatcher.dispatch({
    type: bankConstants.WITHDREW_FROM_ACCOUNT,
    ammount: ammount
  });
}

};

export default BankActions;
```

Store

In the sequence, let's define your BankBalanceStore file. In a Flux application, the store owns state and registers itself with the dispatcher. Every time an action gets dispatched, all the stores are invoked and can decide if they care for that specific action; if one cares, it changes its internal state and emits an event so that the views can get notified that the store has changed.

To emit events, you need an event emitter package from npm. Node.js that has a default event emitter, but it is not supported on browsers. There are many different packages in npm that reimplement a node's event system on the browser; even Facebook has an open source one, which is a simple implementation that prioritizes speed and simplicity. Let's use it: npm install --save fbemitter

Starting with a basic skeleton for your BankAccountStore, you create an event emitter instance and provide an addListener method to subscribe to the store change event. You also import the application dispatcher and register the store, providing a callback that is invoked for every dispatched action. The code is shown in Listing 6-4.

Listing 6-4. Basic plain-js-object Store

```
import {EventEmitter} from 'fbemitter';
import AppDispatcher from './AppDispatcher';
import bankConstants from './constants';

const CHANGE_EVENT = 'change';
let __emitter = new EventEmitter();

let BankBalanceStore = {
```

```
  addListener: (callback) => {
    return __emitter.addListener(CHANGE_EVENT, callback);
  },

};

BankBalanceStore.dispatchToken = AppDispatcher.register((action) => {
  switch (action.type) {
  }

});


export default BankBalanceStore;
```

Notice in the code that you invoked the dispatcher's register method, passing a callback function. This function is called every time a dispatch occurs, and you have the opportunity to decide whether the store does something when certain action types are dispatched.

Additionally, the dispatcher's `register` method returns a dispatch token: an identifier that can be used to coordinate the store's update order, which you will see later on this chapter.

In the sequence, you need to do two more things: create a variable to store the account balance (as well as a getter method to access its value) and make the actual switch statements to respond to the actions CREATE_ACCOUNT, DEPOSIT_INTO_ACCOUNT, and WITHDRAW_FROM_ACCOUNT. Notice that you need to manually emit a change event after changing the internal value of the account balance. The complete code is shown in Listing 6-5.

Listing 6-5. The Complete Code for the BankBalanceStore.js

```
import {EventEmitter} from 'fbemitter';
import AppDispatcher from './AppDispatcher';
import bankConstants from './constants';

const CHANGE_EVENT = 'change';
let __emitter = new EventEmitter();
let balance = 0;

let BankBalanceStore = {

  getState() {
    return balance;
  },

  addListener(callback) {
    return __emitter.addListener(CHANGE_EVENT, callback);
  }

};

BankBalanceStore.dispatchToken = AppDispatcher.register((action) => {
  switch (action.type) {
    case bankConstants.CREATED_ACCOUNT:
      balance = 0;
      __emitter.emit(CHANGE_EVENT);
      break;
```

```
    case bankConstants.DEPOSITED_INTO_ACCOUNT:
      balance = balance + action.ammount;
      __emitter.emit(CHANGE_EVENT);
      break;

    case bankConstants.WITHDREW_FROM_ACCOUNT:
      balance = balance - action.ammount;
      __emitter.emit(CHANGE_EVENT);
      break;
  }

});

export default BankBalanceStore;
```

UI Components

Finally, you need some UI. Your App.js file will import both the store and the actions. It will display the balance that is controlled by the store and call the action creators when the user clicks the withdraw or deposit buttons.

Let's approach this in parts, starting with the store. As shown in Listing 6-6, in the class constructor you define the local state containing a balance key. The value for this key comes from the BankBalanceStore (BankBalanceStore.getState()). In the sequence, you use the lifecycle methods componentDidMount and componentWillUnmount to manage listening for changes in the BankBalanceStore. Whenever the store changes, the handleStoreChange method is called and the component's state gets updated (and, as you already know, as the state changes, the component will re-render itself).

Listing 6-6. Partial Code for the App Component Getting Its State from BankBalanceStore

```
import React, { Component } from 'react';
import { render } from 'react-dom';
import BankBalanceStore from './BankBalanceStore';
import BankActions from './BankActions';

class App extends Component {
  constructor(){
    super(...arguments);
    BankActions.createAccount();
    this.state = {
      balance: BankBalanceStore.getState()
    }
  }

  componentDidMount() {
    this.storeSubscription = BankBalanceStore.addListener( ↵;
      data => this.handleStoreChange (data));
  }
```

```
  componentWillUnmount() {
    this.storeSubscription.remove();
  }

  handleStoreChange(){
    this.setState({balance: BankBalanceStore.getState()});
  }
}
```

In the sequence, let's implement the render function. It takes a text field and two buttons (withdraw and deposit). You also have two local methods to handle the click of those buttons. The methods simply call the action creators and clear the text field. The complete code for App.js is shown in Listing 6-7, and a complementary CSS file for basic styling is shown in Listing 6-8.

Listing 6-7. The Complete App Component

```
import React, { Component } from 'react';
import { render } from 'react-dom';
import BankBalanceStore from './BankBalanceStore';
import BankActions from './BankActions';

class App extends Component {
  constructor(){
    super(...arguments);
    BankActions.createAccount();
    this.state = {
      balance: BankBalanceStore.getState()
    }
  }
  componentDidMount() {
    this.storeSubscription = BankBalanceStore.addListener( ↩;
      data => this.handleStoreChange(data));
  }

  componentWillUnmount() {
    this.storeSubscription.remove();
  }

  handleStoreChange(){
    this.setState({balance: BankBalanceStore.getState()});
  }

  deposit() {
    BankActions.depositIntoAccount(Number(this.refs.ammount.value));
    this.refs.ammount.value = '';

  }

  withdraw() {
    BankActions.withdrawFromAccount(Number(this.refs.ammount.value));
    this.refs.ammount.value = '';
  }
```

```
  render(){
    return (
      <div>
        <header>FluxTrust Bank</header>
        <h1>Your balance is ${(this.state.balance).toFixed(2)}</h1>
        <div className="atm">
          <input type="text" placeholder="Enter Ammount" ref="ammount" />
          <br />
          <button onClick={this.withdraw.bind(this)}>Withdraw</button>
          <button onClick={this.deposit.bind(this)}>Deposit</button>
        </div>
      </div>

    );
  }
}
render(<App />, document.getElementById('root'));
```

Listing 6-8. Basic Styling for the Fake Banking Application

```
body {
  margin: 0;
  font: 16px/1 sans-serif;
  background-color: #318435;
  color: #fff;
  text-align: center;
}
header{
  width:100%;
  padding: 15px;
  text-align: center;
  background-color: #000;
}
h1{
  font-size: 18px;
}
h2{
  font-size: 16px;
}
.atm{
  width: 200px;
  height: 100px;
  border-radius: 10px;
  background-color: #000;
  text-align: center;
  margin: 10px auto 0 auto;
  padding: 20px;
}
.atm input{
  font-size:25px;
  width: 180px
}
```

177

```
.atm button{
  margin: 5px;
  padding: 20px;
}
```

If you are following along, now's a good time to try the withdraw and deposit operations. Make sure you have the browser console open so you can see the all the actions logged by the dispatcher, as shown in Figure 6-5.

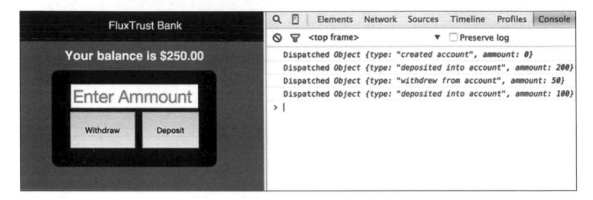

Figure 6-5. *The fake banking app with actions logged*

Flux Utils

Since version 2.1, the Flux library includes base classes for defining stores, as well as a higher order function to use with a container component so it can update its state automatically when relevant stores change. These utilities are valuable because they help reduce the boilerplate in your application.

Flux Utils Stores

The Flux Utils package provides three base classes to implement stores: Store, ReduceStore, and MapStore.

- Store is the simplest one. It is just a small wrapper around a basic store. It helps in coping with boilerplate code but doesn't introduce any concepts or new functionalities.

- ReduceStore is a very special kind of store. Its name comes from the fact that it uses reducing functions to modify its internal state. Reducer is a function that calculates a new state given the previous state and an action, similar to how Array.prototype.reduce works. The state in a ReduceStore must necessarily be treated as immutable, so be careful to only store immutable structures or any of the following:

  - Single primitive values (a string, Boolean value, or a number)

  - An array or primitive values, as in [1,2,3,4]

  - An object of primitive values, as in {name:'cassio', age:35}

  - An object with nested objects that will be manipulated using React immutable helpers

- MapStore is a variation of ReduceStore with additional helper methods to store key value pairs instead of a single value.

Another neat characteristic of ReduceStore (and consequentially MapStore) is that you don't need to manually emit change events: the state is compared before and after each dispatch and changes are emitted automatically.

Let's use the BankBalanceStore from the previous example to exemplify the Flux Util base stores. For comparison purposes, you will first take a look at how the exact same result can be achieved using Flux Util's Store. In the sequence, you will make a much slimmer version using ReduceStore.

Starting with the base Store, the implementation is actually almost identical to your current BankBalanceStore, with two main differences:

- You don't need to create your own instance of an event emitter.

- You don't need to manually register the store with the dispatcher; instead, you create an instance of the store passing the dispatcher as an argument.

This results in a file slightly leaner than your original one, as shown in Listing 6-9.

Listing 6-9. A BankBalanceStore Version Extending Flux Util's Base Store Class

```
import AppDispatcher from './AppDispatcher';
import {Store} from 'flux/utils';
import bankConstants from './constants';

let balance = 0;

class BankBalanceStore extends Store {
  getState() {
    return __balance;
  }

  __onDispatch(action) {
    switch (action.type) {
      case bankConstants.CREATED_ACCOUNT:
        balance = 0;
        this.__emitChange();
        break;

      case bankConstants.DEPOSITED_INTO_ACCOUNT:
        balance = balance + action.ammount;
        this.__emitChange();
        break;

      case bankConstants.WITHDREW_FROM_ACCOUNT:
        balance = balance - action.ammount;
        this.__emitChange();
        break;
    }
  }
}

export default new BankBalanceStore(AppDispatcher);
```

But the implementation really shines using ReduceStore instead of using the regular Store. Besides being cleaner, its functional roots coupled with the use of an immutable data structure allows for a more declarative programming (just like React) and impacts positively in many other areas (like testing, for example).

Let's make yet another implementation of your BankBalanceStore, this time using ReduceStore. To extend ReduceStore, your class needs to implement two methods: getInitialState and reduce. In getInitialState you define the initial state of your store, and in reduce you modify this state as result of actions. A default getState method is already defined, so you don't need to override unless you don't want to treat the ReduceStore state as immutable (which defeats the purpose of using a ReduceStore in the first place, so for practical purposes you will always treat as immutable).

Listing 6-10 shows the complete code for the BankBalanceStore extending ReduceStore. Notice that there's no need to emit change events; they are automatically dispatched for you.

Listing 6-10. BankBalanceStore Extending ReduceStore

```
import AppDispatcher from './AppDispatcher';
import bankConstants from './constants';
import {ReduceStore} from 'flux/utils';

class BankBalanceStore extends ReduceStore {
  getInitialState() {
    return 0;
  }

  reduce(state, action){
    switch (action.type) {

      case bankConstants.CREATED_ACCOUNT:
        return 0;

      case bankConstants.DEPOSITED_INTO_ACCOUNT:
        return state + action.ammount;

      case bankConstants.WITHDREW_FROM_ACCOUNT:
        return state - action.ammount;

      default:
        return state;
    }
  }
}

export default new BankBalanceStore(AppDispatcher);
```

Container Component Higher Order Function

You learned about container components in Chapter 3. They are used to separate business logic non-related to UI rendering (such as data fetching) from its corresponding sub-component. By default, containers are pure, meaning they will not re-render when their state does not change.

■ **Tip**   One note of caution: to use the Flux Util's higher order function, the container component cannot access any props. This is both for performance reasons, and to ensure that containers are reusable and that props do not have to be threaded throughout a component tree.

Let's see this in practice. You will change the app component to automatically subscribe to the BankAccountStore and update its state whenever it changes. You start by removing what won't be needed anymore: you won't need to declare the component's initial state on the constructor. The componentDidMount and componentWillUnmount lifecycle methods can also be removed because the higher order component will take care of subscribing to and unsubscribing from the stores for you. For the same reason, you get rid of the handleStoreChange method. To use this higher order function, your container component must implement two class methods: calculateState (which maps store state to local component's state) and getStores (which returns an array with all the stores the component listens to). Mind that the container higher order function only works with stores that extend Flux Util's Stores. Listing 6-11 shows the updated App.js component, which is now 15% smaller than the original.

Listing 6-11. The App Component Using the Flux Util's Container Higher Order Function

```
import React, { Component } from 'react';
import { render } from 'react-dom';
import {Container} from 'flux/utils';
import BankBalanceStore from './BankBalanceStore';
import BankActions from './BankActions';

class App extends Component {
  constructor(){
    super(...arguments);
    BankActions.createAccount();
  }

  deposit() {
    BankActions.depositIntoAccount(Number(this.refs.ammount.value));
    this.refs.ammount.value = '';

  }

  withdraw() {
    BankActions.withdrawFromAccount(Number(this.refs.ammount.value));
    this.refs.ammount.value = '';
  }

  render(){
    return (
      <div>
        <header>FluxTrust Bank</header>
        <h1>Your balance is ${(this.state.balance).toFixed(2)}</h1>
        <div className="atm">
          <input type="text" placeholder="Enter Ammount" ref="ammount" />
          <br />
```

```
            <button onClick={this.withdraw.bind(this)}>Withdraw</button>
            <button onClick={this.deposit.bind(this)}>Deposit</button>
          </div>
        </div>

    );
  }
}
App.getStores = () => ([BankBalanceStore]);
App.calculateState = (prevState) => ({balance: BankBalanceStore.getState()});

const AppContainer = Container.create(App);

render(<AppContainer />, document.getElementById('root'));
```

Asynchronous Flux

In any decently complex JavaScript web application, you'll likely need to deal with asynchronicity. This can come in basically two forms: from coordinating update order between stores to asynchronous data fetching.

waitFor: Coordinating Store Update Order

In big Flux projects dealing with multiple stores, you may come to a situation where one store depends on data from another store. The Flux dispatcher provides a method called waitFor() to manage this kind of dependency; it makes the store wait for the callbacks from the specified stores to be invoked before continuing execution.

   Using your fake bank application, let's say you have a rewards program that is based on the user's current balance. You could create a new BankRewardsStore to handle the current user's tier on the program, and since the program is solely based on the user balance, for every operation the BankRewardsStore must wait for the BankBalanceStore to finish updating, and then update itself accordingly. Listing 6-12 shows the finished BankRewardsStore.

Listing 6-12. The BankRewards Store

```
import AppDispatcher from './AppDispatcher';
import BankBalanceStore from './BankBalanceStore'
import bankConstants from './constants';
import {ReduceStore} from 'flux/utils';

class BankRewardsStore extends ReduceStore {
  getInitialState() {
    return 'Basic';
  }
  reduce(state, action){
    this.getDispatcher().waitFor([
      BankBalanceStore.getDispatchToken()
    ]);
```

```
  if (action.type === bankConstants.DEPOSITED_INTO_ACCOUNT ||
      action.type === bankConstants.WITHDREW_FROM_ACCOUNT ) {
    let balance = BankBalanceStore.getState();
    if (balance < 5000)
      return 'Basic';
    else if (balance < 10000)
      return 'Silver';
    else if (balance < 50000)
      return 'Gold';
    else
      return 'Platinum';
  }
  return state;
  }
}
export default new BankRewardsStore(AppDispatcher);
```

The BankRewardsStore responds to both DEPOSIT_INTO_ACCOUNT and WITHDRAW_FROM_ACCOUNT action types in the same way: by getting the current balance and simply assigning a tier depending on the balance amount (Basic tier for a balance amount lower than $5,000; Silver tier for a balance amount between $5,000 and $10,000; Gold tier between $10,000 and $50,000; and Platinum tier for a balance amount bigger than $50,000).

Now you can subscribe to this store on your main component and show the user's current tier on the Rewards program. Listing 6-13 shows the updated App.js and Figure 6-6 shows the how the application looks with the update.

Listing 6-13. The Updated App.js Subscribing to the BankRewardsStore

```
import React, { Component } from 'react';
import { render } from 'react-dom';
import {Container} from 'flux/utils';
import BankBalanceStore from './BankBalanceStore';
import BankRewardsStore from './BankRewardsStore';
import BankActions from './BankActions';

class App extends Component {
  constructor(){
    super(...arguments);
    BankActions.createAccount();
  }

  deposit() {
    BankActions.depositIntoAccount(Number(this.refs.ammount.value));
    this.refs.ammount.value = '';
  }

  withdraw() {
    BankActions.withdrawFromAccount(Number(this.refs.ammount.value));
    this.refs.ammount.value = '';
  }
```

```
render(){
  return (
    <div>
      <header>FluxTrust Bank</header>
      <h1>Your balance is ${(this.state.balance).toFixed(2)}</h1>
      <h2>Your Points Rewards Tier is {this.state.rewardsTier}</h2>
      <div className="atm">
        <input type="text" placeholder="Enter Ammount" ref="ammount" />
        <br />
        <button onClick={this.withdraw.bind(this)}>Withdraw</button>
        <button onClick={this.deposit.bind(this)}>Deposit</button>
      </div>
    </div>

  );
  }
}
App.getStores = () => ([BankBalanceStore, BankRewardsStore]);
App.calculateState = (prevState) => ({
  balance: BankBalanceStore.getState(),
  rewardsTier: BankRewardsStore.getState()
});

const AppContainer = Container.create(App);

render(<AppContainer />, document.getElementById('root'));
```

Figure 6-6. *The updated fake bank account with a fake rewards program*

Asynchronous Data Fetching

As you've seen so far, general usage within Flux is straightforward, but the one thing that is not exactly intuitive is where to handle asynchronous requests. Where should you fetch data? How do you make the response go through the Flux data flow?

Although the library does not enforce a specific place to make fetch operations, a best practice that emerged from the community is to create a separate module to wrap all your requests and API calls (a file such as APIutils.js). The API utils can be called from anywhere, but they always make the async requests and then talk to the action creators to dispatch actions (so any store can choose to act on them).

Remember that when you call an asynchronous API, there are two crucial moments in time: the moment you start the call, and the moment when you receive an answer (or a timeout). For that reason, the API utility module will always dispatch at least three different kinds of actions: an action informing the stores that the request began, an action informing the stores that the request finished successfully, and an action informing the stores that the request failed.

Having a separate module wrapping the communication with the API and dispatching different actions in time offers many advantages because it isolates the rest of the system from the asynchronous execution. As soon as the actions get dispatched, the code is executed in a synchronous fashion from the point of view of the stores and the components, and this makes it easier to reason about them.

Let's exemplify this by creating a new application: a site for airline tickets.

AirCheap Application

The application will fetch a list of airports as soon as it loads, and when the user fills the origin and destination airports, the application will talk to an API to fetch airline ticket prices. Figure 6-7 shows the working application.

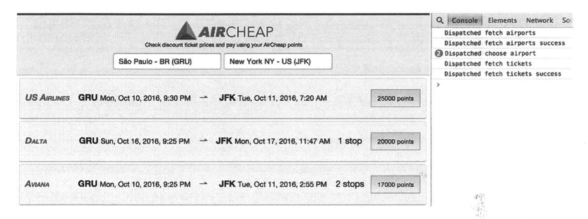

Figure 6-7. *The AirCheap tickets app*

Setup: Project Organization and Basic Files

To start the project in an organized way, you're going to create folders for Flux-related files (action creators, stores, and an API folder for API utility modules) and a folder for React components. The initial project structure will look like Figure 6-8.

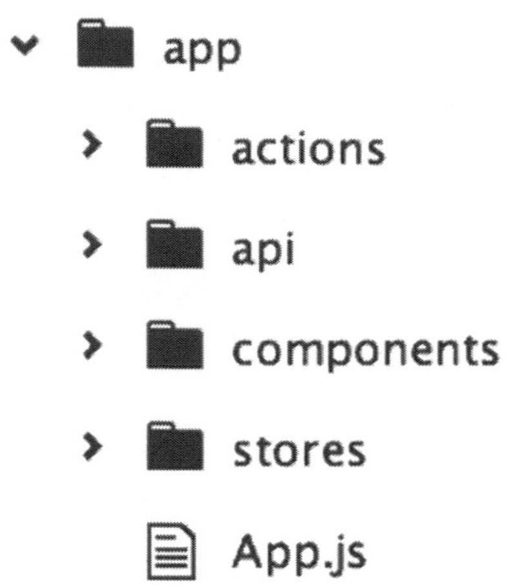

Figure 6-8. The app folder structure for the AirCheap project

Let's start creating the project files, beginning with the AppDispatcher. Remember, the AppDispatcher can be simply an instance of the Flux dispatcher, as shown in Listing 6-14. Some developers prefer to create a dispatchers folder, but since a Flux application will always have a single dispatcher, you will just save the AppDispatcher.js file in the root level of the app folder.

Listing 6-14. Simplest AppDispatcher.js Form

```
import {Dispatcher} from 'flux';
export default new Dispatcher();
```

Of course, you could extend the dispatcher functionality. If you want to log all dispatcher actions, for example, just overwrite the dispatch method as you did in the Fake Bank account app.

Next, let's create your constants.js file. When developing an application in a real-world scenario, you would probably start the constants.js file with just a few constants and increase them as needed, but in your case you already know beforehand all the constants you want to use:

- FETCH_AIRPORTS to name the action you dispatch as the application starts to fetch all the airports. And since this is an async operation, you also create the FETCH_AIRPORTS_SUCCESS and FETCH_AIRPORTS_ERROR constants to represent the success and error on the operation.

- CHOOSE_AIRPORT to name a synchronous action of the user selection an airport (as both origin OR destination).

- The FETCH_TICKETS constant to name the action that you dispatch when both an origin and a destination are selected. This is an asynchronous data fetching operation, so you also need constants to represent success and, eventually, an error on the fetch operation: FETCH_TICKETS_SUCCESS and FETCH_TICKETS_ERROR.

Listing 6-15 shows the final constants.js file.

Listing 6-15. The constants.js File

```
export default {
  FETCH_AIRPORTS: 'fetch airports',
  FETCH_AIRPORTS_SUCCESS: 'fetch airports success',
  FETCH_AIRPORTS_ERROR: 'fetch airports error',
  CHOOSE_AIRPORT: 'choose airport',
  FETCH_TICKETS: 'fetch tickets',
  FETCH_TICKETS_SUCCESS: 'fetch tickets success',
  FETCH_TICKETS_ERROR: 'fetch tickets error'
};
```

Creating the API Helper and ActionCreators for Fetching Airports

Let's create an API helper to deal with the airport and ticket fetching. As discussed earlier, creating a segregated helper module to interact with the API will help keep the actions clean and minimal. For the sake of simplicity, in the case of this sample application, the API helper method will load a static json file in your public folder containing a list of the biggest airports in the world instead of using an actual remote API. You can download the airports.json file and the other public assets for this project from the Apress site (www.apress.com) or from this book's GitHub page (http://pro-react.github.io). In any case, a trimmed down version of the airports.json file is shown in Listing 6-16.

Listing 6-16. A Trimmed Down Version of the public/airports.json File

```
[
  { "code": "ATL", "city": "Atlanta GA", "country": "US" },
  { "code": "LHR", "city": "London", "country": "GB" },
  { "code": "JFK", "city": "New York NY", "country": "US" },
  { "code": "ORD", "city": "Chicago IL", "country": "US" },
  { "code": "HND", "city": "Tokyo", "country": "JP" },
  { "code": "LAX", "city": "Los Angeles CA", "country": "US" },
  { "code": "CDG", "city": "Paris", "country": "FR" },
  { "code": "FRA", "city": "Frankfurt", "country": "DE" },
  { "code": "MAD", "city": "Madrid", "country": "ES" },
  { "code": "SFO", "city": "San Francisco CA", "country": "US" },
  { "code": "GRU", "city": "São Paulo", "country": "BR" },
  { "code": "DME", "city": "Moscow", "country": "RU" }
]
```

In sequence, let's create the api/AirCheapAPI.js file. It contains a function called fetchAirports that loads the airports from the remote json file and calls the actioncreators to dispatch a success or error action. Listing 6-17 shows a first draft of the file.

Listing 6-17. First Attempt at api/AirCheapAPI.js File

```
import 'whatwg-fetch';

let AirCheapAPI = {
  fetchAirports() {
    fetch('airports.json')
    .then((response) => response.json())
    .then((responseData) =>{
```

```
      // Call the AirportActionCreators success action with the parsed data
    })
    .catch((error) => {
      // Call the AirportActionCreators error action with the error object
    });
  }
};
```

export default AirCheapAPI;

■ **Note**   As in earlier examples, you're using the native fetch function to load the json file and importing the whatwg-fetch npm module that provides support for fetch in older browsers. Don't forget to install it with npm install --save whatwg-fetch.

When the API module is called, it will fetch the remote data and success or errors actions itself by talking to the action creators. You don't have the AirportActionCreators yet, but assuming it will contain fetchAirportsSuccess and fetchAirportsError functions, you can complete the AirCheapAPI implementation, as shown in Listing 6-18.

Listing 6-18.   The Complete api/AirCheapAPI.js Dispatching Success and/or Error Actions

```
import 'whatwg-fetch';
import AirportActionCreators from '../actions/AirportActionCreators';


let AirCheapAPI = {
  fetchAirports() {
    fetch('airports.json')
    .then((response) => {
      return response.json()
    })
    .then((responseData) =>{
      // Call the AirportActionCreators success action with the parsed data
      AirportActionCreators.fetchAirportsSuccess(responseData);
    })
    .catch((error) => {
      // Call the AirportActionCreators error action with the error object
      AirportActionCreators.fetchAirportsError(error);
    });
  }
};
```

export default AirCheapAPI;

Moving to the AirportActionCreators, remember that actions are like messages that get dispatched through all stores: they just communicate what happened to the app. There is no place for business logic or computations on an action. With this knowledge, developing an ActionCreator module is pretty straightforward. Listing 6-19 shows the AirportActionCreators file.

Listing 6-19. The actions/AirportActionCreators.js File

```
import AppDispatcher from '../AppDispatcher';
import constants from '../constants';
import AirCheapAPI from '../api/AirCheapAPI';

let AirportActionCreators = {

  fetchAirports() {
    AirCheapAPI.fetchAirports();
    AppDispatcher.dispatch({
      type: constants.FETCH_AIRPORTS,
    });
  },

  fetchAirportsSuccess(response) {
    AppDispatcher.dispatch({
      type: constants.FETCH_AIRPORTS_SUCCESS,
      payload: {response}
    });
  },

  fetchAirportsError(error) {
    AppDispatcher.dispatch({
      type: constants.FETCH_AIRPORTS_ERROR,
      payload: {error}
    });
  }

};

export default AirportActionCreators;
```

AirportStore

The airport store could act on all the possible dispatched actions. It could act on fetchAirports to set a variable indicating that it is currently loading. It could act on fetchAirportsError to set a variable with an appropriate error message and, obviously, it could act on fetchAirportsSuccess to set its internal state to the list of fetched airports.

Let's get started by doing the absolutely minimum: you create the AirportStore.js, inheriting from ReduceStore. Its state will contain the list of airports, starting as an empty array and getting populated as the store acts on fetchAirportsSuccess action. Listing 6-20 shows the complete source code.

Listing 6-20. The actions/AirportStore.js Source File

```
import AppDispatcher from '../AppDispatcher';
import constants from '../constants';
import {ReduceStore} from 'flux/utils';

class AirportStore extends ReduceStore {
  getInitialState() {
    return [];
  }
```

189

```
  reduce(state, action){
    switch (action.type) {

      case constants.FETCH_AIRPORTS_SUCCESS:
        return action.payload.response;

      default:
        return state;
    }
  }
}
export default new AirportStore(AppDispatcher);
```

App Component

Next, let's implement the interface for the AirCheap Application. The user will interact with the application by filling two text fields (Origin and Destination), and to make things easier for the user, you implement an auto-suggest feature that suggests airports as the user types, as shown in Figure 6-9.

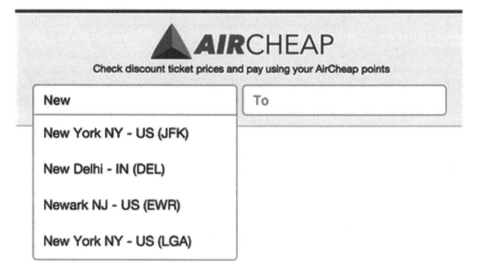

Figure 6-9. *Component with auto suggestions*

There are many auto-suggestion libraries available (as a quick search on npmjs.com reveals). In this example, you use react-auto-suggest, so be sure to install it using NPM (npm install –save react-auto-suggest).

You start by creating a basic structure for your App component. It uses the Flux Util's Container (to listen for store changes and map the stores state to the local component state) and invokes the AirportActionCreator on the lifecycle method componentDidMount to trigger the async loading of the airports. Listing 6-21 shows the basic structure of App.js.

Listing 6-21. The Basic app.js Component Structure

```js
import React, { Component } from 'react';
import { render } from 'react-dom';
import {Container} from 'flux/utils';
import Autosuggest from 'react-autosuggest';
import AirportStore from './stores/AirportStore';
import AirportActionCreators from './actions/AirportActionCreators';

class App extends Component {
  componentDidMount(){
    AirportActionCreators.fetchAirports();
  }

  render() {
    return (
      <div>
        <header>
          <div className="header-brand">
            <img src="logo.png" height="35"/>
            <p>Check discount ticket prices and pay using your AirCheap points</p>
          </div>
          <div className="header-route">
            <Autosuggest id='origin'
                         inputAttributes={{placeholder:'From'}} />

            <Autosuggest id='destination'
                         inputAttributes={{placeholder:'To'}} />
          </div>

        </header>
      </div>
    );
  }
}

App.getStores = () => ([AirportStore]);
App.calculateState = (prevState) => ({
  airports: AirportStore.getState()
});

const AppContainer = Container.create(App);
render(<AppContainer />, document.getElementById('root'));
```

If you run this application now, the react-auto-suggest library will throw an error. It expects a suggestions function to be passed as props. This function gets called every time the user changes the input value of the text field and should return a list of suggestions to be displayed. The function is shown in Listing 6-22.

Listing 6-22. The getSuggestions Function

```
getSuggestions(input, callback) {
  const escapedInput = input.trim().toLowerCase();
  const airportMatchRegex = new RegExp('\\b' + escapedInput, 'i');
  const suggestions = this.state.airports
    .filter(airport => airportMatchRegex.test(airport.city))
    .sort((airport1, airport2) => {
      airport1.city.toLowerCase().indexOf(escapedInput) -  ↵;
      airport2.city.toLowerCase().indexOf(escapedInput)
    })
    .slice(0, 7)
    .map(airport => `${airport.city} - ${airport.country} (${airport.code})`);
  callback(null, suggestions);
}
```

The function receives two parameters: the text inputted by the user and a callback function to call with the suggestions.

In the first lines of the function, you clean up the user input by removing trailing spaces and transforming everything to lowercase. In the following line, you create a regular expression with the escaped user input. This regular expression is then used to filter the list of airports (based on the city name).

Besides filtering the airports, you do three other transformations. You sort the airports so that the occurrences where the word is matched at the beginning appear first, you limit the results to a maximum of seven, and you map the output to a specific format of "city name – country initials (airport code)."

The updated code for the App component with the suggestion function passed as props to the Autosuggest components is shown in Listing 6-23. A matching CSS file with the application style is shown in Listing 6-24.

Listing 6-23. The App Component with Working Airport Suggestions Field

```
import React, { Component } from 'react';
import { render } from 'react-dom';
import {Container} from 'flux/utils';
import Autosuggest from 'react-autosuggest';
import AirportStore from './stores/AirportStore';
import AirportActionCreators from './actions/AirportActionCreators';

class App extends Component {
  getSuggestions(input, callback) {
    const escapedInput = input.trim().toLowerCase();
    const airportMatchRegex = new RegExp('\\b' + escapedInput, 'i');
    const suggestions = this.state.airports
      .filter(airport => airportMatchRegex.test(airport.city))
      .sort((airport1, airport2) => {
        return airport1.city.toLowerCase().indexOf(escapedInput) -  ↵;
        airport2.city.toLowerCase().indexOf(escapedInput)
      })
      .slice(0, 7)
      .map(airport => `${airport.city} - ${airport.country} (${airport.code})`);
    callback(null, suggestions);
  }
```

```
    componentDidMount(){
      AirportActionCreators.fetchAirports();
    }

    render() {
      return (
        <div>
          <header>
            <div className="header-brand">
              <img src="logo.png" height="35"/>
              <p>Check discount ticket prices and pay using your AirCheap points</p>
            </div>
            <div className="header-route">
              <Autosuggest id='origin'
                           suggestions={this.getSuggestions.bind(this)}
                           inputAttributes={{placeholder:'From'}} />

              <Autosuggest id='destination'
                           suggestions={this.getSuggestions.bind(this)}
                           inputAttributes={{placeholder:'To'}} />
            </div>

          </header>
        </div>
      );
    }
}

App.getStores = () => ([AirportStore]);
App.calculateState = (prevState) => ({
  airports: AirportStore.getState()
});

const AppContainer = Container.create(App);

render(<AppContainer />, document.getElementById('root'));
```

Listing 6-24. The AirCheap Application Style Sheet

```
* {
  box-sizing: border-box;
}
body {
  margin: 0;
  font-family: "Helvetica Neue", Helvetica, Arial, sans-serif;
}
header {
  padding-top: 10px;
  border-bottom: 1px solid #ccc;
  border-top: 4px solid #08516E;
  height: 115px;
  background-color: #f6f6f6;
}
```

```css
p {
  margin:0;
  font-size: 10px;
}
.header-brand {
  text-align: center;
}
.header-route {
  margin-top: 10px;
  margin-left: calc(50% - 205px)
}

.react-autosuggest {
  position: relative;
  float: left;
  margin-right: 5px;
}
.react-autosuggest input {
  width: 200px;
  height: 30px;
  padding: 14px 10px;
  font-size: 13px;
  border: 1px solid #aaaaaa;
  border-radius: 4px;
}
.react-autosuggest input[aria-expanded="true"] {
  border-bottom-left-radius: 0;
  border-bottom-right-radius: 0;
}
.react-autosuggest input:focus {
  outline: none;
}
.react-autosuggest__suggestions {
  position: absolute;
  top: 29px;
  width: 200px;
  margin: 0;
  padding: 0;
  list-style-type: none;
  border: 1px solid #aaaaaa;
  background-color: #fff;
  font-size: 13px;
  border-bottom-left-radius: 4px;
  border-bottom-right-radius: 4px;
  z-index: 2;
}
.react-autosuggest__suggestions-section-suggestions {
  margin: 0;
  padding: 0;
  list-style-type: none;
}
```

```css
.react-autosuggest__suggestion {
  cursor: pointer;
  padding: 10px 10px;
}
.react-autosuggest__suggestion--focused {
  background-color: #ddd;
}
.ticket {
  padding: 20px 10px;
  background-color: #fafafa;
  margin: 5px;
  border: 1px solid #e5e5df;
  border-radius: 3px;
  box-shadow: 0 1px 0 rgba(0, 0, 0, 0.25);
}
.ticket span {
  display: inline-block;
}
.ticket-company {
  font-weight: bold;
  font-style: italic;
  width: 13%;
}
.ticket-location {
  text-align: center;
  width: 29%;
}
.ticket-separator {
  text-align: center;
  width: 6%;
}
.ticket-connection {
  text-align: center;
  width: 10%;
}
.ticket-points {
  width: 13%;
  text-align: right;
}
```

If you test the application right now, you should see the autosuggest fields in action: just start typing a few letters. But the application is not finished. After choosing an origin and a destination, nothing else happens. In the next section, let's start implementing the ticket loading.

Finishing the AirCheap application: Loading Tickets

You're fetching the airport data asynchronously as soon as the app component mounts, but there's one more fetch to be done: you need to fetch the actual ticket list when the user chooses the desired origin and destination.

The process is very similar to what you did for fetching airports. You put all the code that handles the actual data fetching in an API helper module. You create action creators to signal the data-fetching steps (loading initiated, loaded data successfully, or error in loading) and make a new store to keep the loaded tickets in its state. The App component is connected to the store and shows the loaded tickets data.

API Helper

For the sake of simplicity, instead of using a real API to return a list of flights and tickets, you load them from a static json file (`flights.json`). Obviously this means that whichever airports the user chooses, the loaded tickets will always be the same, but since your focus is on learning the Flux architecture, this will suffice. The `flights.json` file is shown in Listing 6-25, showing available flight tickets for a trip from São Paulo (GRU) to New York (JFK).

Listing 6-25. The flights.json File

```
[
  {
    "id": "fc704c16fd79",
    "company": "US Airlines",
    "points": 25000,
    "duration": 590,
    "segment": [
      {
        "duration": 590,
        "departureTime": "2016-10-10T21:30-03:00",
        "arrivalTime": "2016-10-11T06:20-04:00",
        "origin": "GRU",
        "destination": "JFK"
      }
    ]
  },
  {
    "id": "3fe21e46fd78",
    "company": "Dalta",
    "points": 20000,
    "duration": 862,
    "segment": [
      {
        "duration": 635,
        "departureTime": "2016-10-16T20:25-03:00",
        "arrivalTime": "2016-10-17T06:00-04:00",
        "origin": "GRU",
        "destination": "YYZ",
        "connectionDuration": 125
      },
      {
        "duration": 102,
        "departureTime": "2016-10-17T08:05-04:00",
        "arrivalTime": "2016-10-17T09:47-04:00",
```

```
          "origin": "YYZ",
          "destination": "JFK"
        }
      ]
    },
    {
      "id": "8bf2b3d7be09",
      "company": "Aviana",
      "points": 17000,
      "duration": 1050,
      "segment": [
        {
          "duration": 515,
          "departureTime": "2016-10-10T21:25-03:00",
          "arrivalTime": "2016-10-11T05:00-04:00",
          "origin": "GRU",
          "destination": "MIA",
          "connectionDuration": 145
        },
        {
          "duration": 192,
          "departureTime": "2016-10-11T07:25-04:00",
          "arrivalTime": "2016-10-11T10:37-04:00",
          "origin": "MIA",
          "destination": "YYZ",
          "connectionDuration": 98
        },
        {
          "duration": 100,
          "departureTime": "2016-10-11T12:15-04:00",
          "arrivalTime": "2016-10-11T13:55-04:00",
          "origin": "YYZ",
          "destination": "JFK"
        }
      ]
    }
]
```

Next, let's edit the AirCheapApi.js module to add methods to fetch the json file and dispatch the corresponding actions. As you did when you first created the AirCheapAPI file, you again assume that you will later implement some methods in the AirportActionCreators (fetchTicketsSuccess and fetchTicketsError). Listing 6-26 shows the updated file.

Listing 6-26. The Updated AirCheapAPI.js File to Fetch Tickets

```
import 'whatwg-fetch';
import AirportActionCreators from '../actions/AirportActionCreators';

let AirCheapAPI = {
  fetchAirports() {
    fetch('airports.json')
```

```
      .then((response) => response.json())
      .then((responseData) =>{
        AirportActionCreators.fetchAirportsSuccess(responseData);
      })
      .catch((error) => {
        AirportActionCreators.fetchAirportsError(error);
      });
    },

    fetchTickets(origin, destination) {
      fetch('flights.json')
      .then((response) => response.json())
      .then((responseData) => {
        AirportActionCreators.fetchTicketsSuccess(responseData);
      })
      .catch((error) => {
        AirportActionCreators.fetchTicketsError(error);
      });
    }
};

export default AirCheapAPI;
```

ActionCreators

Moving on, let's edit the `AirportActionCreators.js` file. Of course you need to add the three necessary action creators for ticket fetching, but let's start implementing another one, the chooseAirport action creator.

You provide the user with two auto-suggestion fields in the interface for selecting origin and destination airports, but so far nothing happens when the user chooses an airport. The chooseAirport action creator will be used for this purpose: it is invoked when either airport (origin or destination) is selected. Listing 6-27 shows the updated AirportActionCreators.

Listing 6-27. Adding Action Creators for Ticket Fetching

```
import AppDispatcher from '../AppDispatcher';
import constants from '../constants'
import AirCheapAPI from '../api/AirCheapApi';

let AirportActionCreators = {

  fetchAirports() {...},
  fetchAirportsSuccess(response) {...},
  fetchAirportsError(error) {...},

  chooseAirport(target, code) {
    AppDispatcher.dispatch({
      type: constants.CHOOSE_AIRPORT,
      target,
      code
    });
  },
```

```
fetchTickets() {
  AirCheapAPI.fetchTickets();
  AppDispatcher.dispatch({
    type: constants.FETCH_TICKETS,
  });
},

fetchTicketsSuccess(response) {
  AppDispatcher.dispatch({
    type: constants.FETCH_TICKETS_SUCCESS,
    payload: {response}
  });
},

fetchTicketsError(error) {
  AppDispatcher.dispatch({
    type: constants.FETCH_TICKETS_ERROR,
    payload: {error}
  });
}
};

export default AirportActionCreators;
```

Stores

You next create two stores. The first store, RouteStore, holds the user selected origin and destination airports. The second store, TicketStore, holds the list of airline tickets that will be fetched when both airports are selected.

Let's start with the RouteStore. It inherits from MapStore, which allows it to hold multiple key-value pairs. There are only two possible keys, origin and destination, and the store responds to the CHOOSE_ AIRPORT action type to update the value of one of these keys with an airport code. Listing 6-28 shows the complete source code.

Listing 6-28. Complete Source Code for the stores/RouteStore.js File

```
import AppDispatcher from '../AppDispatcher';
import constants from '../constants';
import {MapStore} from 'flux/utils';

class RouteStore extends MapStore {
  reduce(state, action){
    switch (action.type) {
      case constants.CHOOSE_AIRPORT:
        // action.target can be either "origin" or "destination"
        // action.code contains the selected airport code
        return state.set(action.target, action.code);
      default:
        return state;
    }
  }
}
export default new RouteStore(AppDispatcher);
```

The TicketStore is very similar to the AirportStore. It inherits from ReduceStore and updates its state when the FETCH_TICKETS_SUCCESS action is dispatched. Listing 6-29 shows the complete source.

Listing 6-29. Source Code for the stores/TicketStore.js File

```
import AppDispatcher from '../AppDispatcher';
import AirportActions from '../actions/AirportActionCreators';
import constants from '../constants';
import RouteStore from './RouteStore';
import {ReduceStore} from 'flux/utils';

class TicketStore extends ReduceStore {
  getInitialState() {
    return [];
  }
  reduce(state, action){
    switch (action.type) {
      case constants.FETCH_TICKETS:
        return [];
      case constants.FETCH_TICKETS_SUCCESS:
        return action.payload.response;
      default:
        return state;
    }
  }
}
export default new TicketStore(AppDispatcher);
```

Notice that the TicketStore also responds to the FETCH_TICKETS action by resetting its state to an empty array. This way, every time you try to fetch different tickets, the interface can be immediately updated to clear any previous tickets that may exist.

Interface Components

Let's begin your work on the interface by creating a new component, the TicketItem.js. It receives the component info as a prop and displays a single ticket row. The component's code is shown in Listing 6-30.

Listing 6-30. The components/TicketItem.js Component

```
import React, { Component, PropTypes } from 'react';

// Default data configuration
const dateConfig = {
  weekday: "short",
  year: "numeric",
  month: "short",
  day: "numeric",
  hour: "2-digit",
  minute: "2-digit"
};
```

```
class TicketItem extends Component {
  render() {
    let {ticket} = this.props;
    let departureTime = new Date(ticket.segment[0].departureTime)  ↩;
                          .toLocaleDateString("en-US",dateConfig);
    let arrivalTime = new Date(ticket.segment[ticket.segment.length-1].arrivalTime)  ↩;
                        .toLocaleDateString("en-US",dateConfig);

    let stops;
    if(ticket.segment.length === 2){
      stops = '1 stop';
    } else if(ticket.segment.length-1 > 1) {
      stops = ticket.segment.length-1 + ' stops';
    }

    return(
      <div className='ticket'>
        <span className="ticket-company">{ticket.company}</span>
        <span className="ticket-location">
          <strong>{ticket.segment[0].origin}</strong>{' '}
          <small>{departureTime}</small>
        </span>
        <span className="ticket-separator">

        </span>
        <span className="ticket-location">
          <strong>{ticket.segment[ticket.segment.length-1].destination}</strong>{' '}
          <small>{arrivalTime}</small>
        </span>
        <span className="ticket-connection">
          {stops}
        </span>
        <span className="ticket-points">
          <button>{ticket.points} points</button>
        </span>
      </div>
    );
  }
}
TicketItem.propTypes = {
  ticket: PropTypes.shape({
    id: PropTypes.string,
    company: PropTypes.string,
    points: PropTypes.number,
    duration: PropTypes.number,
    segment: PropTypes.array
  }),
};

export default TicketItem;
```

In the sequence, let's update the main App component. There are a few things you need to do:

- Make the component listen to updates from the new stores (RouteStore and TicketStore) and calculate its state using both store states. To do this, edit the static methods getStores and calculateState:

```
App.getStores = () => ([AirportStore,RouteStore,TicketStore]);
App.calculateState = (prevState) => ({
  airports: AirportStore.getState(),
  origin: RouteStore.get('origin'),
  destination: RouteStore.get('destination'),
  tickets: TicketStore.getState()
});
```

- Invoke the chooseAirport action creator when the user chooses an origin or destination airport. To do this, you pass a callback to the AutoSuggest's onSuggestionSelected prop. You could have two different callbacks (one for the origin field and other for the destination field), but using JavaScript's bind function you can have just one callback function and pass a different parameter for each field:

```
<Autosuggest id='origin'
             suggestions={this.getSuggestions.bind(this)}
             onSuggestionSelected={this.handleSelect.bind(this,'origin')}
             value={this.state.origin}
             inputAttributes={{placeholder:'From'}} />
<Autosuggest id='destination'
             suggestions={this.getSuggestions.bind(this)}
             onSuggestionSelected={this.handleSelect.bind(this,'destination')}
             value={this.state.destination}
             inputAttributes={{placeholder:'To'}} />
```

The handleSelect function uses a regular expression to separate the airport code from the string and invokes the chooseAirport action creator:

```
handleSelect(target, suggestion, event){
  const airportCodeRegex = /\(([^)]+)\)/;
  let airportCode = airportCodeRegex.exec(suggestion)[1];
  AirportActionCreators.chooseAirport(target, airportCode);
}
```

- Invoke the fetchTickets action creator when the user chooses both an origin and a destination aiport. You can do this on the componentWillUpdate lifecycle method; every time the user selects an airport, you invoke the chooseAirport action creator, and as a consequence the RouteStore dispatches a change event, and the App component will be updated. You check for two things before invoking the action creator: if both origin and destination were chosen and if either one has changed since the last update (so you only fetch once):

```
componentWillUpdate(nextProps, nextState){
  let originAndDestinationSelected =  ↵;
                    nextState.origin && nextState.destination;
  let selectionHasChangedSinceLastUpdate =  ↵;
```

```
                        nextState.origin !== this.state.origin ||
                        nextState.destination !== this.state.destination;
      if(originAndDestinationSelected && selectionHasChangedSinceLastUpdate){
        AirportActionCreators.fetchTickets(nextState.origin,   ↵;
                                        nextState.destination);
      }
    }
```

- Finally, import and implement the Ticket Item component you just created to show the loaded tickets:

```
render() {
  let ticketList = this.state.tickets.map((ticket)=>(
    <TicketItem key={ticket.id} ticket={ticket} />
  ));
  return (
    <div>
      <header>
        <div className="header-brand">...</div>
        <div className="header-route">
          <Autosuggest id='origin' ... />
          <Autosuggest id='destination' ... />
        </div>
      </header>
      <div>
        {ticketList}
      </div>

    </div>
  );
}
```

Listing 6-31 shows the complete updated App component with all the mentioned changes.

Listing 6-31. The Updated App Component

```
import React, { Component } from 'react';
import { render } from 'react-dom';
import ReactDOM from 'react-dom';
import {Container} from 'flux/utils';
import Autosuggest from 'react-autosuggest';
import AirportStore from './stores/AirportStore';
import RouteStore from './stores/RouteStore';
import TicketStore from './stores/TicketStore';
import TicketItem from './components/TicketItem';
import AirportActionCreators from './actions/AirportActionCreators';

class App extends Component {
  getSuggestions(input, callback) {
    const escapedInput = input.trim().toLowerCase();
    const airportMatchRegex = new RegExp('\\b' + escapedInput, 'i');
    const suggestions = this.state.airports
```

```
    .filter(airport => airportMatchRegex.test(airport.city))
    .sort((airport1, airport2) => {
      return airport1.city.toLowerCase().indexOf(escapedInput) -  ↵;
        airport2.city.toLowerCase().indexOf(escapedInput)
    })
    .slice(0, 7)
    .map(airport => `${airport.city} - ${airport.country} (${airport.code})`);
  callback(null, suggestions);
}

handleSelect(target, suggestion, event){
  const airportCodeRegex = /\(([^)]+)\)/;
  let airportCode = airportCodeRegex.exec(suggestion)[1];
  AirportActionCreators.chooseAirport(target, airportCode);
}

componentDidMount(){
  AirportActionCreators.fetchAirports();
}

componentWillUpdate(nextProps, nextState){
  let originAndDestinationSelected = nextState.origin && nextState.destination;
  let selectionHasChangedSinceLastUpdate = nextState.origin !== this.state.origin ||
                                      nextState.destination !== this.state.
destination;
  if(originAndDestinationSelected && selectionHasChangedSinceLastUpdate){
    AirportActionCreators.fetchTickets(nextState.origin, nextState.destination);
  }
}

render() {
  let ticketList = this.state.tickets.map((ticket)=>(
    <TicketItem key={ticket.id} ticket={ticket} />
  ));
  return (
    <div>
      <header>
        <div className="header-brand">
          <img src="logo.png" height="35"/>
          <p>Check discount ticket prices and pay using your AirCheap points</p>
        </div>
        <div className="header-route">
        <Autosuggest id='origin'
                    suggestions={this.getSuggestions.bind(this)}
                    onSuggestionSelected={this.handleSelect.bind(this,'origin')}
                    value={this.state.origin}
                    inputAttributes={{placeholder:'From'}} />

        <Autosuggest id='destination'
                    suggestions={this.getSuggestions.bind(this)}
                    onSuggestionSelected={this.handleSelect.bind(this,'destination')}
```

```
                     value={this.state.destination}
                     inputAttributes={{placeholder:'To'}} />
          </div>

        </header>
        <div>
          {ticketList}
        </div>
      </div>
    );
  }
}

App.getStores = () => ([AirportStore, RouteStore,TicketStore]);
App.calculateState = (prevState) => ({
  airports: AirportStore.getState(),
  origin: RouteStore.get('origin'),
  destination: RouteStore.get('destination'),
  tickets: TicketStore.getState()
});

const AppContainer = Container.create(App);

render(<AppContainer />, document.getElementById('root'));
```

If you test now, the application should be working and loading tickets after the origin and destinations are selected.

Evolving Your Async Data Fetching Implementation

You saw that the best approach for asynchronous API communication within Flux is to encapsulate all API specific code in an API helper module. You invoke the API helper module through an action, and all remote data loaded asynchronously by the API helper module enters the system through an action. This is an elegant solution that follows the Flux principles of single direction data flow and isolates the rest of the system (stores and components) from async code. But it's possible to further evolve this model to remove some boilerplate and decouple the API Helper module from the action creators. You achieve this by implementing a new method in the AppDispatcher: dispatch sync.

AppDispatcher's dispatchAsync

The Flux's dispatcher contains just a few public methods, and generally the most used one is dispatch. As you already know, the dispatch method is used to dispatch an action through all the registered stores.

As you saw in the earlier topics about asynchronous API (and in the sample AirCheap application), for every async operation there are three actions (async operation request, success, and failure). The generic dispatchAsync method expects a promise as a parameter, and the constants represent all steps of the async operation (request, success, failure) and automatically dispatch them based on the promise resolution.

Listing 6-32 shows the updated AppDispatcher with the dispatchAsync method implementation. Notice that you are using the Babel polyfill to make sure the Object.assign works on legacy browsers (make sure to install it using npm install --save babel-polyfill).

Listing 6-32. AppDispatcher with dispatchAsync

```
import {Dispatcher} from 'flux';
import 'babel-polyfill';


class AppDispatcher extends Dispatcher{
  dispatch(action = {}) {
    console.log("Dispatched", action.type);
    super.dispatch(action);
  }

  /**
   * Dispatches three actions for an async operation represented by promise.
   */
  dispatchAsync(promise, types, payload){
    const { request, success, failure } = types;
    this.dispatch({ type: request, payload: Object.assign({}, payload) });
    promise.then(
      response => this.dispatch({
        type: success,
        payload: Object.assign({}, payload, { response })
      }),
      error => this.dispatch({
        type: failure,
        payload: Object.assign({}, payload, { error })
      })
    );
  }
}

export default new AppDispatcher();
```

With this method, you can save a lot of typing in the ActionCreators, since instead of creating three methods for each async operation you can create only one. As an example, Listing 6-33 shows the updated AirportActionCreators file.

Listing 6-33. The Updated (and 50% Smaller) AirportActionCreators.js

```
import AppDispatcher from '../AppDispatcher';
import constants from '../constants'
import AirCheapAPI from '../api/AirCheapApi';

let AirportActionCreators = {

  fetchAirports(origin, destination) {
    AppDispatcher.dispatchAsync(AirCheapAPI.fetchAirports(), {
      request: constants.FETCH_AIRPORTS,
      success: constants.FETCH_AIRPORTS_SUCCESS,
      failure: constants.FETCH_AIRPORTS_ERROR
    });
  },
```

```
  chooseAirport(target, code) {
    AppDispatcher.dispatch({
      type: constants.CHOOSE_AIRPORT,
      target: target,
      code: code
    });
  },

  fetchTickets(origin, destination) {
    AppDispatcher.dispatchAsync(AirCheapAPI.fetchTickets(origin, destination), {
      request: constants.FETCH_TICKETS,
      success: constants.FETCH_TICKETS_SUCCESS,
      failure: constants.FETCH_TICKETS_ERROR
    });
  }

};

export default AirportActionCreators;
```

In the API helper module, not only do you reduce boilerplate, but you also decouple it from the action creators since the API Helper does not need to directly call the success or failure methods. All it has to do is return a promise. Listing 6-34 shows the updated `AirCheapApi.js` file, returning the promise created by the fetch operation and chained to the JSON parsing operation.

Listing 6-34. The Updated AirCheapApi.js File

```
import 'whatwg-fetch';

let AirCheapAPI = {
  fetchAirports() {
    return fetch('airports.json')
    .then((response) => response.json());
  },

  fetchTickets(origin, destination) {
    return fetch('flights.json')
    .then((response) => response.json());
  }
};

export default AirCheapAPI;
```

Kanban App: Moving to a Flux Architecture

You've been working on the Kanban App project since the beginning of this book, and in every chapter you've incrementally added new functionality to it. This chapter, however, will be different. Flux isn't a requisite to bring new functionality to a React project, as you've seen throughout this chapter. Flux is an application architecture that helps make data changes in an app easier to reason about. In converting your Kanban App to a Flux architecture you're not adding features; you're making it more predictable and easier to reason about (and in this sense it certainly helps with adding new functionality in the future).

Refactor: Creating Flux Basic Structure and Moving Files

To get started, make sure to install flux in the project using npm: `npm install --save flux`. Next, let's create folders for Flux's files and move all your components (with the exception of the `App.js` file) to a components folder. The constants and utils files can also remain in the root of the app folder. Figure 6-10 shows the new folder structure.

- **kanbanapp**
  - **app**
    - **actions**
    - **api**
    - **components**
      - Card.js
      - CardForm.js
      - CheckList.js
      - EditCard.js
      - KanbanBoard.js
      - KanbanBoardContainer.js
      - List.js
      - NewCard.js
    - **stores**
    - App.js
    - constants.js
    - utils.js

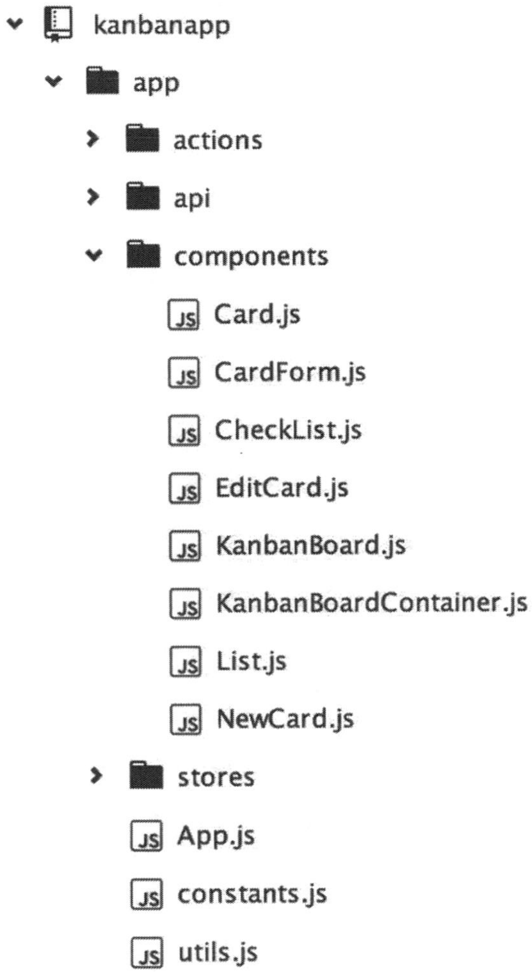

Figure 6-10. The new folder structure for the Kanban app

Fixing Imports

Obviously, you need to update the `import` statement in your components to reflect the new folder structure. Fortunately, the imports are all relative, so you don't need to update every single component. The only affected components are

- `App.js` (where you need to correct all the imported component's paths)

- `KanbanBoardContainer.js` (where you need to update only the utils import)

- `Card.js` and `List.js` (where you need to fix the import of the `constants.js` module)

Listings 6-35 through 6-38 shows the aforementioned files with updated imports.

Listing 6-35. Updated Imports in App.js

```
import React from 'react';
import { render } from 'react-dom';
import { Router, Route } from 'react-router';
import createBrowserHistory from 'history/lib/createBrowserHistory';
import KanbanBoardContainer from './components/KanbanBoardContainer';
import KanbanBoard from './components/KanbanBoard';
import EditCard from './components/EditCard';
import NewCard from './components/NewCard';

render(...);
```

Listing 6-36. Updated Utils Imports in KanbanBoardContainer Component

```
import React, { Component } from 'react';
import update from 'react-addons-update';
import KanbanBoard from './KanbanBoard';

import {throttle} from '../utils';

import 'babel-polyfill'
import 'whatwg-fetch';

const API_URL = 'http://kanbanapi.pro-react.com';
const API_HEADERS = {...};

class KanbanBoardContainer extends Component {
  constructor(){...}
  componentDidMount(){...}
  addCard(card){...}
  updateCard(card){...}
  updateCardStatus(cardId, listId){...}
  updateCardPosition (cardId , afterId) {...}
  persistCardDrag(cardId, status){...}
  addTask(cardId, taskName){...}
  deleteTask(cardId, taskId, taskIndex){...}
  toggleTask(cardId, taskId, taskIndex){...}
  render() {...}
}

export default KanbanBoardContainer;
```

Listing 6-37. Updated Import on the Card Component

```
import React, { Component, PropTypes } from 'react';
import ReactCSSTransitionGroup from 'react-addons-css-transition-group';
import marked from 'marked';
import { DragSource, DropTarget } from 'react-dnd';
import constants from '../constants';
import CheckList from './CheckList';
import {Link} from 'react-router';

let titlePropType = (props, propName, componentName) => {...}
const cardDragSpec = {...}
const cardDropSpec = {...}
let collectDrag = (connect, monitor) => {...}
let collectDrop = (connect, monitor) => {...}

class Card extends Component {...}
Card.propTypes = {...}

const dragHighOrderCard = ...
const dragDropHighOrderCard = ...

export default dragDropHighOrderCard
```

Listing 6-38. Updated Import in the List Component

```
import React, { Component, PropTypes } from 'react';
import { DropTarget } from 'react-dnd';
import Card from './Card';
import constants from '../constants';

const listTargetSpec = {...};
function collect(connect, monitor) {...}

class List extends Component {...}
List.propTypes = {...}

export default DropTarget(CARD, listTargetSpec, collect)(List);
```

Adding Flux Basic Files

Flux is all about actions, stores, and a dispatcher (plus an API helper to handle API async requests). Let's add five new files in the project to cover these:

- An AppDispatcher.js
- A store: CardStore.js, inside the stores folder
- Actions: CardActionCreators.js and TaskActionCreators.js inside the actions folder
- Finally, a KanbanApi.js helper module inside the api folder

You extend the base Flux dispacher with the `DispatchAsync` method you used earlier. As for the `CardStore.js`, `CardActionCreators.js`, `TaskActionCreators.js`, and `KanbanAPi.js` files, you begin with a basic skeleton for each and enhance them in the following sections. Listings 6-39 through 6-43 show the source for all these files, starting with the AppDispatcher.

Listing 6-39. The AppDispatcher

```
import {Dispatcher} from 'flux';
import 'babel-polyfill';

class AppDispatcher extends Dispatcher{
  /**
   * Dispatches three actions for an async operation represented by promise.
   */
  dispatchAsync(promise, types, payload){
    const { request, success, failure } = types;
    this.dispatch({ type: request, payload: Object.assign({}, payload) });
    promise.then(
      response => this.dispatch({
        type: success,
        payload: Object.assign({}, payload, { response })
      }),
      error => this.dispatch({
        type: failure,
        payload: Object.assign({}, payload, { error })
      })
    );
  }
}

export default new AppDispatcher();
```

For the CardStore, you extend Flux's `ReduceStore`.

Listing 6-40. The stores/CardStore.js File Basic Structure

```
import AppDispatcher from '../AppDispatcher';
import constants from '../constants';
import {ReduceStore} from 'flux/utils';

class CardStore extends ReduceStore {
  getInitialState() {
    return [];
  }

  reduce(state, action){
    switch (action.type) {
      default:
        return state;
    }
  }
}
export default new CardStore(AppDispatcher);
```

211

The CardActionCreators and TaskActionCreators start as plain JavaScript objects, but you import the modules that will be used later.

Listing 6-41. The actions/CardActionCreators.js File Basic Structure

```
import AppDispatcher from '../AppDispatcher';
import constants from '../constants';
import KanbanAPI from '../api/KanbanApi';

let CardActionCreators = {

};

export default CardActionCreators;
```

Listing 6-42. The actions/TaskActionCreators.js File Basic Structure

```
import AppDispatcher from '../AppDispatcher';
import constants from '../constants';
import KanbanAPI from '../api/KanbanApi';

let TaskActionCreators = {

};

export default TaskActionCreators;
```

The same goes for the KanbanApi: it also starts as just a plain JavaScript object with the import statements for the modules that will be used later.

Listing 6-43. The api/KanbanApi.js File Basic Structure

```
import 'whatwg-fetch';
import 'babel-polyfill';

let KanbanAPI = {

};

export default KanbanAPI;
```

Moving the Data Fetching to the Flux Architecture

Your project structure is now ready to use Flux, and the first piece of code you're going to port to the new architecture is the initial data fetching. Currently, all API communication (including the initial data fetching) is done in the KanbanBoardContainer, and the cards are kept in the component's state. In the Flux architecture, the KanbanBoardContainer and child components such as the Card component will just fire actions; the API communication will be done by the API helper module and the cards will be kept in the CardStore.

Editing the KanbanBoardContainer

Since you're tackling only the initial data fetching for now, you need to make the following changes to the KanbanBoardContainer:

- Import the CardStore and CardActionCreator modules.

- Make the KanbanBoardContainer listen to change events in the CardStore and map its state to the CardStore state (you can do this manually or using the Flux library Container higher order function). In the process, you remove the local state declared in the class constructor.

- In the ComponentDidMount lifecycle method, instead of directly fetching data, you call an action creator to dispatch an action. This action will trigger a series of effects. The API helper will fetch the remote data, the CardStore will update itself with the new data and dispatch a change event, and finally the KanbanBoardContainer will have its state updated and will trigger a re-render.

The updated KanbanBoardContainer code is shown in Listing 6-44.

Listing 6-44. The Updated KanbanBoardContainer

```
import React, { Component } from 'react';
import update from 'react-addons-update';
import KanbanBoard from './KanbanBoard';
import {throttle} from '../utils';

import {Container} from 'flux/utils';
import CardActionCreators from '../actions/CardActionCreators';
import CardStore from '../stores/CardStore';

// Polyfills
import 'babel-polyfill';
import 'whatwg-fetch';

const API_URL=' http://kanbanapi.pro-react.com'
const API_HEADERS = {...}

class KanbanBoardContainer extends Component {
  constructor{
    super(...arguments);
    this.updateCardStatus = throttle(this.updateCardStatus.bind(this));
    this.updateCardPosition = throttle(this.updateCardPosition.bind(this),500);
  }

  componentDidMount(){
    CardActionCreators.fetchCards();
  }

  addCard(card){...}
  updateCard(card){...}
  updateCardStatus(cardId, listId){...}
```

```
  updateCardPosition (cardId , afterId){...}
  persistCardDrag(cardId, status){...}
  addTask(cardId, taskName){...}
  deleteTask(cardId, taskId, taskIndex){...}
  toggleTask(cardId, taskId, taskIndex){...}

  render() {...}
}

KanbanBoardContainer.getStores = () => ([CardStore]);
KanbanBoardContainer.calculateState = (prevState) => ({
  cards: CardStore.getState()
});

export default Container.create(KanbanBoardContainer);
```

The end objective is to remove the eight methods that deal with card and task manipulations from the KanbanBoardContainer, but for now let's just stick to the plan and only deal with the initial data fetching.

Implementing the FetchCards Action, API Method Call, and Store Callback

So far you've worked on two different Flux projects (Flux Bank and Air Cheap), so the process should be familiar: you need to define an action creator that, when invoked, will call the API Helper, receive a JavaScript promise, and dispatch different actions along the process (init of the fetching process, success or failure). The CardStore will respond to the success action and populate its state with the loaded cards.

FetchCards Constants and Action Creator

As you know, every action needs a constant to identify it. You already have a constants file. Let's add three new constants: FETCH_CARDS, FETCH_CARDS_SUCCESS, and FETCH_CARDS_ERROR (as shown in Listing 6-45).

Listing 6-45. Updated constants.js Source Code

```
 export default {
  CARD: 'card',
  FETCH_CARDS: 'fetch cards',
  FETCH_CARDS_SUCCESS: 'fetch cards success',
  FETCH_CARDS_SUCCESS: 'fetch cards error',
};
```

In the sequence, let's create the fetchCards method in the CardActionCreators. You use the AppDispatcher's DispatchAsync method to make things leaner. Listing 6-46 shows the implemented method.

Listing 6-46. The fetchCards Method Implementation on CardActionCreators

```
import AppDispatcher from '../AppDispatcher';
import constants from '../constants';
import KanbanAPI from '../api/KanbanApi';

let CardActionCreators = {
  fetchCards() {
    AppDispatcher.dispatchAsync(KanbanAPI.fetchCards(), {
      request: constants.FETCH_CARDS,
      success: constants.FETCH_CARDS_SUCCESS,
      failure: constants.FETCH_CARDS_ERROR
    });
  }
};

export default CardActionCreators;
```

Notice that you assume in the code that the KanbanAPI module has a fetchCards method. Let's implement it in the next section.

fetchCards API Method

After the actionCreator (with the corresponding constants), let's move to the kanbanApi. You basically copy the configuration and the fetch method that were used in the KanbanBoardContainer, but in this case, you simply return the fetch promise (instead of manipulating the card's state; this part is now responsibility of the store), as show in Listing 6-47.

Listing 6-47. The KanbanApi Source Code with the fetchCards Method

```
import 'whatwg-fetch';
import 'babel-polyfill';

const API_URL = 'http://kanbanapi.pro-react.com';
const API_HEADERS = {
  'Content-Type': 'application/json',
  Authorization: 'any-string-you-like'
}

let KanbanAPI = {
  fetchCards() {
    return fetch(`${API_URL}/cards`, {headers:API_HEADERS})
    .then((response) => response.json())
  }
};

export default KanbanAPI;
```

CardStore: Responding to FETCH_CARDS_SUCCESS

Finally, let's update the reduce method in the CardStore to respond to the FETCH_CARD_SUCCESS and update its state with the loaded cards, as shown in Listing 6-48.

Listing 6-48. The Updated Reduce Method in the CardStore

```
import AppDispatcher from '../AppDispatcher';
import constants from '../constants';
import {ReduceStore} from 'flux/utils';

class CardStore extends ReduceStore {
  getInitialState() {
    return [];
  }

  reduce(state, action){
    switch (action.type) {
      case constants.FETCH_CARDS_SUCCESS:
        return action.payload.response;

      default:
        return state;
    }
  }
}
export default new CardStore(AppDispatcher);
```

Since the KanbanBoardContainer is already listening to CardStore's changes, your task is complete. If you test now, you should see the cards normally.

Moving All Card and Task Manipulations to the Flux Architecture

In the previous section, you removed the initial data fetching code from the KanbanBoardContainer, but the component still has eight other methods that manipulate cards and tasks. These methods are currently passed down as props through all the component hierarchy and are invoked from the List, Card, and Task components. You created these methods yourself throughout the book, but let's take a brief recap: Table 6-3 lists these methods and what they do.

Table 6-3. *Data Manipulation Methods Currently in KanbanBoardContainer Component*

Method	Description
addCard	Receives an object with card properties as parameters; creates a new card.
updateCard	Receives an object with the updated card properties; updates the properties of the given card. In the refactor, it receives two properties: the original card properties and the changed card properties.
updateCardPosition	Receives the current card id and the card id with which the current card will switch positions. Called during the card drag-and-drop. Switches the positions of the given cards.
updateCardStatus	Receives the current card Id and the new status Id. Called during the card drag-and-drop. Updates the card status.
persistCardDrag	Receives an object containing a given card's ID and the new card status. Called after a card's drag-and-drop. Persists the new card's position and status on the server.
addTask	Receives a card Id and a task name; creates a new task for a given card. In the refactor, you will pass an entire Task object instead of just the task name.
deleteTask	Receives a card Id, a task id, and the task index; deletes the task. In the refactor, you pass the entire card object instead of just the id.
toggleTask	Receives a card id, a task id, and the task index; toggles the task "done" property. In the refactor, you pass the entire card object instead of just the id.

Make all these changes at once. You first replicate all the method functionalities of the Flux architecture (action creators, KanbanApi, and CardStore). Only then do you update the KanbanBoardContainer and all the affected components in the hierarchy (KanbanBoard, List, Card, and Checklist components).

Preparing for the Functionality Migration

Before getting your hands on the action creators, API module, or store, let's do some preparation. You declare all the necessary constants in the constants file. Listing 6-49 shows the updated constants.js file.

Listing 6-49. Necessary Constants Declarations in the constants.js

```
export default {
  CARD: 'card',

  FETCH_CARDS: 'fetch cards',
  FETCH_CARDS_SUCCESS: 'fetch cards success',
  FETCH_CARDS_ERROR: 'fetch cards error',

  CREATE_CARD: 'create card',
  CREATE_CARD_SUCCESS: 'create card success',
  CREATE_CARD_ERROR: 'create card error',

  UPDATE_CARD: 'update card',
  UPDATE_CARD_SUCCESS: 'update card success',
  UPDATE_CARD_ERROR: 'update card error',
```

```
  UPDATE_CARD_STATUS: 'update card status',

  UPDATE_CARD_POSITION: 'update card position',

  PERSIST_CARD_DRAG: 'persist card drag',
  PERSIST_CARD_DRAG_SUCCESS: 'persist card drag success',
  PERSIST_CARD_DRAG_ERROR: 'persist card drag error',

  CREATE_TASK: 'create task',
  CREATE_TASK_SUCCESS: 'create task success',
  CREATE_TASK_ERROR: 'create task error',

  DELETE_TASK: 'delete task',
  DELETE_TASK_SUCCESS: 'delete task success',
  DELETE_TASK_ERROR: 'delete task error',

  TOGGLE_TASK: 'toggle task',
  TOGGLE_TASK_SUCCESS: 'toggle task success',
  TOGGLE_TASK_ERROR: 'toggle task error'
};
```

Action Creators

In sequence, let's implement all the Card and Task manipulation actions. Notice that in the CardActionCreators module you're importing and using the throttle utility function. Listing 6-50 shows the CardActionCreators.js file and Listing 6-51 shows the updated TaskActionCreators.js file.

Listing 6-50. CardActionCreators.js

```
import AppDispatcher from '../AppDispatcher';
import constants from '../constants';
import KanbanAPI from '../api/KanbanApi';
import {throttle} from '../utils';
import CardStore from '../stores/CardStore';

let CardActionCreators = {

  fetchCards() {
    AppDispatcher.dispatchAsync(KanbanAPI.fetchCards(), {
      request: constants.FETCH_CARDS,
      success: constants.FETCH_CARDS_SUCCESS,
      failure: constants.FETCH_CARDS_ERROR
    });
  },

  addCard(card) {
    AppDispatcher.dispatchAsync(KanbanAPI.addCard(card), {
      request: constants.CREATE_CARD,
      success: constants.CREATE_CARD_SUCCESS,
      failure: constants.CREATE_CARD_ERROR
    }, {card});
  },
```

```javascript
  updateCard(card, draftCard) {
    AppDispatcher.dispatchAsync(KanbanAPI.updateCard(card, draftCard), {
      request: constants.UPDATE_CARD,
      success: constants.UPDATE_CARD_SUCCESS,
      failure: constants.UPDATE_CARD_ERROR
    }, {card, draftCard});
  },

  updateCardStatus: throttle((cardId, listId) => {
    AppDispatcher.dispatch({
      type: constants.UPDATE_CARD_STATUS,
      payload: {cardId, listId}
    });
  }),

  updateCardPosition: throttle((cardId , afterId) => {
    AppDispatcher.dispatch({
      type: constants.UPDATE_CARD_POSITION,
      payload: {cardId , afterId}
    });
  },500),

  persistCardDrag(cardProps) {
    let card = CardStore.getCard(cardProps.id)
    let cardIndex = CardStore.getCardIndex(cardProps.id)
    AppDispatcher.dispatchAsync(KanbanAPI.persistCardDrag(card.id, card.status, cardIndex), {
      request: constants.PERSIST_CARD_DRAG,
      success: constants.PERSIST_CARD_DRAG_SUCCESS,
      failure: constants.PERSIST_CARD_DRAG_ERROR
    }, {cardProps});
  }
};

export default CardActionCreators;
```

Listing 6-51. TaskActionCreators.js

```javascript
import AppDispatcher from '../AppDispatcher';
import constants from '../constants'
import KanbanAPI from '../api/KanbanApi';

let TaskActionCreators = {
  addTask(cardId, task) {
    AppDispatcher.dispatchAsync(KanbanAPI.addTask(cardId, task), {
      request: constants.CREATE_TASK,
      success: constants.CREATE_TASK_SUCCESS,
      failure: constants.CREATE_TASK_ERROR
    }, {cardId, task});
  },

  deleteTask(cardId, task, taskIndex) {
```

```
    AppDispatcher.dispatchAsync(KanbanAPI.deleteTask(cardId, task), {
      request: constants.DELETE_TASK,
      success: constants.DELETE_TASK_SUCCESS,
      failure: constants.DELETE_TASK_ERROR
    }, {cardId, task, taskIndex});
  },

  toggleTask(cardId, task, taskIndex) {
    AppDispatcher.dispatchAsync(KanbanAPI.toggleTask(cardId, task), {
      request: constants.TOGGLE_TASK,
      success: constants.TOGGLE_TASK_SUCCESS,
      failure: constants.TOGGLE_TASK_ERROR
    }, {cardId, task, taskIndex});
  }
};

export default TaskActionCreators;
```

KanbanApi

Following with your migration to the Flux architecture, let's update the KanbanApi module, as shown in Listing 6-52.

Listing 6-52. The Updated KanbanApi

```
import 'whatwg-fetch';
import 'babel-polyfill';

const API_URL = 'http://kanbanapi.pro-react.com';
const API_HEADERS = {
  'Content-Type': 'application/json',
  Authorization: 'any-string-you-like'
}

let KanbanAPI = {
  fetchCards() {
    return fetch(`${API_URL}/cards`, {headers:API_HEADERS})
    .then((response) => response.json())
  },

  addCard(card) {
    return fetch(`${API_URL}/cards`, {
      method: 'post',
      headers: API_HEADERS,
      body: JSON.stringify(card)
    })
    .then((response) => response.json())
  },

  updateCard(card, draftCard) {
```

```
      return fetch(`${API_URL}/cards/${card.id}`, {
          method: 'put',
          headers: API_HEADERS,
          body: JSON.stringify(draftCard)
      })
  },

  persistCardDrag(cardId, status, index) {
    return fetch(`${API_URL}/cards/${cardId}`, {
        method: 'put',
        headers: API_HEADERS,
        body: JSON.stringify({status, row_order_position: index})
    })
  },

  addTask(cardId, task) {
    return fetch(`${API_URL}/cards/${cardId}/tasks`, {
      method: 'post',
      headers: API_HEADERS,
      body: JSON.stringify(task)
    })
    .then((response) => response.json())
  },

  deleteTask(cardId, task) {
    return fetch(`${API_URL}/cards/${cardId}/tasks/${task.id}`, {
      method: 'delete',
      headers: API_HEADERS
    })
  },

  toggleTask(cardId, task) {
    return fetch(`${API_URL}/cards/${cardId}/tasks/${task.id}`, {
        method: 'put',
        headers: API_HEADERS,
        body: JSON.stringify({done:!task.done})
    })
  }
 }
};

export default KanbanAPI;
```

CardStore

The final piece in this process is the updated CardStore (shown in Listing 6-53). Notice that besides responding to all the actions to manipulate its state, you also created the helper methods: getCard and getCardIndex.

Listing 6-53. Updated Card Store

```
import AppDispatcher from '../AppDispatcher';
import constants from '../constants';
import {ReduceStore} from 'flux/utils';
import update from 'react-addons-update';
import 'babel-polyfill';

class CardStore extends ReduceStore {
  getInitialState() {
    return [];
  }

  getCard(id) {
    return this._state.find((card)=>card.id == id);
  }

  getCardIndex(id) {
    return this._state.findIndex((card)=>card.id == id);
  }

  reduce(state, action){
    let cardIndex, taskIndex;

    switch (action.type) {
      case constants.FETCH_CARDS_SUCCESS:
        return action.payload.response;

      /*
       * Card Creation
       */
      case constants.CREATE_CARD:
        return update(this.getState(), {$push: [action.payload.card] })

      case constants.CREATE_CARD_SUCCESS:
        cardIndex = this.getCardIndex(action.payload.card.id);
        return update(this.getState(), {
          [cardIndex]: {
            id: { $set: action.payload.response.id }
          }
        });

      case constants.CREATE_CARD_ERROR:
        cardIndex = this.getCardIndex(action.payload.card.id);
        return update(this.getState(), { $splice:[[cardIndex, 1]]});

      /*
       * Card Update
       */
      case constants.UPDATE_CARD:
        cardIndex = this.getCardIndex(action.payload.card.id);
```

```
    return update(this.getState(), {
      [cardIndex]: {
        $set: action.payload.draftCard
      }
    });

case constants.UPDATE_CARD_ERROR:
    cardIndex = this.getCardIndex(action.payload.card.id);
    return update(this.getState(), {
      [cardIndex]: {
        $set: action.payload.card
      }
    });

/*
 * Card Drag'n Drop
 */
case constants.UPDATE_CARD_POSITION:
    if(action.payload.cardId !== action.payload.afterId) {
      cardIndex = this.getCardIndex(action.payload.cardId);
      let card = this.getState()[cardIndex]
      let afterIndex = this.getCardIndex(action.payload.afterId);
      return update(this.getState(), {
        $splice: [
          [cardIndex, 1],
          [afterIndex, 0, card]
        ]
      });
    }

case constants.UPDATE_CARD_STATUS:
    cardIndex = this.getCardIndex(action.payload.cardId);
    return update(this.getState(), {
      [cardIndex]: {
        status: { $set: action.payload.listId }
      }
    });

case constants.PERSIST_CARD_DRAG_ERROR:
    cardIndex = this.getCardIndex(action.payload.cardProps.id);
    return update(this.getState(), {
      [cardIndex]: {
        status: { $set: action.payload.cardProps.status }
      }
    });

/*
 * Task Creation
 */
case constants.CREATE_TASK:
    cardIndex = this.getCardIndex(action.payload.cardId);
```

```
      return update(this.getState(), {
        [cardIndex]: {
          tasks: {$push: [action.payload.task] }
        }
      });

    case constants.CREATE_TASK_SUCCESS:
      cardIndex = this.getCardIndex(action.payload.cardId);
      taskIndex = this.getState()[cardIndex].tasks.findIndex((task)=>(
        task.id == action.payload.task.id
      ));
      return update(this.getState(), {
        [cardIndex]: {
          tasks: {
            [taskIndex]: {
              id: { $set: action.payload.response.id }
            }
          }
        }
      });

    case constants.CREATE_TASK_ERROR:
      let cardIndex = this.getCardIndex(action.payload.cardId);
      let taskIndex = this.getState()[cardIndex].tasks.findIndex((task)=>(
        task.id == action.payload.task.id
      ));
      return update(this.getState(), {
        [cardIndex]: {
          tasks: {
            $splice:[[taskIndex, 1]]
          }
        }
      });

    /*
     * Task Deletion
     */
    case constants.DELETE_TASK:
      cardIndex = this.getCardIndex(action.payload.cardId);
      return update(this.getState(), {
        [cardIndex]: {
          tasks: {$splice: [[action.payload.taskIndex,1]] }
        }
      });

    case constants.DELETE_TASK_ERROR:
      cardIndex = this.getCardIndex(action.payload.cardId);
      return update(this.getState(), {
        [cardIndex]: {
          tasks: {$splice: [[action.payload.taskIndex, 0, action.payload.task]] }
        }
      });
```

```
      /*
       * Task Toggling
       */
      case constants.TOGGLE_TASK:
        cardIndex = this.getCardIndex(action.payload.cardId);
        return update(this.getState(), {
          [cardIndex]: {
            tasks: {
              [action.payload.taskIndex]: { done: { $apply: (done) => !done }}
            }
          }
        });

      case constants.TOGGLE_TASK_ERROR:
        cardIndex = this.getCardIndex(action.payload.cardId);
        return update(this.getState(), {
          [cardIndex]: {
            tasks: {
              [action.payload.taskIndex]: { done: { $apply: (done) => !done }}
            }
          }
        });

    default:
      return state;
    }
  }
}
export default new CardStore(AppDispatcher);
```

Components

Heading back to the components, let's remove all the data manipulation methods from the
KanbanBoardContainer component. Observe that all these methods are grouped into two objects
(taskActions and cardActions) and passed as props through the KanbanBoard, List, Card and CheckList
components. You must remove these methods from the KanbanBoardContainer, and change the proptypes
and render methods of all the mentioned components. And since you also won't pass the cards as props to
the NewCard and EditCart components, you need to edit them as well.

KanbanBoardContainer

Let's tackle one file at a time. Listing 6-54 shows the updated code for the KanbanBoardContainer, without
the constructor and data manipulation methods, but with updated render method (without passing the
methods as props).

Listing 6-54. The Updated KanbanBoardContainer Component

```
import React, { Component } from 'react';
import {Container} from 'flux/utils';
import KanbanBoard from './KanbanBoard';
import CardActionCreators from '../actions/CardActionCreators';
import CardStore from '../stores/CardStore';

class KanbanBoardContainer extends Component {
  componentDidMount(){
    CardActionCreators.fetchCards();
  }

  render() {
    let kanbanBoard=this.props.children && React.cloneElement(this.props.children, {
      cards: this.state.cards,
    });

    return kanbanBoard;
  }
}

KanbanBoardContainer.getStores = () => ([CardStore]);
KanbanBoardContainer.calculateState = (prevState) => ({
  cards: CardStore.getState()
});

export default Container.create(KanbanBoardContainer);
```

KanbanBoard

Next in the hierarchy is the KanbanBoard component. You don't need to pass the taskCallbacks and cardCallbacks objects down to the Lists, and you also don't need to clone the children prop that is provided by the React Router. You cloned the component to inject props into it, but in the Flux architecture they won't be necessary. Listing 6-55 shows the updated KanbanBoard component.

Listing 6-55. The Updated KanbanBoard Component

```
import React, { Component, PropTypes } from 'react';
import { DragDropContext } from 'react-dnd';
import HTML5Backend from 'react-dnd-html5-backend';
import { Link } from 'react-router';
import List from './List';

class KanbanBoard extends Component {
  render() {
    return (
      <div className="app">
        <Link to='/new' className="float-button">+</Link>
```

```
        <List id='todo' title="To Do" cards={
          this.props.cards.filter((card) => card.status === "todo")
        } />

        <List id='in-progress' title="In Progress" cards={
          this.props.cards.filter((card) => card.status == "in-progress")
        } />

        <List id='done' title='Done' cards={
          this.props.cards.filter((card) => card.status == "done")
        } />

        {this.props.children}
      </div>
    )
  }
}
KanbanBoard.propTypes = {
  cards: PropTypes.arrayOf(PropTypes.object)
}

export default DragDropContext(HTML5Backend)(KanbanBoard);
```

List

Moving on, the next component in the hierarchy is the List component. You keep removing the taskCallbacks and cardCallbacks, but in this file you'll also update the hover method in the `listTargetSpec` object; it used to invoke `cardCallbacks.updateStatus`, but now it's going to invoke the updateCardStatus action creator. Listing 6-56 shows the updated source code.

Listing 6-56. The Updated List Component

```
import React, { Component, PropTypes } from 'react';
import { DropTarget } from 'react-dnd';
import Card from './Card';
import constants from '../constants';
import CardActionCreators from '../actions/CardActionCreators';

const listTargetSpec = {
  hover(props, monitor) {
    const dragged = monitor.getItem();
    CardActionCreators.updateCardStatus(dragged.id, props.id);
  }
};

function collect(connect, monitor) {
  return {
    connectDropTarget: connect.dropTarget()
  };
}
```

```
class List extends Component {
  render() {
    const { connectDropTarget } = this.props;

    let cards = this.props.cards.map((card) => {
      return <Card key={card.id} {…card} />
    });

    return connectDropTarget(
      <div className="list">
        <h1>{this.props.title}</h1>
        {cards}
      </div>
    );
  }
}
List.propTypes = {
  id: PropTypes.string.isRequired,
  title: PropTypes.string.isRequired,
  cards: PropTypes.arrayOf(React.PropTypes.object),
  connectDropTarget: PropTypes.func.isRequired
}

export default DropTarget(constants.CARD, listTargetSpec, collect)(List);
```

Card

It's time to update the Card component. The same premise is valid here: you remove any reference to CardCallbacks and TaskCallbacks as well as change any calls to those props to action creator calls. The updated card component is shown in Listing 6-57.

Listing 6-57. The Updated Card Component

```
import React, { Component, PropTypes } from 'react';
import ReactCSSTransitionGroup from 'react-addons-css-transition-group';
import marked from 'marked';
import { DragSource, DropTarget } from 'react-dnd';
import constants from '../constants';
import CheckList from './CheckList';
import {Link} from 'react-router';
import CardActionCreators from '../actions/CardActionCreators';

let titlePropType = (props, propName, componentName) => {...}

const cardDragSpec = {
  beginDrag(props) {
    return {
      id: props.id,
      status: props.status
    };
  },
```

```
  endDrag(props) {
    CardActionCreators.persistCardDrag(props);
  }
};

const cardDropSpec = {
  hover(props, monitor) {
    const draggedId = monitor.getItem().id;
    if(props.id !== draggedId){
      CardActionCreators.updateCardPosition(draggedId, props.id);
    }
  }
}

let collectDrag = (connect, monitor) => {...}
let collectDrop = (connect, monitor) => {...}

class Card extends Component {...}
Card.propTypes = {
  id: PropTypes.number,
  title: titlePropType,
  description: PropTypes.string,
  color: PropTypes.string,
  tasks: PropTypes.array,
  status: PropTypes.string,
  connectDragSource: PropTypes.func.isRequired,
  connectDropTarget: PropTypes.func.isRequired
}

const dragHighOrderCard = DragSource(constants.CARD, cardDragSpec, collectDrag)(Card);
const dragDropHighOrderCard = DropTarget(constants.CARD, cardDropSpec, collectDrop)
(dragHighOrderCard);
export default dragDropHighOrderCard
```

CheckList

In the Checklist component, let's get rid of any TaskCallback calls and insert TaskActionCreator calls. Listing 6-58 shows the updated code.

Listing 6-58. Updated CheckList Component

```
import React, { Component, PropTypes } from 'react';
import TaskActionCreators from '../actions/TaskActionCreators';

class CheckList extends Component {
  checkInputKeyPress(evt){
    if(evt.key === 'Enter'){
      let newTask = {id:Date.now(), name:evt.target.value, done:false};
      TaskActionCreators.addTask(this.props.cardId, newTask);
      evt.target.value = '';
    }
  }
```

```
  render() {
    let tasks = this.props.tasks.map((task, taskIndex) => (
      <li key={task.id} className="checklist__task">
        <input type="checkbox"
               checked={task.done}
               onChange={
                 TaskActionCreators.toggleTask.bind(null, this.props.cardId, task, taskIndex)
               } />
        {task.name}{' '}
        <a href="#"
           className="checklist__task--remove"
           onClick={
             TaskActionCreators.deleteTask.bind(null, this.props.cardId, task, taskIndex)
           } />
      </li>
    ));

    return (
      <div className="checklist">
        <ul>{tasks}</ul>
        <input type="text"
          className="checklist--add-task"
          placeholder="Type then hit Enter to add a task"
          onKeyPress={this.checkInputKeyPress.bind(this)} />
      </div>
    );
  }

}
CheckList.propTypes = {
  cardId: PropTypes.number,
  tasks: PropTypes.arrayOf(PropTypes.object)
}

export default CheckList;
```

NewCard and EditCard

Finally, let's update both the NewCard and EditCard components. In both, you substitute the callback that was passed as props to action creator calls. In the EditCard, you go even further: since the component won't have the cards array as props anymore, it will talk directly to the CardStore to retrieve the selected card details. Listing 6-59 shows the updated NewCard component and Listing 6-60 shows the updated EditCard component.

Listing 6-59. The Updated NewCard.js

```
import React,{Component, PropTypes} from 'react';
import CardForm from './CardForm';
import CardActionCreators from '../actions/CardActionCreators';

class NewCard extends Component {
  componentWillMount(){...}
  handleChange(field, value){...}
```

```
  handleSubmit(e){
    e.preventDefault();
    CardActionCreators.addCard(this.state);
    this.props.history.pushState(null,'/');
  }
  handleClose(e){
    this.props.history.pushState(null,'/');
  }

  render(){...}
}
NewCard.propTypes = {...};

export default NewCard;
```

Listing 6-60. The Updated EditCard.js

```
import React,{Component, PropTypes} from 'react';
import CardForm from './CardForm';
import CardStore from '../stores/CardStore';
import CardActionCreators from '../actions/CardActionCreators';
import 'babel-polyfill'

class EditCard extends Component{
  componentWillMount(){
    let card = CardStore.getCard(parseInt(this.props.params.card_id));
    this.setState(Object.assign({},card));
  }

  handleChange(field, value){...}

  handleSubmit(e){
    e.preventDefault();
    CardActionCreators.updateCard(CardStore.getCard(parseInt(this.props.params.card_id)),
      this.state);
    this.props.history.pushState(null,'/');
  }

  handleClose(e){...}

  render(){...}
}

EditCard.propTypes = {...};

export default EditCard;
```

Removing All Component State

Ideally, you should avoid using and manipulating component state when using Flux. All the component state (even UI-related state) should be kept in stores. This is a good practice and a desirable target when writing Flux applications, but there's nothing inherently wrong in having stateful components with limited, small, UI-related data.

That's precisely the case for the Kanban App so far. You've converted pretty much everything to the Flux architecture, but some components still have local state. The Card component holds a showDetails local state, and the EditCard and NewCard components also have local state for the draft card being manipulated. As we said, this isn't wrong, but for the sake of having a complete Flux port, let's move all those local states to stores and keep the components leaner.

Show/Hide Card Details

Let's start with the showDetails in the Card component. You won't persist this data on the server, but you will use the existing CardStore to keep this value. The CardStore sets its state with the loaded cards data from the Kanban API. You need to add the ShowProperties key for each card, but for simplicity you're not going to do it in the initial data fetch. Instead, you will assume a default value for the cards in which this property hasn't been set yet, and only set this property when the user switches the visibility of the card details. In plain English, if there's no showDetails property in the card, you assume that the details will show. When the user closes the card details for the first time, you then create this property on the desired card and set its value to false.

Card Component

Starting with the Card component, you will

- Get rid of the constructor (since you don't need to set an initial state).

- Call an actionCreator when the user tries to toggle the details visibility.

- Change all references from this.state.showDetails to this.props.showDetails.

- Make sure to show the details only if the property exists (by checking if it is explicitly set to false).

Listing 6-61 shows the updated Card Component.

Listing 6-61. Updated Card Component Without Local State

```
import React, { Component, PropTypes } from 'react';
import ReactCSSTransitionGroup from 'react-addons-css-transition-group';
import marked from 'marked'
import { DragSource, DropTarget } from 'react-dnd';
import constants from '../constants';
import CheckList from './CheckList';
import {Link} from 'react-router';
import CardActionCreators from '../actions/CardActionCreators';

let titlePropType = (props, propName, componentName) => {...};
const cardDragSpec = {...};
const cardDropSpec = {...};
let collectDrag = (connect, monitor) => {...};
let collectDrop = (connect, monitor) => {...};
```

```
class Card extends Component {

  toggleDetails() {
    CardActionCreators.toggleCardDetails(this.props.id);
  }

  render() {
    const { isDragging, connectDragSource, connectDropTarget } = this.props;

    let cardDetails;
    if (this.props.showDetails !== false) {
      cardDetails = (...);
    }

    let sideColor = {...};

    return connectDropTarget(connectDragSource(
      <div className="card" >
        <div style={sideColor}/>
        <div className="card__edit"><Link to={'/edit/'+this.props.id}> </Link></div>
        <div className={
          this.props.showDetails !== false? "card__title card__title--is-open" :
          "card__title"
          } onClick={this.toggleDetails.bind(this)}>
          {this.props.title}
        </div>
        <ReactCSSTransitionGroup transitionName="toggle"
                                 transitionEnterTimeout={250}
                                 transitionLeaveTimeout={250}>
        {cardDetails}
        </ ReactCSSTransitionGroup>
      </div>
    ));
  }
}
Card.propTypes = {...};

const dragHighOrderCard = DragSource(CARD, cardDragSpec, collectDrag)(Card);
const dragDropHighOrderCard = DropTarget(CARD, cardDropSpec, collectDrop)
(dragHighOrderCard);
export default dragDropHighOrderCard
```

Constant and Action Creator

Next, you implement the toggleCardDetails action creator. You need a constant to identify this action, so add a new TOGGLE_CARD_DETAILS to the constants.js file, as show in Listing 6-62.

Listing 6-62. Partial View of the constants.js File with the Addition of the TOGGLE_CARD_DETAILS

```
export default {
  CARD: 'card',

  FETCH_CARDS: 'fetch cards',
  FETCH_CARDS_SUCCESS: 'fetch cards success',
  FETCH_CARDS_ERROR: 'fetch cards error',

  ...

  TOGGLE_CARD_DETAILS: 'toggle card details',

  ...

  TOGGLE_TASK: 'toggle task',
  TOGGLE_TASK_SUCCESS: 'toggle task success',
  TOGGLE_TASK_ERROR: 'toggle task error',
};
```

In the sequence, let's edit the `CardActionCreator` file, as shown in Listing 6-63.

Listing 6-63. Updated CardActionCreator with toggleCardDetails Method

```
import AppDispatcher from '../AppDispatcher';
import constants from '../constants';
import KanbanAPI from '../api/KanbanApi';
import {throttle} from '../utils';
import CardStore from '../stores/CardStore';

let CardActionCreators = {

  fetchCards() {...},

  toggleCardDetails(cardId) {
    AppDispatcher.dispatch({
      type: constants.TOGGLE_CARD_DETAILS,
      payload: {cardId}
    });
  },

  addCard(card) {...},

  updateCard(card, draftCard) {...},

  updateCardStatus: throttle((cardId, currListId, nextListId) => {...}),

  updateCardPosition: throttle((cardId , afterId) => {...},500),

  persistCardDrag(cardProps) {...}
};

export default CardActionCreators;
```

CardStore

Finally, let's update the CardStore. Notice that you check if the showDetails value explicitly equals to false (a test that will fail is the property hasn't been set yet). Listing 6-64 shows the updated file.

Listing 6-64. The Updated CardStore

```
import AppDispatcher from '../AppDispatcher';
import constants from '../constants';
import {ReduceStore} from 'flux/utils';
import update from 'react-addons-update';
import 'babel-polyfill'

class CardStore extends ReduceStore {
  getInitialState() {...}
  getCard(id) {...}
  getCardIndex(id) {...}

  reduce(state, action){
    let cardIndex, taskIndex;

    switch (action.type) {
      case constants.FETCH_CARDS_SUCCESS:
        ...

      /*
       * Card Creation
       */
      case constants.CREATE_CARD:
        ...
      case constants.CREATE_CARD_SUCCESS:
        ...
      case constants.CREATE_CARD_ERROR:
        ...

      /*
       * Card Status Toggle
       */
      case constants.TOGGLE_CARD_DETAILS:
        cardIndex = this.getCardIndex(action.payload.cardId);
        return update(this.getState(), {
          [cardIndex]: {
            showDetails: { $apply: (currentValue) => (currentValue !== false)? false : true }
          }
        });
```

```
      /*
       * Card Update
       */
      case constants.UPDATE_CARD:
        ...
      case constants.UPDATE_CARD_ERROR:
        ...

      /*
       * Card Drag'n Drop
       */
      case constants.UPDATE_CARD_POSITION:
        ...
      case constants.UPDATE_CARD_STATUS:
        ...
      case constants.PERSIST_CARD_DRAG_ERROR:
        ...

      /*
       * Task Creation
       */
      case constants.CREATE_TASK:
        ...
      case constants.CREATE_TASK_SUCCESS:
        ...
      case constants.CREATE_TASK_ERROR:
        ...

      /*
       * Task Deletion
       */
      case constants.DELETE_TASK:
        ...
      case constants.DELETE_TASK_ERROR:
        ...

      /*
       * Task Toggling
       */
      case constants.TOGGLE_TASK:
        ...
      case constants.TOGGLE_TASK_ERROR:
        ...

      default:
        return state;
    }
  }
}
export default new CardStore(AppDispatcher);
```

Edit and New Card Components

The last few components that still have local state are the EditCard and NewCard. In their case, though, the local state is more complex than a single property. It holds a complete card structure. For this reason, you create a completely new store, the DraftStore, that will hold Card information that is being edited.

DraftStore

The DraftStore responds to two actions: CREATE_DRAFT and UPDATE_DRAFT. When the CREATE_DRAFT action is dispatched, the DraftStore updates its internal state to either an empty card object (in the case of a new card) or a copy of an existing card object (in the case of a card edit). This draft card is supplied to a controlled form and an UPDATE_DRAFT action is dispatched for every change.

Let's take a look at the DraftStore source code (as shown in Listing 6-65) before moving to the rest of the implementation.

Listing 6-65. The New DraftStore Source Code

```
import AppDispatcher from '../AppDispatcher';
import constants from '../constants';
import {ReduceStore} from 'flux/utils';
import update from 'react-addons-update';

let defaultDraft = () => {
  return {
    id: Date.now(),
    title:'',
    description:'',
    status:'todo',
    color:'#c9c9c9',
    tasks:[]
  }
};

class DraftStore extends ReduceStore {
  getInitialState() {
    return {};
  }

  reduce(state, action){
    switch (action.type) {
      case constants.CREATE_DRAFT:
        if(action.payload.card){
          return update(this.getState(), {
            $set: action.payload.card
          });
        } else {
          return defaultDraft();
        }
```

237

```
    case constants.UPDATE_DRAFT:
      return update(this.getState(), {
        [action.payload.field]: {
          $set: action.payload.value
        }
      });

    default:
      return state;
    }
  }
}
```

export default new DraftStore(AppDispatcher);

There are a few things worth noticing in the code. First, you have a function called `defaultDraft` that returns a default, clear card object with a temporary ID.

Also, in the `switch` statement in the `reduce` method, when responding to the CREATE_DRAFT action, you check if a card object was passed as payload. This is the case where an existing card is being edited; the card properties are then copied and set as the store state. If no card is passed as parameter (which is the case when the user is creating a new card), the `defaultDraft` method is invoked to create a default empty card that is set as the store state.

The UPDATE_DRAFT action passes two payloads: the field that the user edited, and its new value. In this case, the new value is set in the corresponding property of the draft card in the store's state.

Constants and ActionCreators

There is nothing especially notable here. Just add the new constants and declare the new action creators, as show in Listings 6-66 and 6-67, respectively.

Listing 6-66. Partial Source Code for the Updated constants.js File with CREATE_DRAFT and UPDATE_DRAFT Constants

```
export default {
  CARD: 'card',

  FETCH_CARDS: 'fetch cards',
  FETCH_CARDS_SUCCESS: 'fetch cards success',
  FETCH_CARDS_ERROR: 'fetch cards error',

  ...

  CREATE_DRAFT: 'create draft',
  UPDATE_DRAFT: 'update draft',

  ...

  TOGGLE_TASK: 'toggle task',
  TOGGLE_TASK_SUCCESS: 'toggle task success',
  TOGGLE_TASK_ERROR: 'toggle task error',
};
```

Listing 6-67. Updated CardActionCreators.js

```
import AppDispatcher from '../AppDispatcher';
import constants from '../constants';
import KanbanAPI from '../api/KanbanApi';
import {throttle} from '../utils';
import CardStore from '../stores/CardStore';

let CardActionCreators = {

  fetchCards() {...},
  toggleCardDetails(cardId) {...},
  addCard(card) {...},
  updateCard(card, draftCard) {...},
  updateCardStatus: throttle((cardId, currListId, nextListId) => {...}),
  updateCardPosition: throttle((cardId , afterId) => {...},500),
  persistCardDrag(cardProps) {...},

  createDraft(card) {
    AppDispatcher.dispatch({
      type: constants.CREATE_DRAFT,
      payload: {card}
    });
  },

  updateDraft(field, value) {
    AppDispatcher.dispatch({
      type: constants.UPDATE_DRAFT,
      payload: {field, value}
    });
  }
};

export default CardActionCreators;
```

EditCard and NewCard Components

To finish removing local state from your components, let's update the EditCard and NewCard files. You remove the constructor method and substitute any local state manipulation for action creator calls. Additionally, both components use the Flux library `Container` higher order function to listen to the DraftStore changes and map its state. Listings 6-68 and 6-69 show the updated code.

Listing 6-68. Updated EditCard Component

```
import React,{Component} from 'react';
import CardForm from './CardForm';
import CardStore from '../stores/CardStore';
import DraftStore from '../stores/DraftStore';
import {Container} from 'flux/utils';
import CardActionCreators from '../actions/CardActionCreators';
```

```
class EditCard extends Component{

  handleChange(field, value){
    CardActionCreators.updateDraft(field, value);
  }

  handleSubmit(e){
    e.preventDefault();
    CardActionCreators.updateCard(
      CardStore.getCard(this.props.params.card_id),this.state.draft
    );
    this.props.history.pushState(null,'/');
  }

  handleClose(e){
    this.props.history.pushState(null,'/');
  }

  componentDidMount(){
    setTimeout(()=>{
      CardActionCreators.createDraft(CardStore.getCard(this.props.params.card_id))
    }, 0);
  }

  render(){
    return (
      <CardForm draftCard={this.state.draft}
                buttonLabel="Edit Card"
                handleChange={this.handleChange.bind(this)}
                handleSubmit={this.handleSubmit.bind(this)}
                handleClose={this.handleClose.bind(this)} />
    )
  }
}

EditCard.getStores = () => ([DraftStore]);
EditCard.calculateState = (prevState) => ({
  draft: DraftStore.getState()
});

export default Container.create(EditCard);
```

Listing 6-69. Updated NewCard Component

```
import React,{Component} from 'react';
import CardForm from './CardForm';
import DraftStore from '../stores/DraftStore';
import {Container} from 'flux/utils';
import CardActionCreators from '../actions/CardActionCreators';

class NewCard extends Component{
  handleChange(field, value){
```

```
      CardActionCreators.updateDraft(field, value);
    }

    handleSubmit(e){
      e.preventDefault();
      CardActionCreators.addCard(this.state.draft);
      this.props.history.pushState(null,'/');
    }

    handleClose(e){
      this.props.history.pushState(null,'/');
    }

    componentDidMount(){
      setTimeout(()=>CardActionCreators.createDraft(), 0)
    }

    render(){
      return (
        <CardForm draftCard={this.state.draft}
                  buttonLabel="Create Card"
                  handleChange={this.handleChange.bind(this)}
                  handleSubmit={this.handleSubmit.bind(this)}
                  handleClose={this.handleClose.bind(this)} />
      )
    }
}

NewCard.getStores = () => ([DraftStore]);
NewCard.calculateState = (prevState) => ({
  draft: DraftStore.getState()
});

export default Container.create(NewCard);
```

It certainly was a big refactor in your project, but the end result is a clearer, more organized, and predictable code base. As usual, the complete source code is available at the Apress site (www.apress.com) and on this book's GitHub page (pro-react.github.io).

Summary

In this chapter, you learned what Flux is and which problems it solves. You saw how to integrate Flux in a React application and how to architect complex applications including async API communication.

CHAPTER 7

■ ■ ■

Performance Tuning

React was designed from the ground up with performance in mind. It uses several clever techniques to minimize the number of costly DOM operations required to update the UI, but it also provides tools and methods to fine-tune the performance when required.

In this chapter, you will learn how React's reconciliation process works, how to identify performance bottlenecks with React Perf, and how to use the `shouldComponentUpdate` lifecycle method in your components to short-circuit the re-rendering process for performance improvements.

How the Reconciliation Process Works

Whenever you change the state of a React component, it triggers the reactive re-rendering process. React will construct a new virtual DOM representing your application's state UI and perform a diff with the current virtual DOM to work out what DOM elements should be mutated, added, or removed. This process is called reconciliation.

Batching

In React, whenever you call `setState` on a component, instead of updating it immediately React will only mark it as "dirty" (Figure 7-1 illustrates this process). That is, changes to your component's state won't take effect immediately; React uses an event loop to render changes in batch.

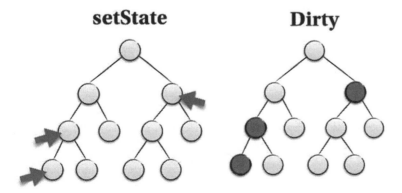

Figure 7-1. *Whenever you call setState on a component, React will only mark it as "dirty."*

243

An event loop is a JavaScript process that keeps on running indefinitely, constantly distributing data around, checking for all the event handlers and lifecycle methods that need to be invoked. By batching the reconciliation process, the DOM is updated only once per event loop, which is key to building a performant application.

Sub-Tree Rendering

When the event loop ends, React re-renders the dirty components as well as their children. All the nested components, even if they didn't change, will have their render method called, as shown in Figure 7-2.

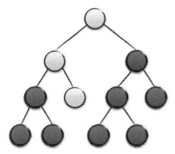

Re-rendered

Figure 7-2. *At the end of the event loop, dirty component trees are re-rendered to the virtual DOM*

This may sound inefficient, but in practice it is actually very fast because React is not touching the actual DOM. All this happens in the in-memory virtual DOM, and JavaScript has become extremely fast in processing this kind of operation on modern browsers.

However, React provides a way to fine-tune this process and prevent sub-trees from re-rendering: the lifecycle method called shouldComponentUpdate. Before re-rendering a child component, React will always invoke its shouldComponentUpdate method. By default, shouldComponentUpdate always returns true, but if you reimplement it and return false, React will skip re-rendering for this component and its children.

Be aware that React is usually quite fast out of the box and this is only needed on occasional circumstances. Using shouldComponentUpdate needlessly is the definition of premature optimization, which is a bad practice that not only wastes time but adds code complexity and more surface area for bugs to appear, especially ones that are hard to debug. Instead of blindly applying shouldComponentUpdate to an application's components, the best approach is to profile your application to detect if and where performance adjustments are necessary.

React Perf

ReactPerf is a profiling tool that gives an overview about an app's overall performance and helps discover optimization opportunities where shouldComponentUpdate lifecycle hooks should be implemented. The Perf object is available as a React add-on and can be used with React in development mode only. You should not include this bundle when building your app for production.

The ReactPerf API is very simple. You invoke two methods: `Perf.start()` when you want to begin measuring the application and `Perf.stop()` to finish measuring. The ReactPerf module also provides three methods to display the relevant data in a nicely formatted table on the browser console after taking the measurements; see Table 7-1.

Table 7-1. *React Perf Methods*

Validator	Description
`Perf.start()` and `Perf.stop()`	Start/stop the measurement. The React operations in between are recorded for analyses below.
`Perf.printInclusive()`	Prints the overall time taken.
`Perf.printExclusive()`	"Exclusive" times don't include the time taken to mount the components: processing props, calling `componentWillMount` and `componentDidMount`, etc.
`Perf.printWasted()`	"Wasted" time is spent on components that didn't actually render anything; in other words, the render stayed the same, so the DOM wasn't touched.

■ **Tip**   While the React Perf add-on provides valuable insight, it still can't detect every single optimization opportunity in your application. Use it along with the Browser's developer tools besides testing and debugging the application yourself.

The Performance Test Application

To experiment with ReactPerf and later implement `shouldComponentUpdate`, you will create a simple React application that displays a clock. It will contain three components: the main App component, a Clock component, and a Digit component.

Starting bottom-up, the Digit component will receive a numeric value as a property, check if it is less than 10 (to add a trailing zero character) and render it. Listing 7-1 shows the complete code.

Listing 7-1. Digit.js source Code

```
import React, { Component, PropTypes } from 'react';

class Digit extends Component {
  render() {
    let digitStyle={
      display:'inline-block',
      fontSize: 20,
      padding: 10,
      margin: 5,
      background: '#eeeeee'
    };
```

245

```
    let displayValue;
    if(this.props.value < 10){
      displayValue = '0' + this.props.value;
    } else {
      displayValue = this.props.value;
    }

    return (
      <div style={digitStyle}>{displayValue}</div>
    );
  }
}

Digit.propTypes = {
  value: PropTypes.number.isRequired
}
```

export default Digit;

In sequence, let's create the Clock component. It will receive three properties (hours, minutes, and seconds) and render three Digit components, one for each. Listing 7-2 shows the Clock.js code.

Listing 7-2. The Clock.js Code

```
import React, { Component, PropTypes } from 'react'
import Digit from './Digit';

class Clock extends Component {
  render() {
    return(
      <div>
        <Digit value={this.props.hours} />{' : '}
        <Digit value={this.props.minutes} />{' : '}
        <Digit value={this.props.seconds} />
      </div>
    );
  }
}

Clock.propTypes = {
  hours: PropTypes.number.isRequired,
  minutes: PropTypes.number.isRequired,
  seconds: PropTypes.number.isRequired
}
```

export default Clock;

Finally, let's work on the App component implementation. It will be a stateful component and have a getTime method that returns an object containing individual properties for hour, minutes, seconds, and milliseconds. This method will be used on both the constructor function (to initialize the component state) and on the componentDidMount lifecycle method (to set the application state to an updated value repeatedly). In the render function, you display a Clock component. Listing 7-3 shows the complete code.

Listing 7-3. The App Component

```
import React, { Component } from 'react';
import { render } from 'react-dom';
import Clock from './Clock';

class App extends Component {
  constructor(){
    super(...arguments);
    this.state = this.getTime();
  }

  componentDidMount(){
    setInterval(()=>{
      this.setState(this.getTime());
    },500);
  }

  getTime(){
    let now = new Date();
    return {
      hours: now.getHours(),
      minutes: now.getMinutes(),
      seconds: now.getSeconds()
    };
  }

  render(){
    return (
      <div>
        <Clock hours={this.state.hours}
               minutes={this.state.minutes}
               seconds={this.state.seconds} />
      </div>
    );
  }
}

render(<App />, document.getElementById("root"));
```

When testing the application, you should see something like Figure 7-3.

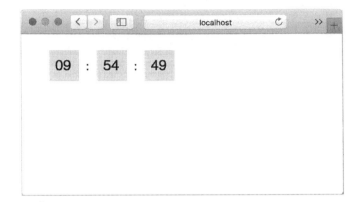

Figure 7-3. *The performance test application*

Installing and Using ReactPerf

Now that your sample application is done, let's install ReactPerf and profile it to look for performance optimization opportunities. The ReactPerf is provided as an add-on, so make sure to install it using npm install --save react-addons-perf before continuing.

Next, let's import the Perf module into your App component. You will start measuring the performance just before the app render, and stop measuring right after it. Then you will invoke printInclusive (to present a list of all the rendered components instances and time taken) and printWasted (to present component instances that were rendered without any changes). The updated code is shown in Listing 7-4.

Listing 7-4. Using ReactPerf to Profile the Performance Test Application

```
import React, { Component } from 'react';
import { render } from 'react-dom';
import Perf from 'react-addons-perf';
import Clock from './Clock';

class App extends Component {...}

Perf.start();
render(<App />, document.getElementById("root"));
Perf.stop();
Perf.printInclusive();
Perf.printWasted();
```

Testing the application on the browser now outputs the information shown in Figure 7-4 to the console.

In Figure 7-4, the lines marked with the number 1 denote the printInclusive output. It shows that your application has

- A single App instance

- A single Clock instance, nested inside the App component

- Three Digit instances, nested inside the Clock component

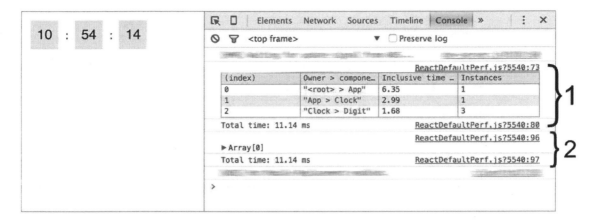

Figure 7-4. *React Perf output*

The console lines marked with the number 1 also shows the initialization and rendering time of each component in the tree index and the total application time.

The lines marked with the number 2 indicate the output from the `printWasted` method call. It contains an empty array because the method didn't find any wasted time at all.

But there is a problem with the measurements you took: by stopping the profiling immediately after the first render, you didn't analyze any state changes. You simply took a snapshot of the initial state of the application. To fix that, you will use a timer to measure the application for a little over a second before outputting any results. Listing 7-5 shows the updated code and Figure 7-5 shows the new output in the browser console.

Listing 7-5. Profiling for Over a Second Before Showing Results

```
import React, { Component } from 'react';
import { render } from 'react-dom';
import Clock from './Clock';
import Perf from 'react-addons-perf';

class App extends Component {...}
Perf.start()
render(<App />, document.getElementById("root"));
setTimeout(()=>{
  Perf.stop();
  Perf.printWasted();
},1500)
```

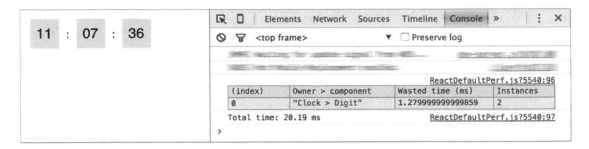

Figure 7-5. *The output from printWasted after a little more than a second of measurement*

Also, notice in the code above that you only kept the `printWasted` output.

Notice that now the ReactPerf detected two unnecessary renders of the Digit component. What happened here? To understand, let's recap the steps that happened.

- You started the test when the clock was marking 11:07:35.

- During the profiling, the state changed and triggered a re-render of the clock component to display the value of the time as 11:07:36

- The Clock, in turn, rendered all three digits, even the ones that didn't change.

The two instances that the ReactPerf detected were the re-render of the hour and the minute digits; because their value didn't change, they were needlessly updated.

Notice, however, that these components were only updated in the virtual DOM. Due to React's diffing process, they never mutating the real DOM. Furthermore, the amount of "wasted" time rendering the two digit components was less than two milliseconds, which can be considered negligible and has no performance impact. There is absolutely no reason to implement `shouldComponentUpdate` here.

Forcing an Impact on Performance

Let's make a few changes in the app to purposely create a performance problem: you're going to add a tenth of seconds field to your Clock component, update the App component every tenth of a second, and, to make sure it has an impact on performance, render 200 clocks on screen. Listing 7-6 shows the updated App component and Listing 7-7 shows the updated Clock component. The Digit component does not need any update.

Listing 7-6. Updated App Running Every Tenths-of-a-Second and Rendering 200 Clocks

```
import React, { Component } from 'react';
import { render } from 'react-dom';
import Clock from './Clock';
import Perf from 'react-addons-perf';

class App extends Component {
  constructor(){...}

  componentDidMount(){
    setInterval(()=>{
      this.setState(this.getTime());
    },10);
  }
}
```

```
  getTime(){
    let now = new Date();
    return {
      hours: now.getHours(),
      minutes: now.getMinutes(),
      seconds: now.getSeconds(),
      tenths: parseInt(now.getMilliseconds()/10),
    };
  }

  render(){
    let clocks=[];
    for (var i = 0; i < 200; i++) {
      clocks.push(<Clock hours={this.state.hours} minutes={this.state.minutes}
seconds={this.state.seconds} tenths={this.state.tenths} />)
    }

    return (
      <div>
        {clocks}
      </div>
    );
  }
}

Perf.start()
render(<App />, document.getElementById("root"));
setTimeout(()=>{
  Perf.stop();
  Perf.printWasted();
},2000)
```

Listing 7-7. The Updated Clock Component

```
import React, { Component, PropTypes } from 'react'
import Digit from './Digit';

class Clock extends Component {
  render() {
    return(
      <div>
        <Digit value={this.props.hours} />{' : '}
        <Digit value={this.props.minutes} />{' : '}
        <Digit value={this.props.seconds} />{' . '}
        <Digit value={this.props.tenths} />
      </div>
    );
  }
}
```

```
Clock.propTypes = {
  hours: PropTypes.number.isRequired,
  minutes: PropTypes.number.isRequired,
  seconds: PropTypes.number.isRequired,
  tenths: PropTypes.number.isRequired
}
```

export default Clock;

Now, when running in the browser you will notice that the app performance is sluggish. That was purposeful, but if you are on a fast machine and are not observing any difference, feel free to increase the loop count. The ReactPerf measurements confirm it: there's now a lot of time wasted by computing Digit components whose render didn't change. As shown in Figure 7-6, you now have a very noticeable performance hit of more than 0.6 seconds. Just for reference, the FPS meter is also displayed; currently the application is running at 15 fps.

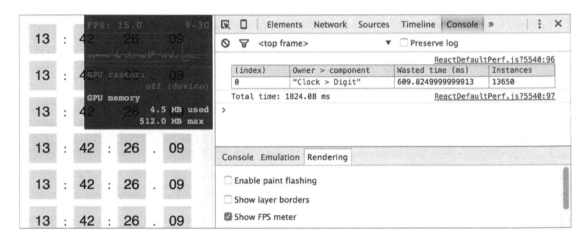

Figure 7-6. *ReactPerf shows you're now spending 609 ms computing unchanged Digit components*

shouldComponentUpdate

React provides the shouldComponentUpdate lifecycle method, which is triggered before the rerendering process starts and provides the possibility of not computing a render tree entirely. The method receives nextProps and nextState as arguments, and you should return either true or false to tell React if the component needs to be re-rendered. It defaults to true, but if you return false, the component is considered clean, and therefore no diffing or rendering is performed.

In the Clock application, all you have to do when implementing shouldComponentUpdate on the Digit component is a straight comparison between the new and old values that come in as props, as shown in Listing 7-8.

Listing 7-8. shouldComponentUpdate Implementation on the Digit Component

```
import React, { Component, PropTypes } from 'react'

class Digit extends Component {

  shouldComponentUpdate(nextProps, nextState) {
    // Don't trigger a re-render unless the digit value has changed
    return nextProps.value !== this.props.value;
  }

  render() {...}
}

Digit.propTypes = {...}

export default Digit;
```

As you can see in Figure 7-7, React Perf now outputs an empty array as wasted rendering instances. The performance impact is immediately perceivable in the browser (to prove this, the FPS meter is shown again; now the application runs twice as fast as before).

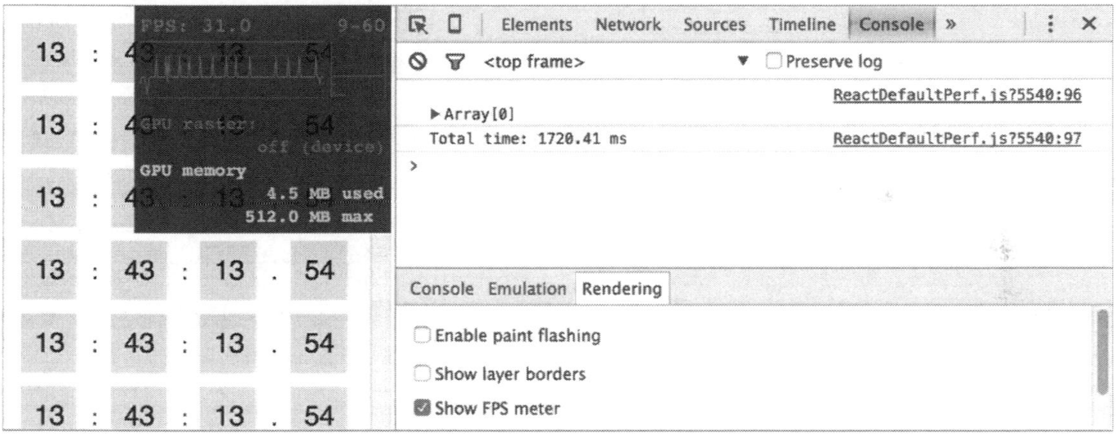

Figure 7-7. The Clock application after implementing shouldComponentUpdate on the Digit component

React will invoke the shouldComponentUpdate function pretty often, so keep in mind that the any tests and comparisons you may want to implement need to be really fast or it will defeat the purpose of improving the app performance.

Comparing single values (as you did in the earlier example) is really fast, so it works, but trying to compare values deeply nested inside objects is a very expensive operation, and it won't work.

That's when using immutable values pays of; it makes tracking changes and comparing entire objects cheap, fast, and reliable.

In Chapter 3, you studied React's immutability helpers. They help to make mutations on JavaScript objects, but instead of changing the value inside an object directly, they always return an entirely new object with the mutated value. This means that a shallow compare between the old and the new objects is enough to determine if there's a change, even if the changed value is deeply nested inside.

■ **Tip**   While React immutability helpers provide a nice mechanism to deal with default JavaScript data structures (that aren't immutable) in immutable way, you might want to consider using a library that provides true immutable collections for JavaScript. Using immutable data structures not only leads to better performance optimizations in React, but also helps you achieve better data consistency and improved code quality.

There are many different libraries that provide Immutable collections for JavaScript, including Facebook's own Immutable-js.

Immutable-js implements highly efficient immutable data structures such as Lists, Maps, Sets, and others. More information about Immutable-js is available on the library's site at `https://facebook.github.io/immutable-js/`.

shallowCompare Add-on

React provides an add-on called `shallowCompare` to be used with `shouldComponentUpdate`. It shallow compares both the props and state of the object and returns if they have changed.

The `shallowCompare` add-on is not a silver bullet, but it does helps achieve a performance boost if your app fits these criteria:

- The component where you want to apply the shallow compare is "pure" (in other words, it renders the same result given the same props and state).

- You are using immutable values or React's immutability helper to manipulate state.

Kanban App: Implementing shouldComponentUpdate with the shallowCompare Add-on

The Kanban application has a pretty good performance overall, but there's a moment where it can get a little sluggish: when dragging cards around. That's because every time you change a card's position or list, all the cards get rerendered. To fix this, let's implement the `shouldComponentUpdate` lifecycle method with the `shallowCompare` add-on on the Card component.

To get started, install `react-addons-shallow-compare` from npm:

```
npm install --save react-addons-shallow-compare
```

Next, edit the Card component to import `shallowCompare` and implement `shouldComponentUpdate`, as shown in Listing 7-9.

Listing 7-9. shouldComponentUpdate Implementation on the Card Component

```
import React, { Component, PropTypes } from 'react';
import ReactCSSTransitionGroup from 'react-addons-css-transition-group';
import marked from 'marked';
import { DragSource, DropTarget } from 'react-dnd';
import constants from '../constants';
import CheckList from './CheckList';
import {Link} from 'react-router';
import CardsActionCreators from '../actions/CardsActionCreators';
```

```
import shallowCompare from 'react-addons-shallow-compare';

let titlePropType = (props, propName, componentName) => {...};
const cardDragSpec = {...};
const cardDropSpec = {...};
let collectDrag = (connect, monitor) => {...};
let collectDrop = (connect, monitor) => {...};

class Card extends Component {
  toggleDetails() {...}

  shouldComponentUpdate(nextProps, nextState) {
    return shallowCompare(this, nextProps, nextState)
  }

  render() {...}
};
Card.propTypes = {...};

const dragHighOrderCard = DragSource(constants.CARD, cardDragSpec, collectDrag)(Card);
const dragDropHighOrderCard = DropTarget(constants.CARD, cardDropSpec, collectDrop)
(dragHighOrderCard);
export default dragDropHighOrderCard;
```

Summary

In this chapter, you got a better understanding of the assumptions that were made in order to make the React's reconciliation algorithm fast. You saw that while it's fast enough in the vast majority of use cases, it is possible to manually improve a component's performance by implementing the shouldComponentUpdate lifecycle method to prevent it (and its entire UI sub-tree) from rerendering.

CHAPTER 8

■ ■ ■

Isomorphic React Applications

To put it simply, a single page application is merely an empty HTML body that uses JavaScript to bring the page to life. While there are lots of benefits to this approach, there is also one visible downside: by the time the browser is able to download and run the application's JavaScript (and ask the server for the initial data), users will experience a flash of blank page before seeing any content.

Isomorphic JavaScript applications (also called universal JavaScript applications) are applications whose code is (entirely or partially) shared between client and the server. By running the application's JavaScript on the server, the page can get prepopulated before being sent to the browser, so the user can immediately see the content even before the JavaScript runs on the browser. When the local JavaScript runs, it will take over further navigation, giving the user the snappy interaction expected of a single page application with the quick first load of server-rendered pages.

In this approach, not only do users get a better experience because the application loads and renders faster, but other benefits arise as side effects: you get progressive enhancement for free (the app doesn't stop working completely when JS fails) along with better accessibility and search engine indexability.

Node.js and Express

In order to run and prepopulate React applications on the server, you will use Node.js and Express. You've been using Node.js and Node's package manager (npm) since the first chapter of this book. As you've seen before, Node.js is a JavaScript runtime that allows the execution of JavaScript applications outside the browser. Although it became an important tool for local development/package management of client-side JavaScript projects, it really shines as a server-side solution for JavaScript, and in particular, in building network programs such as web servers, making it similar to PHP and Python.

Express is a Node.js web application server framework, designed for building single-page, multi-page, and hybrid web applications. It is so commonly used that it's considered the de facto standard server framework for Node.js.

The next section provides a quick introduction to Express and won't cover anything related to React. If you are already familiar with Express, feel free to skip this section.

Node.js and Express "Hello World"

It is beyond the scope of this book to cover Node.js and Express, but to get familiarized with the basic setup before moving forward with universal React applications, let's build a plain Node.js and Express "Hello World" application. Starting with a blank, new folder, you will create a `package.json` project file (using `npm init -y` command to accept all defaults) and a `server.js` file.

Next, let's install the project's dependencies: the Express framework and Babel (the compiler that lets you use the latest features of JavaScript). To install Express using npm, use the command `npm install --save express`.

The Babel installation is a little more complex. Out of the box, the babel-core package doesn't do anything. In order to actually do anything to your code you need to enable plug-ins (or combination of plug-ins, called presets). In this example, you will use the ES6 preset: `npm install --save babel-core babel-preset-es2015`.

Finally, you also want to install the babel-cli package, which can be used to compile files from the command line. To install the Babel compiler command line globally, use the command `npm install --global babel-cli`.

Configuring Babel

Note that Babel needs to be configured on a project basis in order to work. The easiest way to configure Babel is to create a `.babelrc` file on the root folder of your project. In your case, the configuration includes simply setting the ES6 preset on this project. Listing 8-1 shows the final `.babelrc` configuration file.

Listing 8-1. The .babelrc Configuration File

```
{
  "presets": ["es2015"]
}
```

Creating the Express Server

Create a new `server.js` file so you can start coding your server-side application. At this point, the project structure should look like Figure 8-1.

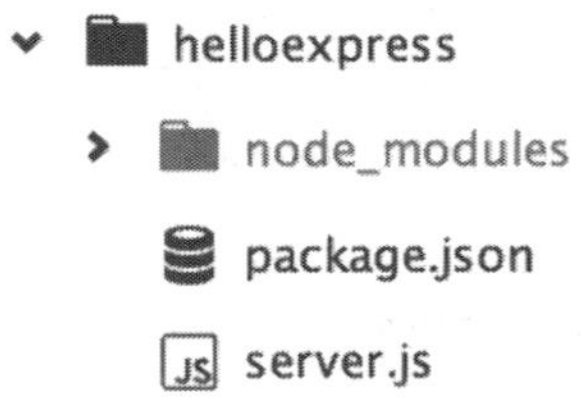

Figure 8-1. *Bare-bones Node.js and Express project*

In the `server.js` file you require Express and you create an instance of the Express server. By convention, you typically use an "app" constant to point to the `express.Server`, like so:

```
import express from 'express';
const app = express();
```

In the sequence, you can set up one or more routes for your application. A route consists of a path (string or regexp), a callback function, and an HTTP method. The callback function accepts two parameters: request and response. The request object contains information about the HTTP request that raised the event (including query string, parameters, body, HTTP headers, etc.). In response to the request, you use the response object to send back the desired HTTP response to the client browser.

Your Hello World example calls app.get(), which represents the HTTP GET method, with the path "/", followed by the callback function that uses the response object to send a string back to the browser:

```
app.get('/', (request, response) => {
  response.send('<html><body><p>Hello World!</p></body></html>');
});
```

Finally, you can make the server start listening to a given port. In the following code, you call listen(), specifying port 3000 and a callback method that will be invoked while the server is running:

```
app.listen(3000, ()=>{
  console.log('Express app listening on port 3000');
});
```

The complete source code for the server.js file is shown in Listing 8-2.

Listing 8-2. Source Code for the server.js File

```
import express from 'express';
const app = express();

app.get('/', (request, response) => {
  response.send('<html><body><p>Hello World!</p></body></html>');
});

app.listen(3000, ()=>{
  console.log('Express app listening on port 3000');
});
```

Running the Server

To start the server in debug mode (to see the logs generated by Express), type the following command on the terminal:

```
DEBUG=express:* babel-node server.js
```

With the server running, you can point your browser to localhost:3000. The results should be similar to Figure 8-2.

Figure 8-2. *Running the Node.js and Express server and testing on the browser*

To make things easier and save some typing, you can pass this command as the start script on package.json file. This way the next time you want to start the server locally you only need to type npm start. Listing 8-3 shows the updated package.json.

Listing 8-3. The Updated package.json

```
{
  "name": "helloexpress",
  "version": "0.0.1",
  "description": "Hello world sample application in Node.js + Express",
  "scripts": {
    "start": "DEBUG=express:* babel-node server.js"
  },
  "author": "Cássio Zen",
  "license": "ISC",
  "dependencies": {
    "babel": "^5.8.29",
    "express": "^4.13.3"
  }
}
```

Using Templates

Sending string responses using response.send is a quick way to get started with Express, but for any realistic job it can became cumbersome to format all responses this way and deliver complete HTML structures. Express supports the use of templates for this reason. A template is HTML markup, enhanced with tags that will either insert variables or run programming logic. Express supports a variety of template formats. For this example you will use a template format called EJS.

First, make sure to install EJS as a dependency of the application with npm install --global ejs. Next, you need to configure your application to use EJS templates. This can be done using the set method:

```
app.set('view engine', 'ejs');
```

By default, template files must be saved in a views folder. Create a new views folder with an index.ejs template file, as shown in Figure 8-3.

- ▾ 📁 helloexpress
  - › 📁 node_modules
  - ▾ 📁 views
    - 🖼 index.ejs
  - ⚙ .babelrc
  - 🅾 package.json
  - 🇯🇸 server.js

Figure 8-3. Template folder and index.ejs template file

To instruct your application to render a template instead of sending a string, you use the response. render method, passing the template name and an object that will be accessible from inside the template to display dynamic values. Listing 8-4 shows the complete index.js source code with all the updates you made to use templates and render server.js. Listing 8-5 shows the index.ejs source code.

Listing 8-4. The Updated server.js Rendering a Template

```
import express from 'express';
const app = express();

app.set('view engine', 'ejs');

app.get('/', (request, response) => {
  response.render('index',{message:'Hello World'});
});

app.listen(3000, ()=>{
  console.log('Express app listening on port 3000');
});
```

Listing 8-5. The views/index.ejs Template File

```html
<!DOCTYPE html>
<html>
  <head>
    <meta charset="utf-8">
    <title>Express Template</title>
  </head>
  <body>
    <h1><%= message %></h1>
  </body>
</html>
```

Serving Static Assets

Express comes with built-in middleware to serve static content. The express.static() middleware takes one argument that refers to the root directory from which the static assets are to be served. To serve static files from a public folder, for example, just add the following line to the server code:

```
app.use(express.static(__dirname + '/public'));
```

Isomorphic React Basics

Now that you're familiar with Express, let's move on to render an actual React component on the server. React and the React-DOM package offer built-in support for rendering components in the server through the ReactDOMServer.renderToString method. It renders a given component and generates annotated markup to be sent to the browser. On the browser, React can pick up the annotated markup and only attach event handlers, allowing you to have a very performant first-load experience.

Creating the Project Structure

An isomorphic React project structure has different requirements than those of a client-side–only application. For this reason, instead of using the React App Boilerplate app you've been using so far as the base for new projects, you will create a project structure from scratch in this case.

Starting in a new folder, the first thing to do is to create a package.json project file. You can create one quickly by running npm init -y. The project structure will contain two folders at the root level: a public folder (for static assets that will be served to the browser) and an app folder (where you will save React components and other project files that will be shared by both client and server). Inside the app folder you create a components folder to keep your project organized.

The project starts with three files: server.js, index.ejs, and browser.js. The server.js file will contain server-side JavaScript code (where you will set up an Express server and render the components). The browser.js file will contain client-side JavaScript code. The index.ejs file will contain the basic HTML page structure that will be sent to the browser. Figure 8-4 shows the project structure files and folders.

- ▾ 📁 universal-react
  - ▾ 📁 app
    - ❯ 📁 components
  - ❯ 📁 public
  - 🗋 browser.js
  - 🗋 index.ejs
  - 🗋 package.json
  - 🗋 server.js

Figure 8-4. *The project structure*

The Contacts App Files

In this project, you will use an example similar to one from Chapter 3, a contactList component with a search bar. The project files won't be identical, though; you will create a simplified component hierarchy to focus on the server-side rendering and receive the array of contacts through a prop named `initialData`. The component hierarchy will contain

- **ContactsApp**: The main component
  - **SearchBar**: Shows an input field so user can filter the contacts
  - **ContactList** : Loops through data creating a series of ContactItems

Figure 8-5 shows the desired output.

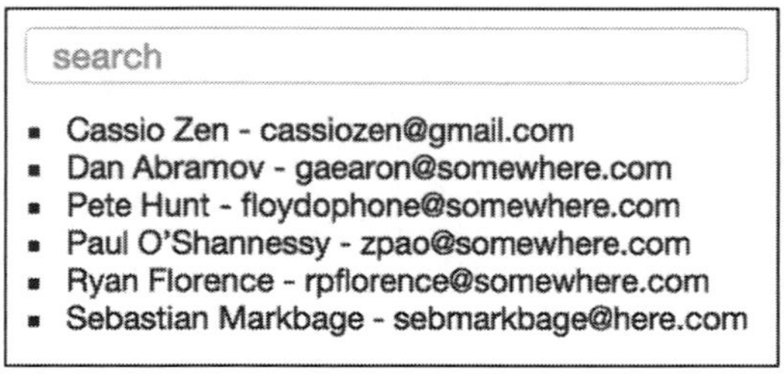

```
search

■ Cassio Zen - cassiozen@gmail.com
■ Dan Abramov - gaearon@somewhere.com
■ Pete Hunt - floydophone@somewhere.com
■ Paul O'Shannessy - zpao@somewhere.com
■ Ryan Florence - rpflorence@somewhere.com
■ Sebastian Markbage - sebmarkbage@here.com
```

Figure 8-5. *The Contacts app*

In total, the React project has four files, three components and an external JSON file containing the contacts list. You create all the component files in the components folder; the source code is shown in Listings 8-6 through 8-8). The json file will be saved in the public folder, and its content is shown in Figure 8-6.

The ContactList component receives an array of contacts and the filterText. It filters the contacts and loops through the array, rendering each contact's information (Listing 8-6).

Listing 8-6. app/components/ContactList.js

```
import React, {Component, PropTypes} from 'react';

class ContactList extends Component {
  render(){
    var filteredContacts = this.props.contacts.filter(
      (contact) => contact.name.indexOf(this.props.filterText) !== -1
    );
    return(
      <ul>
        {filteredContacts.map(
          (contact) => <li key={contact.email}>{contact.name} - {contact.email}</li>
        )}
      </ul>
    )
  }
}
ContactList.propTypes = {
  contacts: PropTypes.arrayOf(PropTypes.object),
  filterText: PropTypes.string.isRequired
}

export default ContactList;
```

The SearchBar component renders a controlled form component to the user and calls a callback on every change. The value inputted by the user is used to filter the contact list (Listing 8-7).

Listing 8-7. app/component/SearchBar.js

```
import React, {Component, PropTypes} from 'react';

class SearchBar extends Component {
  handleChange(event){
    this.props.onUserInput(event.target.value)
  }

  render(){
    return <input type="search"
                  placeholder="search"
                  value={this.props.filterText}
                  onChange={this.handleChange.bind(this)} />
  }
}
```

```
SearchBar.propTypes = {
  onUserInput: PropTypes.func.isRequired,
  filterText: PropTypes.string.isRequired
}

export default SearchBar;
```

The ContactApp renders the ContactList and SearchBar components. It receives the initial contact list through the initialData prop, and attributes this prop value to its own state (Listing 8-8).

Listing 8-8. app/components/ContactsApp.js

```
import React, {Component, PropTypes} from 'react';
import ContactList from './ContactList';
import SearchBar from './SearchBar';

class ContactsApp extends Component {
  constructor(){
    super(...arguments);
    this.state = {
      contacts: this.props.initialData || [],
      filterText: ''
    }
  }

  handleUserInput(searchTerm){
    this.setState({filterText:searchTerm})
  }

  render(){
    return(
      <div>
        <SearchBar filterText={this.state.filterText}
                   onUserInput={this.handleUserInput.bind(this)} />
        <ContactList contacts={this.state.contacts}
                   filterText={this.state.filterText}/>
      </div>
    )
  }
};

ContactsApp.propTypes = {
  initialData: PropTypes.any
};

export default ContactsApp;
```

Finally, Figure 8-6 shows the contacts.json file in the application's root folder.

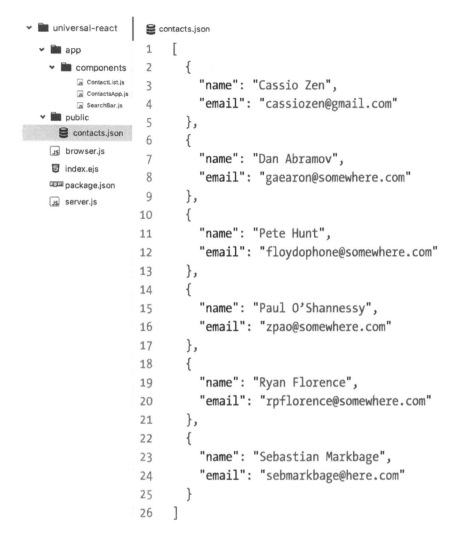

```
universal-react          contacts.json
  app                 1    [
    components         2      {
      ContactList.js   3        "name": "Cassio Zen",
      ContactsApp.js   4        "email": "cassiozen@gmail.com"
      SearchBar.js     5      },
    public             6      {
      contacts.json    7        "name": "Dan Abramov",
    browser.js         8        "email": "gaearon@somewhere.com"
    index.ejs          9      },
    package.json      10      {
    server.js         11        "name": "Pete Hunt",
                      12        "email": "floydophone@somewhere.com"
                      13      },
                      14      {
                      15        "name": "Paul O'Shannessy",
                      16        "email": "zpao@somewhere.com"
                      17      },
                      18      {
                      19        "name": "Ryan Florence",
                      20        "email": "rpflorence@somewhere.com"
                      21      },
                      22      {
                      23        "name": "Sebastian Markbage",
                      24        "email": "sebmarkbage@here.com"
                      25      }
                      26    ]
```

Figure 8-6. *The contacts.json file in the root folder of the project structure*

Rendering React Components on the Server

With the app structure and the sample components ready, you can now write the server script. To start, install all the dependencies for server-side development: the Express server, the EJS template format, and the React packages. To install all at once, use the command `npm install --save express ejs react react-dom`.

You also need to install Babel, so use the ES6 syntax and JSX. To install the latest Babel version with support for ES6 and JSX as well as its peer dependency (webpack), use `npm install --save webpack babel-core babel-loader babel-preset-es2015 babel-preset-react`.

Finally, you need to install the babel compiler command line. For convenience, you can install it globally using the command `npm install --global babel-cli`.

Babel Configuration

Babel needs to be configured on a project basis in order to work. The easiest way to configure Babel is to create a `.babelrc` file on the root folder of your project. In your case, the configuration includes simply setting the ES6 preset on this project. Listing 8-9 shows the final `.babclrc` configuration file.

Listing 8-9. The .babelrc Configuration File

```
{
  "presets": ["es2015","react"]
}
```

Express App

The template file is pretty straightforward: just the basic HTML tags with a root `div` where the dynamic content will be inserted. Listing 8-10 shows the source code.

Listing 8-10. The index.ejs Template File

```html
<!DOCTYPE html>
<html>
  <head>
    <meta charset="utf-8">
    <title>Isomorphic React</title>
  </head>
  <body>
    <div id="root"><%- content %></div>
  </body>
</html>
```

Next, in the `server.js` JavaScript file you set up an Express server with the following considerations:

- The Express server will be configured to
  - Use EJS as template format and look for the template files in the root folder.
  - Serve static assets from the `public` folder.
- Your ContactApp components need a list of contacts. This list could come from a database or an API server, but for simplicity purposes you will load from the json file you saved in the `public` folder.

The server code is shown in Listing 8-11.

Listing 8-11. The Basic Express App with a Contact List

```javascript
import express from 'express';
import contacts from './public/contacts.json';

const app = express();

app.set('views', './')
app.set('view engine', 'ejs');
app.use(express.static(__dirname + '/public'));
```

```
app.get('/', (request, response) => {
  response.render('index',{
    content: 'Hello'
  });
});

app.listen(3000, ()=>{
  console.log('Express app listening on port 3000');
});
```

Everything is wired up and working. You can test right now, but the result is just a "hello" string on the browser. To start the server, use node_modules/.bin/babel-node server.js.

Rendering React Components

Now comes the interesting part: rendering the React component on the server. There are a few things to consider here:

- As mentioned, you will use a react-dom method called renderToString to generate annotated markup from the component and send to the browser.

- You won't use JSX on the Express server. As mentioned in Chapter 2, to instantiate React components outside JSX, you need to wrap the component in a factory before calling it.

Listing 8-12 shows the updated server code.

Listing 8-12. The Express Application Rendering a React Component

```
import fs from 'fs';
import express from 'express';
import React from 'react';
import { renderToString } from 'react-dom/server';
import ContactsApp from './app/components/ContactsApp';

const app = express();
app.set('views', './')
app.set('view engine', 'ejs');
app.use(express.static(__dirname + '/public'));

const contacts = JSON.parse(fs.readFileSync(__dirname + '/public/contacts.json', 'utf8'));

const ContactsAppFactory = React.createFactory(ContactsApp);

app.get('/', (request, response) => {
  let componentInstance = ContactsAppFactory({initialData:contacts});
  response.render('index',{
    content: renderToString(componentInstance)
  });
});
```

```
app.listen(3000, ()=>{
  console.log('Express app listening on port 3000');
});
```

If you run the server and test on the browser, you will see that the component was rendered correctly and that the generated HTML contains all the necessary annotations the client-side React will need to mount the component on the browser. Your result should look like Figure 8-7.

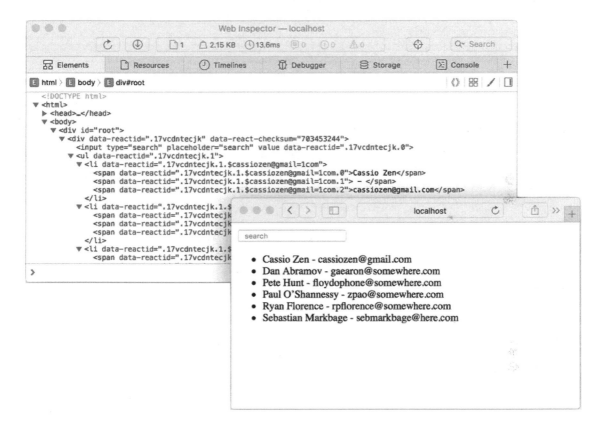

Figure 8-7. *Server-side rendered React component*

Notice, however, that right now there is no interactivity in the browser. The component is static and is not filtering the contacts. This happens because you didn't create or send any JavaScript to run on the browser; you only created server-side JavaScript. The browser is simply receiving and showing an HTML page with no dynamic content so far.

Mounting React on the Client

You are creating an isomorphic project setup that allows you to use the same component code to render both on the server and the client, but you're not done just yet because you only rendered on the server so far. You need to provide a JavaScript file to the browser to make React mount on top of the prerendered components and hook up event listeners.

Client-side Setup

You already have an empty JavaScript file (browser.js) for the purpose of generating the client-side JavaScript, but this file needs to be compiled and packed before being sent to the browser.

In all the examples of this book you used webpack with Babel to do this process, and it won't be different now. Create a webpack configuration file in the root folder. It will be very simple since you're not going to use advanced features such as the webpack's development server, just basic setup to pack the browser.js file and output a bundle.js file in the public folder, as shown in Listing 8-13.

Listing 8-13. The webpack.config.js File

```
module.exports = {
  entry: [
    './browser.js'
  ],
  output: {
    path: './public',
    filename: "bundle.js"
  },
  module: {
    loaders: [{
      test: /\.jsx?$/,
      loader: 'babel'
    }]
  }
};
```

With this configuration in place, you can run webpack -p to generate the client-side bundled JavaScript file.

Passing the Component's initialData

Now that you have a configuration file in place to compile and pack the browser.js file into a bundle.js file on the public folder, you need to update your template file to load this client-bundled JavaScript file.

That's not the only update you need on the template file, though. Mounting React on top of a server-rendered component is different from every other client render in that you need to provide the exact same props that were used to render the component on the server; otherwise React will be forced to rerender the entire DOM (React will give you a warning for this). What is needed is a mechanism for passing the same props used on the server render to the client. You can achieve this by creating a script tag in the HTML template and just dumping all the props inside. The client JavaScript can then parse and use the exact same props.

In plain English, you need two script tags in the template file: one contains the initial data needed by the React components (all the data and props), and the other is used to load the client JavaScript. Listing 8-14 shows the updated index.ejs file.

Listing 8-14. The Updated index.ejs Template File with Two Script Tags

```
<!DOCTYPE html>
<html>
  <head>
    <meta charset="utf-8">
    <title>Isomorphic React</title>
  </head>
```

```
<body>
  <div id="root"><%- content %></div>

  <script id="initial-data" type="application/json">
    <%- reactInitialData %>
  </script>
  <script type="text/JavaScript" src="bundle.js"></script>
</body>
</html>
```

Listing 8-15 shows the server.js with the updated render call, passing the array of contacts that will be needed by the client side script to instantiate the ContactsApp component locally.

Listing 8-15. The Updated server.js File Populating the Context Script Tag with a JSON-Formatted List of Contacts

```
import fs from 'fs';
import express from 'express';
import React from 'react';
import { renderToString } from 'react-dom/server'
import ContactsApp from './app/components/ContactsApp'

const app = express();
app.set('views', './')
app.set('view engine', 'ejs');
app.use(express.static(__dirname + '/public'));

const contacts = JSON.parse(fs.readFileSync(__dirname + '/public/contacts.json', 'utf8'));

const ContactsAppFactory = React.createFactory(ContactsApp);

app.get('/', (request, response) => {
  let componentInstance = ContactsAppFactory({contacts:contacts});
  response.render('index',{
    reactInitialData: JSON.stringify(contacts),
    content: renderToString(componentInstance)
  });
});

app.listen(3000, ()=>{
  console.log('Express app listening on port 3000');
});
```

browser.js

The browser.js file is analogous to the server.js file: you import the desired components and render it. You even need to pass the exact same props that were passed to the component when it was rendered on the server. If you pass different props, the client-side React won't be able to "mount" on top of the prerendered component, assign event listeners, and assume interactivity. Fortunately, the server is passing the props it used inside a script tag with an id of initialData; the client-side JavaScript can parse and use them. Listing 8-16 shows the complete source.

271

Listing 8-16. The browser.js File

```
import React from 'react';
import { render } from 'react-dom';
import ContactsApp from './app/components/ContactsApp';

let initialData = document.getElementById('initial-data').textContent;
if(initialData.length>0){
  initialData = JSON.parse(initialData);
}

render(<ContactsApp initialData={initialData} />, document.getElementById('root'));
```

To avoid any errors in circumstances where no initialData is needed, notice that you are checking if the initial data script tag contains any content before parsing it.

Before running the server to test, make sure to compile and pack the browser.js to public/bundle.js using the command webpack -p. See Figure 8-8.

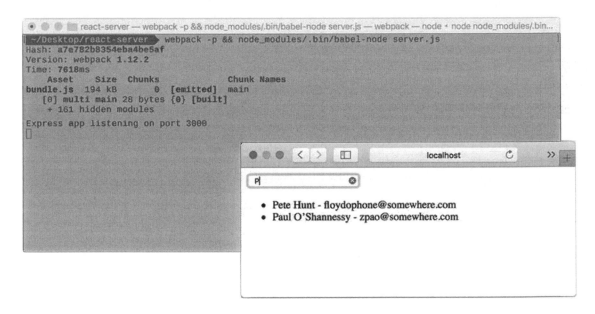

Figure 8-8. *React on client-side mounting a server-prerendered component*

Routing

React Router is the de facto routing solution for React applications, and since it's 1.0 release it supports server rendering out of the box. The routing setup in the server, though, is a little bit different than in a client because, besides matching routes to components, you also want to send 500 responses for errors and 30x responses for redirects.

To facilitate these needs, you drop one level lower than the <Router> API with

- Match to match the routes to a location without rendering

- RoutingContext for synchronous rendering of route components

Setting Up Internal Routes

You will continue working on the ContactsApp example, but now you're going to implement a new route called Home. Start by installing the React Router. Be aware that the examples in this book are using React Router 1.0.0. You also need to install its dependency history. Make sure to install both using `npm install --save react-router history`.

Next, set up your routes file. Since the routes are going to be shared between the client and the server, you save it in the app folder. Initially, you set up three routes: a new parent App route, a new Home index route, and a route called Contacts to show your existing ContactsApp. Listing 8-17 shows the source code.

Listing 8-17. The app/routes.js

```
import React from 'react';
import { Route, IndexRoute } from 'react-router'
import App from './components/App'
import Home from './components/Home'
import ContactsApp from './components/ContactsApp'

export default (
  <Route path="/" component={App}>
    <IndexRoute component={Home} />
    <Route path="contacts" component={ContactsApp} />
  </Route>
);
```

In this route, you're assuming you have two new components: App and Home. Let's create both in the app/components folder, as shown in Listings 8-18 and 8-19.

Listing 8-18. The app/components/app File

```
import React, {Component} from 'react';
import { Link } from 'react-router'

class App extends Component {
  render(){
    return(
      <div>
        <nav>
          <Link to='/'>Home</Link>{' '}
          <Link to='/contacts'>Contacts</Link>
        </nav>
        <div>
          {this.props.children}
        </div>
      </div>
    )
  }
};

export default App;
```

Listing 8-19. The app/components/home File

```
import React, {Component} from 'react';

class Home extends Component {
  render(){
    return <h1>Home</h1>;
  }
};

export default Home;
```

Dynamic Data Fetching

Until now, your project only contained a single entry point: the ContactsApp component. Every time you loaded your application in the browser, the server prefetched the contacts list and sent a prepopulated component to the browser. In an application with multiple routes, the server needs to detect which data is needed by the component that maps the current route. It doesn't make sense, for example, to always load the contacts list if the user is at the Home route. On the other hand, if the user starts navigating at the Home and goes to the Contact route, the component won't be prepopulated, so it needs to be able to fetch data from the server as needed.

In other words, you need an approach that allows

- Data prefetching on the server only for the component that maps to the current route

- Data fetching on the client in case the user navigates to a different route where data is needed but wasn't prefetched

While there isn't a single correct way of declaring a component's data fetching needs in a way that can be fulfilled both on the server and on the client, a popular approach is to create a static method on the component's class to declare the data needed by that component. The static method is accessible even when the component is not instantiated, which is crucial for prefetching.

To exemplify, let's change the way your sample isomorphic application handles data fetching. The ContactsApp is the only component that needs data, so you declare a static method to fetch remote data. If the user enters the application on the Contacts route, the server will then run this method and pass the results as props to the component. If the user enters the application through any other route and later navigates to the Contacts route, the browser will run this method to fetch data on demand.

To start, you install the isomorphic-fetch npm package. It's a clever package that uses Node's default fetch on the server and implements a polyfill for the browser: `npm install --save isomorphic-fetch`.

Next, let's update the ContactsApp component to create the static `requestInitialData` method.

You also implement the `componentDidMount` lifecycle method that is only called on the browser to check if whether the `initialData` was provided by the server or not (in which case it invokes the `requestInitialData` method to fetch the initial data now). Listing 8-20 shows the updated code.

Listing 8-20. The Updated Component

```
import React, {Component, PropTypes} from 'react';
import fetch from 'isomorphic-fetch';
import ContactList from './ContactList';
import SearchBar from './SearchBar';
```

```
class ContactsApp extends Component {
  constructor(){
    super(...arguments);
    this.state = {
      contacts: this.props.initialData || [],
      filterText: ''
    }
  }

  componentDidMount(){
    if (!this.props.initialData) {
      ContactsApp.requestInitialData().then(contacts => {
        this.setState({ contacts });
      });
    }
  }

  handleUserInput(searchTerm){
    this.setState({filterText:searchTerm})
  }

  render(){
    return(
      <div>
        <SearchBar filterText={this.state.filterText}
                   onUserInput={this.handleUserInput.bind(this)} />
        <ContactList contacts={this.props.initialData}
                     filterText={this.state.filterText}/>
      </div>
    )
  }
};

ContactsApp.propTypes = {
  initialData: PropTypes.any
};

ContactsApp.requestInitialData = () => {
        return fetch('http://localhost:3000/contacts.json')
        .then((response) => response.json());
};

export default ContactsApp;
```

Rendering Routes

Now you're going to make big changes in both server.js and browser.js to render the routes on both client and server.

Rendering Routes on the Server

Starting with server.js, you make the changes in steps. The first step is to change the "get" entry point from "/" to "*" so all routes will invoke the callback. You also configure the error, not found, and redirect routes. For existing routes, you render the appropriate component. Listing 8-21 shows these changes.

Listing 8-21. First Step of Updates to server.js

```
import fs from 'fs';
import express from 'express';
import React from 'react';
import { renderToString } from 'react-dom/server';
import { match, RoutingContext } from 'react-router';
import routes from './app/routes';

const app = express();

app.set('views', './');
app.set('view engine', 'ejs');
app.use(express.static(__dirname + '/public'));

const contacts = JSON.parse(fs.readFileSync(__dirname + '/public/contacts.json', 'utf8'));

let renderRoute = (response, renderProps) => {
  // The actual rendering will be moved here
};

app.get('*', (request, response) => {
  match({ routes, location: request.url }, (error, redirectLocation, renderProps) => {
    if (error) {
      response.status(500).send(error.message);
    } else if (redirectLocation) {
      response.redirect(302, redirectLocation.pathname + redirectLocation.search);
    } else if (renderProps) {
      renderRoute(response, renderProps);
    } else {
      response.status(404).send('Not found');
    }
  });
});

app.listen(3000, ()=>{...});
```

A few additional things to notice on this code:

- The ContactsApp import and factory were removed (since this will be managed by the router now).

- For better organization, you move the response.render method outside the routing and to a new function called renderRoute (which you implement in the next step).

In the next step, let's reimplement the component rendering. React Router provides an object called RoutingContext with the hierarchy of all the components that must be rendered for the current route. It's possible to pass the RoutingContext directly to React's renderToString to generate the markup for all the components, but this won't work in your case because you also need to prefetch data and pass it as props to the components that implement the requestInitialData static method.

What you do, instead, is loop through all the components inside RoutingContext to check if any of them implements requestInitialData. If you find a component that does, you prefetch the data and pass it as props to the internal component by overriding the function used in the RoutingContext to instantiate the internal components. Listing 8-22 shows the updated code.

Listing 8-22. The Second Step of Updates to server.js

```
import ...;

const app = express();
app.set(...)
app.set(...);
app.use(...);
const contacts = JSON.parse(...);

// Helper function: Loop through all components in the renderProps object
// and returns a new object with the desired key
let getPropsFromRoute = ({routes}, componentProps) => {
  let props = {};
  let lastRoute = routes[routes.length - 1];
  routes.reduceRight((prevRoute, currRoute) => {
    componentProps.forEach(componentProp => {
      if (!props[componentProp] && currRoute.component[componentProp]) {
        props[componentProp] = currRoute.component[componentProp];
      }
    });
  }, lastRoute);
  return props;
};

let renderRoute = (response, renderProps) => {
  // Loop through renderProps object looking for 'requestInitialData'
  let routeProps = getPropsFromRoute(renderProps, ['requestInitialData']);
  if (routeProps.requestInitialData) {
    // If one of the components implements 'requestInitialData', invoke it.
    routeProps.requestInitialData().then((data)=>{
      // Ovewrite the react-router create element function
      // and pass the pre-fetched data as initialData props
```

```
      let handleCreateElement = (Component, props) =>(
        <Component initialData={data} {...props} />
      );
      // Render the template with RoutingContext and loaded data.
      response.render('index',{
        reactInitialData: JSON.stringify(data),
        content: renderToString(
          <RoutingContext createElement={handleCreateElement} {...renderProps} />
        )
      });
    });
  } else {
    // No components in this route implements 'requestInitialData'.
    // Simply render the template with RoutingContext and no initialData.
    response.render('index',{
    reactInitialData: null,
    content: renderToString(<RoutingContext {...renderProps} />)
    });
  }
};

app.get('*', (request, response) => {...});
app.listen(3000, ()=>{...});
```

The complete source code for the updated server.js file is shown in Listing 8-23.

Listing 8-23. The Complete Updated Source Code for the server.js File

```
import fs from 'fs';
import express from 'express';
import React from 'react';
import { renderToString } from 'react-dom/server';
import { match, RoutingContext } from 'react-router';
import routes from './app/routes';
const app = express();

app.set('views', './')
app.set('view engine', 'ejs');
app.use(express.static(__dirname + '/public'));

const contacts = JSON.parse(fs.readFileSync(__dirname + '/public/contacts.json', 'utf8'));

let getPropsFromRoute = ({routes}, componentProps) => {
  let props = {};
  let lastRoute = routes[routes.length - 1];
  routes.reduceRight((prevRoute, currRoute) => {
    componentProps.forEach(componentProp => {
      if (!props[componentProp] && currRoute.component[componentProp]) {
        props[componentProp] = currRoute.component[componentProp];
      }
    });
  }, lastRoute);
```

```
    return props;
};

let renderRoute = (response, renderProps) => {
  let routeProps = getPropsFromRoute(renderProps, ['requestInitialData']);
  if (routeProps.requestInitialData) {
    routeProps.requestInitialData().then((data)=>{
      let handleCreateElement = (Component, props) =>(
        <Component initialData={data} {...props} />
      );
      response.render('index',{
        reactInitialData: JSON.stringify(data),
        content: renderToString(
          <RoutingContext createElement={handleCreateElement} {...renderProps} />
        )
      });
    });
  } else {
    response.render('index',{
    reactInitialData: null,
    content: renderToString(<RoutingContext {...renderProps} />)
    });
  }
};

app.get('*', (request, response) => {
  match({ routes, location: request.url }, (error, redirectLocation, renderProps) => {
    if (error) {
      response.status(500).send(error.message);
    } else if (redirectLocation) {
      response.redirect(302, redirectLocation.pathname + redirectLocation.search);
    } else if (renderProps) {
      renderRoute(response, renderProps);
    } else {
      response.status(404).send('Not found');
    }
  });
});

app.listen(3000, ()=>{
  console.log('Express app listening on port 3000');
});
```

Rendering routes on the Browser

Next, you need to make similar adjustments to the browser.js client file: render a route and check if there is initialData, passing it as props to the correct component. Again you rely on React Router's createElement prop to override the default function used to instantiate React elements to pass the initialData as props for the component that implements requestInitialData static methods. Listing 8-24 shows the updated code.

Listing 8-24. The Updated browser.js Code

```
import React from 'react';
import { render } from 'react-dom';
import { Router } from 'react-router';
import { createHistory } from 'history';
import routes from './app/routes';

let handleCreateElement = (Component, props) => {
  if(Component.hasOwnProperty('requestInitialData')){
    let initialData = document.getElementById('initial-data').textContent;
    if(initialData.length>0){
      initialData = JSON.parse(initialData);
    }
    return <Component initialData={initialData} {...props} />;
  } else {
    return <Component {...props} />;
  }
}

render((
  <Router history={createHistory()} createElement={handleCreateElement}>{routes}</Router>
), document.getElementById('root'))
```

If you test right now starting on the Home route ("/"), you will notice that the contact app will fetch data from the browser when you navigate to its route. However, if you access the application directly into the /contacts route, the server will prefetch the contacts data and send a populated component to the browser.

Summary

In this chapter, you learned about the benefits of isomorphic applications, which includes a better perceived performance, search engine optimization, and graceful degradation (the app works even if the local JavaScript is disabled). You now know how to render React components on the server and how to "mount" on the browser prerendered react components.

CHAPTER 9

Testing React Components

As our applications grow more complex and we continue to add new features, we need to verify that our new implementations haven't introduced bugs to our existing functionalities. Automated testing provides a living documentation of expected behaviors and allows us to develop with more confidence, knowing that any problems will be immediately apparent.

In this chapter, we will introduce Jest (React's preferred testing framework) and TestUtils, a set of methods that makes it easy to test React components in any common JavaScript testing framework.

Jest

Jest is React's recommended testing framework. It is based on the popular Jasmine framework and adds a few helpful features:

- It runs your tests with a fake DOM implementation (so that your tests can run on the command line).

- It has support for JSX out of the box.

Jest Test Project Structure

To use Jest on a project, only two things are necessary: a test task configured in the `package.json` file and a `__tests__` folder that is the default location for Jest test files. To illustrate, let's create a new folder and set up this structure.

In a new folder, create a `package.json` project file (npm init -y) and install Jest and babel-jest (npm install –save-dev jest-cli babel-jest).

Next, edit the `package.json` file to set up the test task using Jest and babel-jest. Listing 9-1 shows the updated file.

Listing 9-1. Package.json File with Test Task Configured to Use babel-jest

```
{
  "name": "testsample",
  "version": "0.0.1",
  "description": "",
  "main": "index.js",
  "author": "",
  "license": "ISC",
```

```
  "devDependencies": {
    "babel-jest": "^5.3.0",
    "jest-cli": "^0.6.1"
  },
  "scripts": {
    "test": "jest"
  },
  "jest": {
    "scriptPreprocessor": "<rootDir>/node_modules/babel-jest"
  }
}
```

It is worth noticing in Listing 9-1 the usage of the `<rootDir>` config param. It points to the root directory that Jest should scan for tests and modules within. When used inside the `package.json`, the value for this config param defaults to the directory of the `package.json`.

Finally, create a __tests__ folder (notice the double underscore characters at the beginning and end) to complete the basic structure.

Getting Started

Before moving to React, let's set up a Jest test environment using a plain JavaScript object. Consider a scenario where you want to test the following `sum.js` file in the root folder of the project (as shown in Listing 9-2).

Listing 9-2. sum.js

```javascript
let sum = (value1, value2) => (
  value1 + value2
)

export default sum;
```

In the __tests__ folder, create a `sum-test.js` file, as shown in Listing 9-3.

Listing 9-3. sum-test.js

```javascript
jest.autoMockOff();

describe('sum', function() {
  it('adds 1 + 2 to equal 3', function() {
    var sum = require('../sum');
    expect(sum(1, 2)).toBe(3);
  });
});
```

Now you can run the tests using the test task you set up in the earlier section (npm test). The output is shown in Figure 9-1.

```
[$ npm test                                                                ]

> jest-getting-started@1.0.0 test /Users/cassiozen/jest-getting-started
> jest

Using Jest CLI v0.6.1
 PASS  __tests__/sum_test.js (0.427s)
1 test passed (1 total in 1 test suite, run time 0.872s)
```

Figure 9-1. *Test passed*

■ **Note**   In the first line of your test file, notice that you disabled Jest's auto-mocking (with `jest.autoMockOff`).

Automatic mocking allows the isolation of a module from its dependencies. The intention is to be able to test only a unit of code in isolation without relying on the implementation details of its dependencies.

However, not all code can be tested without relying on its dependencies (especially in existing code bases where code wasn't generated with testing in mind). In these cases, a better strategy is to disable auto-mocking and explicitly set mock on for some specific modules.

React Test Utilities

React comes with a suite of built-in test utilities that facilitates the process of testing components. The test utilities are provided as a separated add-on package on npm. Install it using `npm install --save-dev react-addons-test-utils`.

Rendering a Component for Testing

The most-used React test utilities method is `renderIntoDocument`. As the name suggests, it renders a component into a detached DOM node; this allows you to make assertions about the generated DOM without inserting the actual component in the page. In the most basic form, you can do something like this:

```
let component = TestUtils.renderIntoDocument(<MyComponent />);
```

You can then use `findDOMNode()` to access the raw DOM element and test its values.

Example Using renderIntoDocument and Jest

To exemplify, let's create a new project using the default structure you saw in the "Jest Test Project Structure" section. Create a CheckboxWithLabel component in the root folder and a `CheckboxWithLabel_test.js` file in the `__tests__` folder. Figure 9-2 shows the project structure.

▾ 📁 testing-react

   ▾ 📁 _tests_

      📄 CheckboxWithLabel_test.js

   ▸ 📁 node_modules

    📄 CheckboxWithLabel.js

    📦 package.json

Figure 9-2. *React project structure with tests*

Next, update the package.json file to include the jest test task configuration. It will be a little different from the previous version because you will include a React-specific configuration. Listing 9-4 shows the updated package.json.

Listing 9-4. Package.json File with Test Task Configured to Use babel-jest and Test React Applications

```
{
  "name": "testing-react",
  "version": "1.0.0",
  "description": "",
  "main": "index.js",
  "keywords": [],
  "author": "",
  "license": "ISC",
  "devDependencies": {
    "babel-jest": "^5.3.0",
    "jest-cli": "^0.6.1",
    "react": "^0.14.1",
    "react-addons-test-utils": "^0.14.1",
    "react-dom": "^0.14.1"
  },
  "scripts": {
    "test": "jest"
  },
  "jest": {
    "scriptPreprocessor": "<rootDir>/node_modules/babel-jest",
    "unmockedModulePathPatterns": [
      "<rootDir>/node_modules/react",
      "<rootDir>/node_modules/react-dom",
      "<rootDir>/node_modules/react-addons-test-utils",
      "<rootDir>/node_modules/fbjs"
    ]
  }
}
```

The React component is pretty straightforward: you implement a simple checkbox that swaps between two labels, as shown in Listing 9-5.

Listing 9-5. CheckboxWithLabel.js

```
import React, {Component} from 'react';

class CheckboxWithLabel extends Component {

  constructor() {
    super(…arguments);
    this.state = {isChecked: false};
    this.onChange = this.onChange.bind(this);
  }

  onChange() {
    this.setState({isChecked: !this.state.isChecked});
  }

  render() {
    return (
      <label>
        <input type="checkbox"
               checked={this.state.isChecked}
               onChange={this.onChange} />
        {this.state.isChecked ? this.props.labelOn : this.props.labelOff}
      </label>
    );
  }
}

export default CheckboxWithLabel;
```

In the test code, you start by using React's TestUtils renderIntoDocument to get a detached DOM node with your component. Immediately after that you use ReactDOM.findDOMNode() to access the raw DOM element from your component. Finally, you make an assertion, expecting that the component label starts with the "off" label. Listing 9-6 shows the test file.

Lisitng 9-6. CheckboxWithLabel_test.js

```
jest.autoMockOff();

import React from 'react';
import ReactDOM from 'react-dom';
import TestUtils from 'react-addons-test-utils';

const CheckboxWithLabel = require('../CheckboxWithLabel');

describe('CheckboxWithLabel', () => {
```

```
// Render a checkbox with label in the document
var checkbox = TestUtils.renderIntoDocument(
  <CheckboxWithLabel labelOn="On" labelOff="Off" />
);

var checkboxNode = ReactDOM.findDOMNode(checkbox);

it('defaults to Off label', () => {
  // Verify that it's Off by default
  expect(checkboxNode.textContent).toEqual('Off');
});

});
```

Running the npm test, your test passes. Notice that we were only able to write our tests using ES6 syntax because we've using babel-jest (included as a dependency in the package.json project file), as shown in Figure 9-3.

```
Using Jest CLI v0.6.1
PASS __tests__/CheckboxWithLabel_test.js (0.865s)
1 test passed (1 total in 1 test suite, run time 1.429s)
```

Figure 9-3. *Test result*

Transversing and Finding Children

Having a component rendered into a DOM node is the first step in testing React components, but in most cases you will want to transverse the component's rendered tree to find and make assertions on specific children. React's TestUtils provide six functions for this purpose, as shown in Table 9-1.

Table 9-1. *Utility Functions for Transversing and Finding Children in the Component's Rendered Tree*

Function	Description
scryRenderedDOMComponentsWithClass	Finds all instances of components in the rendered tree that are DOM components with the class name matching className.
findRenderedDOMComponentWithClass	Like scryRenderedDOMComponentsWithClass() but expects there to be one result, and returns that one result, or throws an exception if there is any other number of matches besides one.
scryRenderedDOMComponentsWithTag	Finds all instances of components in the rendered tree that are DOM components with the tag name matching tagName.
findRenderedDOMComponentWithTag	Like scryRenderedDOMComponentsWithTag() but expects there to be one result, and returns that one result, or throws an exception if there is any other number of matches besides one.
scryRenderedComponentsWithType	Finds all instances of components with type equal to componentClass.
findRenderedComponentWithType	Same as scryRenderedComponentsWithType() but expects there to be one result and returns that one result, or throws an exception if there is any other number of matches besides one.

Let's add a new test to your sample project to exemplify the use of the find utilities. Use the findRenderedDOMComponentWithTag function to get the input element and verify that it is not checked by default. Listing 9-7 shows the updated source code.

Listing 9-7. The Updated Source Code for CheckboxWithLabel_test.js

```
jest.autoMockOff();

import React from 'react';
import ReactDOM from 'react-dom';
import TestUtils from 'react-addons-test-utils';

const CheckboxWithLabel = require('../CheckboxWithLabel');

describe('CheckboxWithLabel', () => {

  // Render a checkbox with label in the document
  var checkbox = TestUtils.renderIntoDocument(
    <CheckboxWithLabel labelOn="On" labelOff="Off" />
  );

  var checkboxNode = ReactDOM.findDOMNode(checkbox);

  it('defaults to Off label', () => {
    // Verify that it's Off by default
    expect(checkboxNode.textContent).toEqual('Off');
  });

  it('defaults to unchecked', () => {
    // Verify that the checkbox input field isn't checked by default
    let checkboxElement = TestUtils.findRenderedDOMComponentWithTag(checkbox, 'input');
    expect(checkboxElement.checked).toBe(false);
  });
});
```

Simulating Events

One of the most useful utilities in React's TestUtils is the Simulate function, which lets you trigger user events like mouse clicks, for example. Let's add a new test to your previous project, simulating a click to change the CheckboxWithLabel text. Listing 9-8 shows the updated test file.

Listing 9-8. The Updated Source Code for CheckboxWithLabel_test.js

```
jest.autoMockOff();

import React from 'react';
import ReactDOM from 'react-dom';
import TestUtils from 'react-addons-test-utils';

const CheckboxWithLabel = require('../CheckboxWithLabel');
```

287

```
describe('CheckboxWithLabel', () => {

  // Render a checkbox with label in the document
  var checkbox = TestUtils.renderIntoDocument(
    <CheckboxWithLabel labelOn="On" labelOff="Off" />
  );

  var checkboxNode = ReactDOM.findDOMNode(checkbox);

  it('defaults to Off label', () => {
    // Verify that it's Off by default
    expect(checkboxNode.textContent).toEqual('Off');
  });

  it('defaults to unchecked', () => {
    // Verify that the checkbox input field isn't checked by default
    let checkboxElement = TestUtils.findRenderedDOMComponentWithTag(checkbox, 'input');
    expect(checkboxElement.checked).toBe(false);
  });

  it('changes the label after click', () => {
    // Simulate a click and verify that it is now On
    TestUtils.Simulate.change(
      TestUtils.findRenderedDOMComponentWithTag(checkbox, 'input')
    );
    expect(checkboxNode.textContent).toEqual('On');
  });
});
```

Shallow Rendering

Shallow rendering is a new feature introduced in React 0.13 that lets us output a component's virtual tree without generating a DOM node. This way we can inspect how the component would be built, but without actually rendering it. The advantages of this approach over using renderIntoDocument includes removing the need for a DOM in the test environment (which is consequentially much faster), and the fact that is allows us to test React components in true isolation from other component classes. It does this by allowing us to test the return value of a component's render method, without instantiating any subcomponents.

In its current state, shallow rendering is still an experimental feature, but it is starting to gain traction and will be the recommended way to test components in the future.

Basic Usage

Using shallow rendering is straightforward. You begin by creating an instance of the shallow renderer and then use it to render a component and grab the output. Listing 9-9 shows a sample implementation, assuming you're testing a component called <MyComponent />.

Listing 9-9. Basic shallowRenderer Usage

```
import React from 'react';
import TestUtils from 'react-addons-test-utils';

const CheckboxWithLabel = require('./MyComponent);

const shallowRenderer = TestUtils.createRenderer();

shallowRenderer.render(<MyComponent className="MyComponent">Hello</MyComponent>);
const component = shallowRenderer.getRenderOutput();
```

This gives you an object that represents the React component and looks roughly like Listing 9-10 (with some properties omitted for brevity).

Listing 9-10. Shallow Render Outputted Object

```
{
  "type": "div",
  "props": {
    "className": "MyComponent",
    "children": {
      "type": "h1",
      "props": {
        "children": "Hello "
      }
    }
  }
}
```

You can now create tests that make assertions on this component representation:

```
expect(component.props.className).toEqual('MyComponent');
```

When you looked at the structure of the object returned from the shallow renderer, you may have noticed the children property. This will contain any text, DOM elements, or other React components that might make up the component being tested.

To exemplify, start rewriting the tests in your previous example to use shallow rendering. Remove the old test cases and start creating a new one to check if the checkboxes default to unchecked with the label "Off." Listing 9-11 shows the updated source code.

Listing 9-11. The CheckboxWithLabel_test File Now Using react-shallow-testutils

```
jest.autoMockOff();

import React from 'react';
import ReactDOM from 'react-dom';
import TestUtils from 'react-addons-test-utils';

const shallowRenderer = TestUtils.createRenderer();
const CheckboxWithLabel = require('../CheckboxWithLabel');
```

```
describe('CheckboxWithLabel', () => {

  shallowRenderer.render(<CheckboxWithLabel labelOn="On" labelOff="Off" />);
  const checkbox = shallowRenderer.getRenderOutput();

  it('defaults to unchecked and Off label', () => {
    // Verify that it's Off by default
    const inputField = checkbox.props.children[0];
    const textNode = checkbox.props.children[1];
    expect(inputField.props.checked).toBe(false);
    expect(textNode).toEqual('Off');
  });

});
```

This works fine for simple components but it can feel quite brittle to traverse heavily nested objects and select array elements this way.

React Shallow Test Utils

As mentioned, shallow rendering is still in the early stages of development and is lacking some functionality in React 0.13 and 0.14. (including the ability to return a mounted instance of the component and support for TestUtils's transversing and finding functions). Much of this will be available by default in React 0.15, but for now you can install a npm package called react-shallow-testutils to get access to these functions. Install it with npm install --save-dev react-shallow-testutils.

The first great capability provided by the react-shallow-testutils package is the ability to access not only the object representing the component, but also the mounted component.

Let's use the instance to rewrite the previous test. Instead of manually referencing the array of elements, create the expected render method output in the test and then compare that with your component. Listing 9-12 shows the updated test.

Listing 9-12. An Alternative Approach for the Same Test

```
jest.autoMockOff();

import React from 'react';
import ReactDOM from 'react-dom';
import TestUtils from 'react-addons-test-utils';
import ShallowTestUtils from 'react-shallow-testutils';

const shallowRenderer = TestUtils.createRenderer();
const CheckboxWithLabel = require('../CheckboxWithLabel');

describe('CheckboxWithLabel', () => {

  // Render a checkbox with label in the document
  shallowRenderer.render(<CheckboxWithLabel labelOn="On" labelOff="Off" />);

  const checkbox = shallowRenderer.getRenderOutput();
  const component = ShallowTestUtils.getMountedInstance(shallowRenderer);
```

```
  it('defaults to unchecked and Off label', () => {
    const expectedChildren = [
      <input type="checkbox" checked={false} onChange={component.onChange} />,
      "Off"
    ];
    expect(checkbox.props.children).toEqual(expectedChildren);
  });

});
```

You may have noticed the previous example referred to an onChange method: onChange={component.onChange}.

Here you use the component mounted instance that react-shallow-testutils provided for you to ensure that you are testing against the same function that your React component uses.

If you want to call a mountedInstance method that will end changing the component state, make sure to call shallowRenderer.getRenderOutput again to get the updated render. For example, let's implement a new test in your example project calling the component's onChange. Listing 9-13 shows the updated file.

Listing 9-13. Calling a Method on the Mounted Component

```
jest.autoMockOff();

import React from 'react';
import ReactDOM from 'react-dom';
import TestUtils from 'react-addons-test-utils';
import ShallowTestUtils from 'react-shallow-testutils';

const shallowRenderer = TestUtils.createRenderer();
const CheckboxWithLabel = require('../CheckboxWithLabel');

describe('CheckboxWithLabel', () => {

  // Render a checkbox with label in the document
  shallowRenderer.render(<CheckboxWithLabel labelOn="On" labelOff="Off" />);

  let checkbox = shallowRenderer.getRenderOutput();
  const component = ShallowTestUtils.getMountedInstance(shallowRenderer);

  it('defaults to unchecked and Off label', () => {
    const expectedChildren = [
      <input type="checkbox" checked={false} onChange={component.onChange} />,
      "Off"
    ];
    expect(checkbox.props.children).toEqual(expectedChildren);
  });

  it('changes the label after click', () => {
    component.onChange();
    checkbox = shallowRenderer.getRenderOutput();
    expect(checkbox.props.children[1]).toEqual('On');
  });
});
```

If you run the tests again with npm test, the result will look like Figure 9-4.

```
[$ npm test                                                            ]

> testing-react@1.0.0 test /Users/cassiozen/testing-react
> jest

Using Jest CLI v0.6.1
 PASS  __tests__/CheckboxWithLabel_test.js (0.76s)
2 tests passed (2 total in 1 test suite, run time 1.189s)
```

Figure 9-4. *Two tests passed*

Summary

In this chapter, you saw how React components can be tested using React's Test Utils. You can either generate the component DOM tree into a detached DOM node (using renderIntoDocument) or use shallow rendering to output a component's virtual tree without actually rendering it. After having a representation of the component, you can use any testing framework to make assertions about the component's props, nodes, etc. You also learned about Jest, the testing framework made by Facebook that is the preferred way to test React projects.

Index

■ S

Get the eBook for only $5!

Why limit yourself?

Now you can take the weightless companion with you wherever you go and access your content on your PC, phone, tablet, or reader.

Since you've purchased this print book, we're happy to offer you the eBook in all 3 formats for just $5.

Convenient and fully searchable, the PDF version enables you to easily find and copy code—or perform examples by quickly toggling between instructions and applications. The MOBI format is ideal for your Kindle, while the ePUB can be utilized on a variety of mobile devices.

To learn more, go to www.apress.com/companion or contact support@apress.com.